SHYLOCK'S VENICE

SHYLOCK'S VENICE

The Remarkable History of Venice's Jews and the Ghetto

HARRY FREEDMAN

BLOOMSBURY CONTINUUM
LONDON · OXFORD · NEW YORK · NEW DELHI · SYDNEY

BLOOMSBURY CONTINUUM
Bloomsbury Publishing Plc
50 Bedford Square, London, WC1B 3DP, UK
29 Earlsfort Terrace, Dublin 2, Ireland

BLOOMSBURY, BLOOMSBURY CONTINUUM and the Diana logo are trademarks
of Bloomsbury Publishing Plc

First published in Great Britain 2024

A catalogue record for this book is available from the British Library

Library of Congress Cataloguing-in-Publication data has been applied for

ISBN: HB: 978-1-3994-0727-4; eBook: 978-1-3994-0726-7; ePDF: 978-1-3994-0725-0

2 4 6 8 10 9 7 5 3

Typeset by Deanta Global Publishing Services, Chennai, India
Printed and bound in Great Britain by CPI Group (UK) Ltd, Croydon CR0 4YY

MIX
Paper | Supporting
responsible forestry
FSC® C013604

To find out more about our authors and books visit www.bloomsbury.com
and sign up for our newsletters

To Remi

For the wonderful future you have ahead of you.

By the same author

Contents

Introduction		I
1	Crossing the Lagoon	7
2	Confrontation and Segregation	29
3	Crossing Boundaries	49
4	Concord and Dispute	71
5	More Trouble	89
6	Stability and Friction	107
7	The Lion Who Roared	123
8	Music and Culture in the Ghetto	147
9	Politics and Diplomacy	161
10	Edging Towards Modernity	175
11	Decline	195
Epilogue		211
Acknowledgements		214
Notes		216
Bibliography		230
Index		238
A Note on the Author		248

Introduction

Venice is an improbable place. A lagoon dotted with small, silty islands strung together to create a city. Not just any old city. A city that for centuries was one of the wealthiest and most powerful states in Europe. An empire without an emperor; a republic in an age of kingdoms and duchies and principalities. A seagoing state of merchant adventurers who built one of the most beautiful cities in the world; so beautiful that 14 million people visit it each year. An island city-state so pleasing to the eye, so exquisite its architecture, so enchanting its waterscape, that in the glory years of the Republic it styled itself *La Serenissima*, the Most Serene.

A financially astute trading centre governed by a patrician regime, Venice treated its Jews better than almost anywhere else in Europe. That's not saying much. The Venetians were dreadful, frightful, horrific to their Jews. But even so, if you were a Jew in times gone by and you had to live in Europe, you couldn't choose better than La Serenissima. For all its faults.

This is a book about the Venice Ghetto. The word ghetto is used today to describe an area whose residents share the same economic status, ethnicity or background. The impoverished quarters of major cities where refugees and immigrants crowd together are called ghettos. So are districts where those of a similar origin or faith choose to live. Even those who dwell in mansions within gated communities may think of themselves as living in a ghetto of sorts. But none of these places is anything like the Venice Ghetto, the very first ghetto in the world. Prison is a more appropriate word for the area in which the Jews of Venice were forced to live. Or, if we are feeling generous, open prison, since the barred gates were opened during daylight hours and the ghetto inhabitants could come and go freely. Provided they returned by nightfall.

There was nothing particularly unusual about confining the Jews in Venice into one part of the city; most cities had quarters where those of the same nationality lived. Greeks, Armenians, Turks, Dalmatians, Albanians and Germans all dwelt in their own districts of Venice. German merchants were obliged to live in the *Fondaco dei Tedeschi*, where they were free to come and go as they pleased, though the Turks in the *Fondaco dei Turchi* did have constraints placed upon their movements. But Turkey was often a hostile power and the Turkish merchants tended to stay in Venice only for short periods, conducting their business, doing who knows what else and leaving again. One can understand why the Venetians might have been wary of them. The Jews though, barricaded at night in their prison ghetto, were not a hostile community. Far from it, they were only allowed to be in the city because they were useful to the Venetians. The Jews did what the Venetians were prohibited by religion from doing. They lent money, typically as pawnbrokers, and helped the city's many poor to put food on the table.

Moneylending was one of very few trades that Jews were allowed to practise in Christian Europe. It was also the stick with which they were beaten. The myth of the avaricious Jewish moneylender, the conspiracy theory of the world-dominating Jewish banker, only exists because Christians were forbidden to lend to each other on interest. Jews were forbidden too, under the same biblical stricture. But by the twelfth century, rabbis were coming round to the view that Jews should be allowed to charge interest. They had little choice. They couldn't earn a proper living. They were forbidden from joining the guilds, the trade associations to which all merchants and craftsmen had to belong, and they were excluded from all the professions, with the occasional exception of medicine.

The first Jewish moneylenders opened shop in Venetian territory at the end of the thirteenth century. The Venetians licensed them to lend to the poor, charged them fees for the privilege of doing so, and regulated the rate of interest they could levy. They resented and distrusted the Jews, accusing them of deicide, telling them that they had been rejected and cursed by God for their failure to recognize the divinity of Christ; it was these sins which justified their status as serfs. This attitude towards the Jews was no different from any in Europe. But unlike in other countries the Venetians never expelled the Jews, nor confiscated their belongings. They didn't slaughter Jewish men, rape women, or forcibly baptize children. That wasn't the Venetian way. Rather, they took money from them through taxation. That was how the Venetians did things. That's why Venice was the best place in Europe for Jews to live.

It was for reasons of economic utility that the Venetians first permitted Jewish moneylenders to settle in the city. It was for similar reasons that they later permitted Jewish merchants to reside in the ghetto. A decline in the Venetian economy during the sixteenth century had forced the government to review their trade policies. Jewish merchants based in Turkey handled much of the trade to and from the empire; the Venetians valued their contribution to the economy, but the merchants themselves were discouraged by the petty restrictions and bureaucracy the Republic imposed upon foreign traders. Trading with Venice was so difficult that when they arrived with their cargoes they could not even find a place in the city to stay. Realizing that it was in their own interest to make life easier for the Jewish merchants, the Venetian government expanded the ghetto and set aside lodgings for them to rent when in town.

The merchants soon brought their families and in time their temporary lodgings became permanent. In their robes and turbans they brought colour to the ghetto and their liquidity provided a certain amount of financial relief. But like the moneylenders the merchants were few in number, there were never enough of them to drag the ordinary, barely employed residents of the ghetto out of their poverty.

Confined to their compound, taxed to the hilt, barred from nearly every field of employment, forbidden to own property, obliged to wear a distinguishing yellow badge or cap, we might conclude that life for the Jews of Venice was miserable. As indeed it was. And yet, something remarkable happened in the Venice Ghetto.

For centuries the university at the nearby town of Padua had been the scholarly heart of the Republic. As one of the only institutions in Europe that would admit Jewish students, its medical school had long been a magnet for the ambitious. Padua had a *yeshiva* too, a school for rabbinic training. There had never been a lack of opportunity for the bright and scholarly among the Jews of Venice. But the establishment of the ghetto broadened the intellectual horizon for those who were not naturally attracted to formal education. Quite unexpectedly, almost as soon as it was established, the ghetto became the centre of a Jewish cultural renaissance.

We may never fully understand why it happened. Certainly the zeitgeist had much to do with it. These were the closing years of the Italian Renaissance, and even in their ghetto the Jews could not help but be touched by cultural upheavals in the outside world. The fact that Venice was Europe's preeminent centre of printing also helped; scholars flocked from far and wide to have their works immortalized in print. And the concentration in such a small space of so many minds, all raised in a Jewish culture that emphasized education, must have made a contribution too.

Whatever the reasons, the Venice Ghetto was arguably the place where the Jewish enlightenment began, where for the first time Jews, ironically enough, stepped out of what has been called their 'ghetto mentality' and began to engage with the world around them.

The Jewish enlightenment is traditionally said to have begun in Germany in the eighteenth century. That, it is claimed, is when Jews first started to study secular subjects, engage with contemporary culture, and integrate with the world around them. But such things were already happening in the Venice Ghetto two centuries earlier. Not, it is true, for everybody; many residents of the ghetto were too downtrodden to give much thought to anything other than scraping a few coins together or how to protect their children from plague and hunger. But a few, not many, wrote books on science, philosophy and medicine. Some composed music or wrote poetry, delved into antique writings, or printed new editions of ancient manuscripts. Ghetto intellectuals conversed with Italian scholars and corresponded with European humanists. There was even a renowned artist, Moses dal Castellazzo; an occupation that in those days was the least Jewish of all cultural activities. If Florence was the home of the Italian Renaissance, Venice saw the flowering of its Jewish counterpart.

The ghetto occupies a distinctive place in the history of European antisemitism. The Venetians had been the first to effectively imprison their Jews, but as the years passed they grew noticeably more tolerant, more willing to engage with them culturally and in commerce. They still despised Jews of course, they weren't that enlightened; they continued to treat them as outsiders, cursing them as deicides, fearing the supernatural powers they irrationally credited them with. But over the two centuries of the ghetto's existence the anti-Jewish polemics grew fewer and the calls to expel them from the city died down. The hand of the Venetian State weighed less heavily: always anxious to exact as much money from the ghetto as it could, in its latter years the Republic became more open to negotiation and compromise. Maybe the change was brought about by the zeitgeist; by a world that was opening up, where communications were improving and attitudes towards foreign cultures and nations were generally becoming more tolerant. Maybe it was because the ghetto contained people of note, intellectuals and merchants who commanded a degree of respect, who made tangible contributions to the prosperity and cultural well-being of Venice. Although it never became as tolerant towards its Jews as Amsterdam, whose story was very different, in its latter years the Venetian Republic displayed noticeably little hostility to its Jews. It stands out as an example of a city that not only came to terms with the fact that Venetians had to live with an indigenous Jewish population but, recognizing their economic utility, encouraged other Jews to join them. Provided, of course, that the newcomers too were also economically useful.

In the following pages we will read about life in the Venice Ghetto during the three centuries when Jews were confined there. We will meet its outstanding characters, the torchbearers of the Jewish renaissance. Leon Modena, who preached Judaism to princes and bishops, corresponded with Christian Talmudists, and brought music to the ghetto. Simone Luzzatto, whose manifesto on religious tolerance was read in Amsterdam and London, and Leone Ebreo the philosopher of love. We will hear how the poet Sara Copia Sulam was exploited by the Venetian guests she invited to her ghetto salon and read about Elia Levita, the author of courtly romances who lived for ten years in the home of a Cardinal, learning from him and teaching him. We will cross paths with Elijah Halfon, adviser to Henry VIII and Anselmo del Banco whose name tells us his profession, along with a sprinkling of mystics, alchemists, odd bods and false messiahs. Oh, and of course, Shylock, the most famous Venetian Jew of all.

I

Crossing the Lagoon

DON ISAAC ABARBANEL ARRIVES IN VENICE

In 1492 King Ferdinand and Queen Isabella expelled their Jewish subjects from Spain. Most fled to the ports, desperate to cross the Mediterranean, to seek out new lives for themselves in lands they had scarcely heard of. The vessels they crowded onto were often unseaworthy, captained by men hoping to profit from the misery of the refugees, crewed by those hoping to extort what they could. Some of the exiles were murdered for their possessions before they were even able to set foot on the boats. Others managed to set sail, only to be sold into slavery on the north coast of Africa. A good few were driven by the winds back to Spain or drowned at sea. Only a small proportion of the refugees survived.

Those who did survive then fled to towns and communities across the Mediterranean. Many headed to the Ottoman Empire, where they would be at liberty to practise their religion and to live free of the persecutions and expulsions they had endured in Christian Europe. Some settled in Italy. One who did was Don Isaac Abarbanel (or Abravanel, scholars and experts cannot agree how he pronounced his name).

Don Isaac is well known in Jewish circles today for his biblical commentaries and his works of humanist philosophy, but his reputation in the late fifteenth century was for financial acumen and diplomacy. He was born in 1437 into a wealthy, aristocratic Jewish family in Lisbon. He followed his father into the Portuguese royal court where he became one of King Alfonso V's leading financiers. Don Isaac (Don is a courtesy title) was the principal contributor to a substantial loan of 12 million reals raised on behalf of the king. And in 1471, when as part of a territorial grab the Portuguese army seized the Moroccan city of Arzila from the Islamic Wattasid dynasty, they sold members of the local population into slavery. Among them were 220 Jews. Don Isaac paid a considerable ransom from his own funds to free them.[1]

But when King Alfonso died in 1481, and the Duke of Bragança led an unsuccessful rebellion against the new monarch, João II, Abarbanel was accused of conspiracy. Sentenced to death, and with his wealth confiscated, he fled across the border to Spain, carrying only his reputation with him. He set himself up as a tax farmer – collecting taxes on commission – and won contracts to supply the Spanish army. He became fabulously wealthy again and ended up once more as a financier to royalty, this time to King Ferdinand and Queen Isabella of Spain. He helped to pay for their conquest of Granada and for the forced conversion they imposed upon the Muslim population. So immersed was Abarbanel in the Spanish court that he was taken completely by surprise in 1492 when the king and queen announced that all Jews in their kingdom were to be expelled. Abarbanel did his best; he petitioned the king three times and when that failed tried to bribe him, but to no avail. He and his family were expelled from Spain with their fellow Jews, sailing on the same dangerous and unseaworthy vessels, sharing the indignities they suffered, until they disembarked as refugees on foreign shores. In the Abarbanel family's case the foreign shore was Naples.

Isaac Abarbanel was one of the first Jewish Bible commentators to try to make scriptural passages relevant to the lives of his readers. His commentaries examine the historical and literary aspects of the text; unlike earlier exegetes he discusses entire stories and narratives rather than just explaining the meaning of individual words and sentences. From time to time he writes about himself. Abarbanel described his experience of being driven from Spain in the commentary he wrote to the biblical Book of Kings. He peppered his account with quotations taken from Moses's *Song at the Red Sea*[2]:

> On one day 300,000 enfeebled people, young and old, children and women, myself among them, departed from all the king's domains, going wherever the wind would take them . . . Some went to the nearby kingdoms of Portugal and Navarre . . . Some made their way by sea, a pathway in the mighty waters. Yet even the hand of God was against them, to confound and destroy them. For many of the wretches were sold as slaves in foreign lands and many drowned in the sea, sinking like lead in the powerful currents. And some were cast into both fire and water, for the ships caught alight . . . I chose the way of those who went by sea, and I am in exile. I came with my household . . . here to the praiseworthy city of Naples whose kings are kings of righteousness.[3]

We should take the figure of 300,000 refugees with a grain of salt, but the rest of his description tallies with accounts from other contemporary sources. Of course, these days Abarbanel's story would have been different. Supremely wealthy exiles do not flee along with the masses into death-trap boats on the Mediterranean. They board private jets and continue their charmed lives elsewhere in the world.

Down and out in Naples was not the end of Don Isaac Abarbanel's story. He remade his fortune once again and became a trusted associate of King Ferrante (Ferdinand I). When the Kingdom of Naples fell to the French, Abarbanel fled with the royal court to Messina in Sicily. From there he went to Corfu and then to Monopoli in Apulia. As he travelled he found time to complete his commentaries on the books of the Bible, and to compose theological and philosophical tracts. Even in flight, Abarbanel was rarely idle.

Don Isaac finally settled in Venice in 1503. It seems that he went there with a specific purpose in mind, alert to a new financial opportunity. Five years earlier the Portuguese explorer Vasco da Gama had sailed down the west coast of Africa, rounded the Cape of Good Hope, and discovered that India could be reached by sea. His discovery meant that those engaged in the lucrative trade in spices and silks from India to Europe no longer needed to board a ship to cross the Indian Ocean, disembark with their wares when reaching the Arabian peninsula, and endure a lengthy and dangerous journey across desert and mountain before boarding a ship once more at Alexandria, Constantinople or Antioch to sail homeward across the Mediterranean. Instead, they could ship their wares the whole way in one boat, saving themselves time, money and considerable danger. But the new sea route threatened to undermine the Venetian economy. Venice had grown prosperous and formidable as a seafaring nation, its boats and merchants dominating the Mediterranean shipping routes between Europe and the East. Should the spice traders circumvent the Mediterranean, Venice would lose a considerable part of its income. In straitened circumstances, it would become diminished militarily and find itself at the greater mercy of its perennial enemy, the Turks.

Venice was a powerful republic, with an empire covering a large chunk of north-eastern Italy, the Dalmatian Coast, Cyprus, Crete and several Greek islands. But its best days lay behind it. The fall of Constantinople in 1453, where Venice once had a large merchant community, had been a turning point, and the city had recently suffered a humiliating defeat in the Turkish–Venetian War (1499–1503). The threat to Venice's maritime trade due to Vasco da Gama's new sea route to India was yet another reversal in what seemed to be a never-ending stream of misfortunes.

Venice's setback was Don Isaac's opportunity. As a result of Vasco da Gama's discovery the Portuguese were now offering to transport Venetian merchandise to and from India, effectively cutting out the ships owned by the Republic's merchants. The Venetian government had set up a commission to find ways of preventing a catastrophic economic collapse, but the situation appeared bleak. Although he was long estranged from the Portuguese court, Don Isaac had once been a powerful member of its elite. He believed he understood its workings, its interests, and how best to deal with it. He travelled to Venice, where his son Joseph was already living, and obtained an introduction to the Council of Ten, the most powerful of the Republic's various governing bodies. He put himself forward as an intermediary, offering to negotiate a deal with Portugal. According to the hyperbolic account of his sixteenth-century biographer, the Council of Ten were so impressed with what Don Isaac had to say that they admitted him into their inner circle, revealing to him all their hidden secrets.

Documents in the Venetian archive provide a more sober account of what happened. They record that Don Isaac offered to send his nephew to Lisbon to seek a solution to the dispute. The Council of Ten replied that if he returned from Portugal with an agreement to which they could assent, Don Isaac could 'rest assured that the gratitude of our State will not pass over him'.[4]

The Council of Ten was one of the governing legislatures of the Venetian Republic. Unlike other Italian cities dominated by autocrats, like the Medicis of Florence or the Sforzas of Milan, where nepotism and corruption were endemic, Venice had a well-ordered, long-established and stable system of governance. It was not a democracy, most people had little or no political power, but among the ruling class, the noble families who had governed Venice for generations, power was distributed relatively equitably. The main governing body was the Great Council, a large and unwieldy assembly with a membership that sometimes exceeded 2,000, a gathering far too large to do much more than oversee constitutional matters. Day-to-day governance was devolved into the hands of the Senate, whose 120 members elected by the Grand Council sat together with a number of ex-officio dignitaries and officers of state.

The executive arm of the Senate, similar to a modern-day cabinet, was the *Collegio*. It was made up of sixteen *savii or* sages, of whom six, known as *Savii Grandi*, acted as the Republic's ministers. The role of chair of the *Collegio* was rotated between the six *Savii Grandi* each week. Power never rested with any individual long enough for them to abuse it.

At the apex of this pyramid of governance sat the *Doge*, or duke. Appointed for life, his role was mainly as a figurehead, one whose every public appearance was conducted with exaggerated Venetian magnificence, in a display of the pomp and splendour at which the city still excels today. Politically, however, his ability to make decisions was restrained by six councillors, the *Signoria*, who acted as a brake on his ambitions. Without their approval on any issue, he was unable to act.

Even the Church was subordinate in administrative matters to the Venetian government, powerless to interfere in matters of state. Venice had always managed to keep Rome at arm's length, fiercely guarding its independence while remaining ecclesiastically loyal and professing submission. Even the bishops in Venice were chosen by the Senate, Rome could only confirm their appointment.

There was one anomaly within this carefully constructed pyramid of power. The Council of Ten, to whom Don Isaac had sent his proposal, did not sit neatly within the hierarchy. Set up in 1310 to protect the citizens of Venice from the abuse of personal power, the semi-autonomous Council of Ten was elected by the Great Council and supplemented by the Doge and his *Signoria*, making the Council of Ten effectively a council of seventeen. Three members of the Council were appointed as *capi* to preside over its discussions; their post was rotated monthly among the Council's members.

The Council of Ten were extraordinarily powerful. More agile than the Senate, they could cut through red tape, take decisions quickly, and proactively intervene in matters on which the security of the Republic rested, which needed delicate handling or extreme secrecy. The Senate constrained them as best they could. Membership of the Council was for one year only, and when a member's year was up he could not be re-elected until another twelve months had passed. Nor could two members of the same family sit on the Council at the same time. And in the month during which they held office the three *capi* were forbidden to have any contact with the outside world. Confined to the Doge's Palace, the seat of the Serenissima's government, they were thus insulated from all threats of and attempts at bribery.[5]

THE TEDESCHI

The rulers of Venice dealt with Don Isaac as courteously as they would have done with any other wealthy, foreign courtier, particularly one armed with a proposal that might benefit them. The fact that Don Isaac was a Jew does not seem to have influenced their relationship with him. They would not have been so pragmatic with any of his co-religionists. Relations between the Venetian authorities and the Jews living in their territories were never good; even at their very best they were little more than tolerable. Nevertheless, despite all the restrictions and burdens that the Venetians placed upon them, the Serenissima was one of the better places for a Jew to live.

The earliest Jews to settle in the Venetian territories were of German origin. The Venetians referred to them as Tedeschi, an Italian word meaning German. When the Black Death raged through Europe in the mid-fourteenth century, a plague for which the Jews were blamed, burnt alive and slaughtered in their thousands, the Tedeschi fled southwards over the Alps and into Italy. For most of the fourteenth and fifteenth centuries the Venetian authorities confined them to the *terraferma*, the Republic's extensive mainland territories. The borders of these lands stretched beyond Padua and Verona to Bergamo in the west, to the Friuli region in the north, and eastwards around the Adriatic all the way to the Dalmatian coast. Mestre, on the edge of the *terraferma*, on the western bank of the lagoon directly opposite Venice, was the closest place to the island city that the Tedeschi Jews were allowed to live.

These days Mestre is effectively a suburb of the island city of Venice, a cheaper place to live and for tourists to stay. It offers easy access to the city across the Ponte della Libertà, a four-kilometre road bridge built by the fascist Italian dictator Mussolini in the 1930s. Running alongside the road is a far older railway bridge, built in 1846. These days one can cross from Mestre to Venice by road or rail. Until the railway bridge was built the only way to cross the lagoon from Mestre was by boat.

Because of the inconvenience of the sea journey across the lagoon, Jews who entered the city had permission from the

Venetian authorities to remain overnight. But an edict laid down in 1215 had been very clear that if Jews were to spend time in the city of Venice, they would have to conform to a set of rules. Most importantly, they were under no circumstances to have sexual relations with Christians. Nor were they to stay in the city for more than 15 days at a time. In order to ensure that they observed the regulations fully and to humiliate them, they were obliged to wear circles of yellow fabric on their clothing, badges identifying them as Jews.

But badges are easy to conceal. By 1496 it was apparent that some Jews were covering up their badges and staying longer in the city than they should. So the badge was upgraded to a yellow hat. From now on Jews were obliged to wear yellow head-coverings as identification. And the time they were allowed to spend in the city was reduced. Instead of being able to stay for 15 days consecutively they were now limited to spending no more than 15 days in any one year. This tightening of the rules was just one in a string of restrictions of varying degrees of severity that the Venetian Senate imposed on the Jews over the years.[6]

Venice was not unusual in placing restrictions on its Jews. Venetian Jews were restricted in where they could live, in having to wear a yellow hat and even, as we shall see, the work they could do. But in comparison with elsewhere Venice was benevolent towards its Jews. There were cities and countries that refused to allow them in altogether. Don Isaac had been expelled from Spain in 1492 along with all other Jews who refused to convert to Christianity, but he wouldn't have been any better off had he remained in his native Portugal. In 1496, four years after they evicted the Jews from Spain, King Ferdinand and Queen Isabella betrothed their daughter Isabella to King Manuel of Portugal. A condition of the betrothal was that all Jews be driven out from Portugal, including those who had crossed into the country from Spain four years earlier.

Spain and Portugal were by no means the first places to expel their Jewish inhabitants. Jews had been expelled from Naples in 1288 and from the whole of England in 1290. During the thirteenth and fourteenth centuries they were repeatedly expelled from parts of

France, but often only for a few years. After a while they would be readmitted, only to be subsequently massacred or expelled again. Repeatedly banishing the Jews and confiscating their goods each time was a lucrative business opportunity for the French nobility.

THE CHANGING FACE OF ANTISEMITISM

Religion lay at the heart of anti-Jewish feeling in Europe. Not only had the Jews killed Christ but their stubborn and obtuse rejection of his divinity, their refusal to convert to Christianity, was impeding his return. That is how early European antisemitism is often explained. But hatred of Jews pre-dates the death of Christ. The Church's vilification of the synagogue was erected on deep foundations which had nothing to do with religion. It is a moot question as to whether medieval and early modern Christian antisemitism would have been quite so virulent had there never been such a thing as pre-Christian antisemitism.

In 38 CE, anti-Jewish riots broke out in the Greek city of Alexandria on the Nile delta. The city was within the Roman Empire. They were unconnected to religion, the riots were a secular outburst, a protest against the special political rights Jews enjoyed in the city. The Jewish population of Alexandria had been granted special rights because they did not fit neatly into either of the city's two established political categories: they were neither Greek citizens nor were they Egyptians. Instead of being bound by the obligations imposed on either group they had their own unique political status, with specific privileges and fealties. In the minds of those rioting in Alexandria the Jews were outsiders, they were different, not part of the acceptable social structure. Their otherness was nothing to do with religion.

Not enough attention has been paid by contemporary scholars of antisemitism to its psychological roots. Like all racism, antisemitism began as hatred and fear of the outsider, only later was it imbued with anti-Jewish stereotypes and illustrated with specific accusations against Jews. The Irish philosopher Richard Kearney, in a wide-ranging study of Otherness, suggests that there are three types of outsider. There is the stranger with whom we share a reciprocal disconnection: we are strangers to them just as they are strangers to us, each dwelling beyond the other's experience. There are monsters, those terrifying alien creatures of myth and fantasy who remind us that we can never be secure in ourselves; that danger lurks around every corner. And there are gods, whose powers and abilities exceed our own, against whom we are impotent.[7]

These three types of outsider have, at different times and places, all served as archetypes for the Jew-hater's image of the Jew. In his study of anti-Jewish hatred the first-century Jewish–Roman historian Josephus recorded a legend in which a group of strangers (in his account they were lepers) were exiled from ancient Egyptian society. Seeking vengeance, they returned under the leadership of a man who brought a series of plagues upon the Egyptian people and their Pharaoh.[8] The man's name was Moses. In this corruption of the biblical narrative Moses is presented as the stranger who exists at the limit of our experience, the Jew Moses who looks and acts just like we do but who will destroy everything we believe in and care about.

Then there is the outsider as monster, the fearful creature who will prevail over us if we do not subdue him first. These monsters will raise their heads frequently in this book, they are the Jews whose touch the Christians of Venice feared would infect them with pestilential disease, whose gaze would pollute their souls. These are the monsters that need to be dealt with and subdued before they can wreak their damage. Just like the Jews.

One of the very earliest images of Jews as monsters was portrayed by the Stoic philosopher Posidonius of Apameia. He claimed that when the Greek king Antiochus IV Epiphanes invaded Jerusalem in 168 BCE, he found a Greek prisoner in the Temple miserably sitting in front of a splendid feast. The prisoner told him that every year the Jews would capture and fatten a Greek citizen, kill him, and eat him as part of an anti-Hellenist ritual. This is the Jew as monster but with a polemical twist because the invading King Antiochus IV is himself vilified as a monster in the Jewish tradition. It was his desecration of the Temple that led to the successful revolt of the Maccabees and the establishment of the Jewish Hasmonean kingdom. Not so, implies Posidonius's polemic. The Jewish defamation of Antiochus is a distraction, to deflect attention from their own monstrosity. Had Antiochus not entered the Temple he would never have found the Greek sacrificial victim, and the Jews would never have been exposed as monsters.[9]

Finally, there is the outsider as a god, with superpowers far beyond the abilities of ordinary people. It is how contemporary antisemites think of Jews, who are said to control the banks, manipulate the media, and run the world. It is quite flattering. If only it were true.

Nor were the Alexandrian riots the first example of anti-Jewish racism. Three centuries earlier the biblical book of Esther introduced an anti-hero named Haman. He told his king that he should wipe out all the Jews in Persia because they had different customs and laws. Haman's antisemitism was not about religion. But hatred of Jews in medieval and early modern Europe most certainly was.

Christian Europe reviled the Jews. They excluded them from nearly every profession and field of employment. The only profession Jews were generally permitted to take up was that of physician. The Jewish connection with medicine went back for centuries; it was a bond that Christian rulers saw no advantage to themselves in breaking.

Jews had other uses apart from medicine. Like underclasses throughout history, they were available to do the work that the majority population could not or would not do. Not menial tasks, there were plenty of penurious Christians available to perform those. But society was becoming economically more sophisticated; traders and merchants needed access to money to finance their commercial activities, the poor required it to feed their families or to tide themselves over from time to time. The Bible forbade the lending of money on interest. The Church frowned on those Christian bankers and moneylenders who were prepared to flout the law against lending on interest, who were oblivious to the harm they were doing to their souls. There was no need for Christians to lend to other Christians and to charge them interest. It was far better to allow such sinful tasks to be done by Jews.

The origins of Jewish involvement in banking and moneylending, and the antisemitic accusation that Jews control finance, goes back to medieval times, when it was the only field of work that most Jews were permitted to enter. Typical Jewish moneylenders were local operators, lending small sums to those who had an article of value to deposit, often little more than rags. Although they are often referred to as moneylenders, they do not conform to our modern image of the payday loan merchant who lends unsecured sums on onerous terms. They are better described as pawnbrokers, only lending money against pledges which were redeemed when the loan was repaid. Occasionally they might lend only on the security of a written bond, but this was the exception rather than the rule.

These moneylenders were not wealthy people. Their profits were severely curtailed by local regulations that set the interest rates they could charge, they were taxed heavily, and their overheads were high because of the number of people attached to their households. Their limited incomes were often the only source of outside money flowing into a Jewish community, they had to fund an entire entourage. Often as many as ten or twelve people, employees, religious functionaries, tutors and menial workers were all dependent for their sustenance on one struggling moneylender.[10]

Some of the pawnbrokers, particularly those whose families had a history of moneylending and had accumulated capital, managed to make the transition from lending small amounts to the poor into something approaching a modern conception of a bank. They provided loans for commerce and trade and often branched out into other activities as blacksmiths, goldsmiths, tailors, even manufacturers of gunpowder.[11] They did become extremely wealthy, but they were few and far between. As the authorities imposed ever higher taxes and limited the rates of interest the Jews could charge, opportunities diminished for others to join their ranks. The idea that moneylending brought untold riches to Jewish communities, that every Jew was a Shylock, is one of the principal canards which underpin centuries of antisemitism.

FLEEING TO VENICE

The first Jewish moneylenders to be allowed to operate on Venetian territory arrived in 1298. They were admitted because the Venetian government wanted to clamp down on Christian usurers who were lending money in contravention of biblical law and doing so at extortionate rates. The Venetian authorities granted a licence to the newly arrived Jewish moneylenders, charged them a fee for the privilege, determined the rate of interest that they could charge, and restricted them to dwelling in Mestre, keeping them out of the city but close at hand. The arrangement was inconvenient, both for the pawnbrokers and their Venetian clients, who either had to wait for those days when the moneylender was allowed into the city, or else cross the lagoon whenever they needed to deposit a pledge or borrow money.

The Jews of Venice lived in Mestre for two hundred years. But their sojourn came to an abrupt end when Venice was attacked by the League of Cambrai. The League was an alliance between the Holy Roman Emperor, the King of France, the Pope and a host of smaller European states and principalities, formed with the intention of regaining territories that Venice had recently seized. The name Cambrai derives from the north-eastern French town in which the alliance was formalized. In April 1509 the first French troops entered Venetian territory and proceeded to overrun the *terraferma*. Within two months all the principal towns in the Venetian lands had surrendered and the Venetian army had been pushed back to Mestre.

Foreseeing a situation of this gravity, and conscious that if the Jewish moneylenders were ever taken captive the pledges and deposits they were holding would be lost, the Senate had recently granted the Jews of Mestre a charter allowing them to enter the city of Venice in the event of war. Now, with the League's army at their backs, the Jews fled for their lives across the lagoon and into the city.

Eliyahu Capsali was a student in the Talmudic college, or yeshiva, in the university town of Padua in the *terraferma* when the

League of Cambrai invaded. Capsali was a member of a prominent rabbinic family in the Venetian colony of Candia, the island we know today as Crete. He had travelled to Padua to spend a few years studying, just as his father had done before him. When he returned to Candia he wrote a history of Venice starting with the election in 697 of its first Doge, Paoluccio Anafesto. We now know that Anafesto didn't exist, that he was a mythical character, but Capsali wasn't to know that; in Venetian folk history Anafesto's election was when the history of the Republic began.

As part of his history Capsali wrote at length about his experiences during the League of Cambrai's invasion. He explained how the Venetian authorities had imposed taxes to pay for the costs of the war, first raising a levy on property rents and then introducing a poll tax. Then, Capsali tells us, they imposed additional taxes on the Jews, 'melting their hearts like water because they did not have the wherewithal to pay the taxes and levies day after day and month after month'. He described the build-up to war in great detail, reporting on conversations, real or imagined, between senior officers, describing the excitement in Padua as the Venetian army marched through the streets, remarking that the whole town was kept awake by the cries and shouts of the soldiers as they passed.[12]

It seems implausible that a foreign rabbinic student in his late teens or early twenties who knew few local people, would be able to gather quite as much information as Capsali did about the progress of the war. But his account is detailed and many of the events he describes match what is known from other sources. He must have spoken to many people and kept detailed records. He even describes the appearance of the white-robed King Louis XII of France, with his crown on his head, who invigorated the French troops fighting on behalf of the League of Cambrai and led them to an overwhelming victory against the Venetians at Agnadello on 14 May 1509. Like most pre-modern historians, Capsali exaggerates when it comes to numbers. He says that 28,000 Venetians died in the battle at Agnadello. Modern historians put the figure at around 4,000.[13]

Around a fortnight after Agnadello, news reached Capsali's yeshiva in Padua that Verona had fallen to the forces of the Holy

Roman Emperor, Maximilian I. The Jews of Padua were terrified. In flowery language interwoven with biblical quotes Capsali relates that when they heard the news:

> most of the Jews who were there hurriedly fled towards Venice carrying their possessions bundled up in their garments. They came to Venice for they were in fear of their lives, vulnerable to every blow and mishap. They took counsel and fled into Venice where the government gave them permission to stay, and they rented houses, each person as they saw fit, until Venice was full of many Jews, over 1,000 householders. For they did not just come from Padua but also from other communities throughout Italy, like a multitude of locusts.[14]

The Jews settled across the city, renting homes to the north and east of the Rialto. The wealthy Hayyim Meshullam, a member of Venice's leading banking family, rented the opulent Ca' Bernardo *palazzo* on the Grand Canal. Hayyim Meshullam was known for his philanthropy; in his history Eliyahu Capsali described how he provided cooked meals of meat and rice three times each week for the poor of Padua and supplied them with wood for fuel in winter. Nevertheless, renting the Ca' Bernardo palace was an ostentatious display that did nothing to endear Meshullam to the local population. Capsali acknowledged as much, saying that the palace became a 'chastizing plague' to the Jews of Venice.

The Jews had fled into Venice in fear of their lives. They were expected to leave once the danger had passed. However, it didn't take long for the financially astute Venetian authorities to recognize the economic benefits of letting them stay. The Jewish pawnbrokers were holding dozens of pledges deposited by their clients in return for loans; it made far more sense for them to stay in the city with their deposits than to have them go back to Mestre where they ran the risk of being plundered should another invading army rampage through. It was also more convenient for the poor of the city to be able to borrow money on the spot, rather than putting up with the cost and bother of travelling to Mestre.

Most importantly, by granting the Jews a charter allowing them to live in Venice for a limited period of time the government could impose a charge upon them, adding much needed funds to the treasury. To that end in 1511 the Senate levied a tax of 5,000 ducats on the Jewish subjects of the Republic, at a time when a labourer might earn one ducat a week and the rent on a typical family dwelling was around 25 ducats a year. Two-thirds of the Senate's levy was to be paid by those living in the city itself.

From now on Jewish life in Venice would be regulated by charter and taxation. The charters gave the Jews the right to live and lend money in the city, the tax they paid brought funds into the Republic's treasury. It was a far from ideal arrangement. The charters came up for renewal frequently and the level of taxation had to be renegotiated every time, as did the interest rate the Jews were allowed to charge on their loans. Since there was never a guarantee that an expiring charter would be renewed, Jewish life in Venice was always insecure. If the charter was not renewed, the Jews would be obliged to leave the city and their homes.

As odd as it may seem to us, the principle of taxing an entire community collectively, rather than levying charges on individual members, was not unusual in early modern Europe. It benefited both the authorities and the community that was being taxed. In return for a single, communal payment the authorities gave the community the right to impose its own fiscal and juridical rules upon its members and to live according to its own customs and laws.[15]

The sudden influx of Jewish refugees into the city did not go down well with the local Catholic preachers. They were used to living in a city without Jews; they were offended by their presence, railed against them and demanded they be expelled. The chronicler Marin Sanudo, whose extensive diaries are one of the chief sources of information about life in early sixteenth-century Venice, was present at a sermon preached by the friar Ruffino Lovato of Padua during Easter in 1509. He heard the friar say that it was lawful to strip Jews of their money and leave them with nothing to live on. This was several weeks before the invasion by the League of Cambrai and the mass flight of Jews into the city. Two years later Sanudo heard the friar preach again, this time in a part of Venice where there was now a large Jewish population. The friar's demands that the Jews be expelled from Venice were so virulent that the Jewish community complained to the Senate. The cleric was rebuked but a fortnight later he was at it again, accusing the Jews of killing Christ and trying to stir up a pogrom. He was by no means the only zealot to preach in this way.[16]

THE CULTURAL RENAISSANCE BEGINS

Don Isaac Abarbanel was dead by this time; he had died in Venice in 1508. But his son Joseph still lived in the city. An eminent physician who treated many of the Venetian elite, he lived a more privileged life than most members of the Jewish community. As did his brother Judah Leon, more commonly known by his Italian name Leone Ebreo, Leon the Hebrew. Like his father he had settled in Naples when he first arrived in Italy, travelling from there to Genoa, Barletta and eventually Venice.[17] It was in the Serenissima that he began work on the book which would pave the way for the cultural renaissance that came to characterize Jewish Venice. A cultural revolution in which, for the first time in Christian Europe, Jewish scholars, philosophers, musicians and poets stepped beyond the narrow cultural confines of Judaism and actively engaged with the world beyond. It wasn't the first Jewish cultural revolution; there had once been a similar renaissance in Spain. But that had been 500 years earlier and in those days Spain was a Muslim, not a Christian, society.

Judah Leon was born in 1460, the oldest of five children. He received an outstanding education; his father, who could afford to pay for the very best tutors, wanted his children to attain the same high intellectual standards that he had achieved. Unlike most fifteenth-century Jewish children, who were given just a basic Hebrew education, Don Isaac's children were tutored in both Jewish and secular subjects. Among them the philosophy of the ancient Greeks and the Arabic scholars who followed them; the fields in which Judah Leon would make his name.

Of all Don Isaac's five children, Judah Leon was the one whose career was the most illustrious and whose name is best known. He inherited his father's intellect, comported himself with the family's aristocratic bearing, studied medicine, and had been appointed physician to the King and Queen of Spain. They must have thought highly of him because when they expelled the Jews in 1492 they asked him to stay behind. Once the royal couple realized that Judah Leon preferred loyalty to his family and people over the luxury of the royal court, they ordered their servants to kidnap his one-year-old son, thinking this would force him to remain in the country.

Judah Leon got wind of the plot to kidnap his baby son and had him smuggled over the border to Portugal, planning to reunite with him when he had settled his affairs. He must have dismissed from his mind the death sentence that the Portuguese king had decreed against his father. But the King of Portugal had not forgotten. When he heard that Don Isaac's grandson was in the country, he had the boy seized and baptized as a Christian.

As far as anyone knows, that was the last time Judah Leon saw or heard of his son. The Hebrew poem he composed expressing his grief has gone down as a classic of early modern Jewish verse:

Time with his pointed shafts has hit my heart
and split my guts, laid open my entrails,
landed me a blow that will not heal,
knocked me down, left me in lasting pain . . .
He did not stop at whirling me around,
exiling me while yet my days were green,
sending me stumbling, drunk, to roam the world . . .
He scattered everyone I care for northward,
eastward, or to the west, so that
I have no rest from constant thinking, planning –
and never a moment's peace, for all my plans.[18]

Judah Leon fled Spain and travelled to Naples with his family. He continued to practise as a physician, replacing his elite Spanish medical practice with one of similar stature in Italy.[19] His reputation today rests upon his scholarship and writing although, like his father, he only pursued his intellectual and literary activities as an adjunct to his professional career.

Unlike his father, though, Judah Leon almost certainly didn't write in Hebrew.[20] His sole surviving work, *Dialoghi d'amore (Dialogues of Love)*, was probably written in a Tuscan dialect of Italian, although some scholars maintain that the original version was either in Latin or the Jewish–Spanish dialect Ladino. Whatever language he wrote in, it is evident from his style that Judah Leon intended his book to be read primarily by Christians. Even so, he made no attempt to conceal his Jewish identity, he referred frequently to Hebrew teachings and traditions, he even claimed that Plato had been taught by 'our ancient fathers'.[21] His publishers, however, were more reticent about his Jewishness. The book sold so well that in later editions the printers added a note to say that Leone had abandoned his Jewish faith and converted to Christianity. It wasn't true, but throughout history outsiders have resorted to subterfuge to help them look less foreign. The question of whether Leone Ebreo was a Jewish philosopher or a philosopher who happened to be a Jew is still debated in academic circles today.[22]

Dialoghi d'amore is composed as three discussions, between a man Philo and his student Sophia, revolving around the subject of love. Philo, the teacher, is the lover, Sophia his beloved. The first of the discussions explores the relationship between love and desire, the second the universality of love and the third its origins. The premise of the book is that love animates and maintains the universe, that it is the basis of the relationship between God, the cosmos and humanity. This is the starting point for a wide range of topics synthesizing Aristotelian and Platonic thought, drawing Aristotle closer to the views of Plato. Plato's views, Leone insisted, were derived from the *prisca theologia*, the ancient, divine theology that could be traced back through Jeremiah and Moses to Adam.

Dialoghi d'amore proved highly popular. By 1607 it had gone through twenty-five editions and had been translated into Latin,

Hebrew, French and Spanish. Its popularity was as much due to its style as its content; it was an entertaining philosophical discussion written from a mystical, astrological perspective. The Spanish author Cervantes quoted it in his books *Don Quixote* and *La Galatea*; the poet John Donne, theologian Giordano Bruno and philosopher Baruch Spinoza were all influenced by it. Leone Ebreo was the first Jewish secular philosopher to write a popular work for a non-Jewish audience.

Leone Ebreo did not live to see the publication of *Dialoghi d'amore*; by the time it was first issued in Rome in 1535 he was already dead. And none of the other books he is believed to have written have survived. They may never even have been published. His grandson, named Judah Abarbanel, claimed to possess a manuscript of a work by his grandfather called *De Harmonia Mundi* that had been composed specifically for the outstanding Renaissance philosopher Pico della Mirandola. Pico, whose short life ended just two years after Leone arrived in Italy, in 1492, was the greatest and most erudite scholar of the Renaissance. Leone Ebreo was not far behind. Had they met the two men would have had much to talk about.

Leone Ebreo may never have conversed with Pico, but we can be pretty sure he had discussions with Abraham de Balmes, with whom he shared a similar background. Both men practised as physicians in Naples before moving to Venice; both were philosophers, both wrote for Christian and Jewish readers.

Unlike Leone, de Balmes lived his whole life in Italy. He had been born around 1460 or 1470 in Lecce before moving to Naples to study and practise medicine. He stayed there until the Jews were expelled in 1510. Then he made his way north to Venice.

On his arrival in the city, de Balmes was hired by Cardinal Grimaldi, a collector of art and literature, a distinguished patron of Renaissance scholarship and a student of Kabbalah, the Jewish mystical tradition that was a popular topic of study among elite Christian scholars. The Cardinal employed de Balmes as his personal physician, but their interests were so closely meshed that we can imagine his primary motivation for employing him was scholarly.

The most valuable thing that a man like de Balmes could offer the wealthy Grimaldi was access to knowledge that would have been inaccessible to the Cardinal. For centuries Christian scholars in Europe had been cut off from the revival in Greek philosophy and science taking place in the Arab-speaking world, because they could not read or understand Arabic. But Jews living in Islamic lands spoke Arabic and they knew Hebrew, just as Jews in Christian lands did. Hebrew became a bridge between Arabic and Latin. Arabic-speaking Jews translated texts into Hebrew for their own purposes. Hebrew scholars in Europe would then eventually translate them into Latin.

In 1210 Samuel ibn Tibbon translated an Arabic version of Aristotle's *Meteorology* into Hebrew. He did the same with original works of Arabic philosophy, by Averroes, Al-Farabi, Avicenna, Maimonides and others. Translation became a family business, his son Moses ibn Tibbon took up the baton after his father. By the fifteenth century dozens of works of Arabic philosophy had been translated into Hebrew. Abraham de Balmes was one of a handful of Jews in Christian Europe who then translated the Hebrew versions into Latin.

De Balmes is credited with translating at least fourteen works by Averroes, the twelfth-century Spanish Islamic philosopher whose prolific commentaries on Aristotle helped revive the study of Greek philosophy in the Middle Ages. He also translated treatises by the lesser-known Islamic philosophers Avempace and Al-Farabi.[23] For the first time Christian scholars had access to works of Arabic philosophy, brought to them through the medium of Hebrew translators. Having a Hebrew scholar like Abraham de Balmes in his home must have been immensely satisfying to Cardinal Grimaldi.

Leone Ebreo and Abraham de Balmes were erudite scholars who moved easily between the worlds of Jewish and Christian scholarship. They were among the pioneers of the literary revolution starting to break out in the Jewish circles of Venice; the first Jews to write primarily for Italians rather than for their own people. But Ebreo and de Balmes lived privileged lives in Venice; they were both doctors who counted several of the nobility among their patients and they were each fortunate enough to benefit from unique personal circumstances. Leone came from a wealthy aristocratic family, de Balmes lived under the patronage of Cardinal Grimaldi, whose own father had been elected Doge, or duke, of Venice. The vast majority of the city's Jews did not share such good fortune. Living in poverty, reviled by the Christian majority, obliged to wear a distinguishing yellow cap, never knowing when they might be expelled once again from the city, their lives were difficult. And they were about to get worse.

Confrontation and Segregation

Jews paid a heavy price for the right to live in Venice. Although the annual toll of 5,000 ducats imposed on them in 1511 was significantly lower than the 14,000-ducat tax they'd had to pay when they fled into the city two years earlier, the discount didn't last long. A year later the Senate put the annual tax up again, to 10,000 ducats.

The most prominent member of the Jewish community was the banker Asher Meshullam. It is unlikely that he was ever appointed to a formal leadership role, but he was considered to be the head of the community, the man the Venetian authorities held responsible when they wanted to impose a particular demand upon their Jews, or when taxes were due to be paid.

Like many Italian Jews, indeed like many Jews today, Asher Meshullam had both a Hebrew and a vernacular name. The Italians called him Anselmo del Banco, his profession becoming his family name. His brother Hayyim, who had caused a stir by renting the Ca' Bernardo palace when the Jews had first arrived in the city, was known in Italian as Vita or Vivian del Banco; Hayyim being the Hebrew for life.

It was Anselmo del Banco who took it upon himself to challenge the Senate's decision to raise the tax to 10,000 ducats. He informed them that the Jewish community could not and would not pay it. The Senate, refusing to be dictated to by a Jew, no matter how wealthy, threw him into prison along with his brother Vita. They underestimated Anselmo; he was no fool and he held the trump card. Even if the Venetians were loath to admit it, the much-reviled Jewish banks and pawnshops were essential for the smooth functioning of the Republic's economy. Without them the poor of the city would have been unable to survive. Anselmo told the Senate that if they didn't agree to reduce the proposed tax on the Jews, he would close the banks. A stalemate ensued.

One year later, in 1513, the charter granted to the Jews to live and operate their pawnshops in the city came up for renewal. Asher Meshullam, who had still not consented to the proposed 10,000-ducat annual tax, took the opportunity to renew the negotiations. After he made it clear that his family and that of another banker would pay the bulk of the tax themselves, an annual figure of 6,500 ducats was agreed for all Jews in the city. Asher Meshullam was made both taxpayer and tax collector: apart from personally paying a large proportion of the tax himself, he was held responsible for collecting the rest of the money from the Jewish community.[1]

The figure of 6,500 ducats was only a basic sum, it did not absolve the Jews from paying additional taxes or making loans to the Senate as and when they were demanded. Nevertheless, the new charter guaranteed them the right to reside in Venice for the next five years. For the first time since they had arrived the Jews began to feel that their tenure in the city was becoming secure. It was, but not quite in the way they imagined.

On Good Friday in 1515, six years after the flight of the Jews into Venice, the chronicler Marin Sanudo wrote in his diary that he did not wish to ignore 'a depraved custom' he had become aware of. He noted with satisfaction that when the Jewish refugees had first arrived in Venice they had kept a low profile during Holy Week, a time of year when anti-Jewish feelings tended to intensify. They would remain out of sight, Sanudo wrote, from Palm Sunday until after Easter. But that year Jews had been out on the streets in great numbers, and it was a 'very bad thing'. He complained that they had not been rebuked for their insolence because the Republic was still at war and Jews had an important role to play in the economy of the city. 'Thus they do whatever they want,' he grumbled. 'The preacher at the Frari, Fra Giovan Maria di Arezzo, thunders against them . . . [he] concludes that it is all right to take everything the Jews have and put it towards the defence of the state, since they are our servants.'[2]

Marin Sanudo was not the only one to be offended by the presence of Jews on the street during Easter. Two weeks later, on 23 April, a proposal was put to the Senate that the Jewish community be segregated from the rest of the population. It was suggested that they be forced to relocate to the Giudecca, an island in the Venetian lagoon. It was thought, probably incorrectly, that the island acquired its name, meaning Jewish quarter, because of a colony of Jews who had lived there long ago.

Anselmo del Banco led the protests against the proposed segregation, but it seems that he was less concerned about the idea of separating the Jewish community from the rest of the population; what worried him more was the proposed location. He argued that the site was too exposed, that the Jews would be at the mercy of the troops who were quartered on the island. Perhaps sarcastically, he suggested that the Jews be moved to the holiday island of Murano.

The Giudecca proposal was not adopted but the idea of segregating the Jews did not go away. During Lent the following year Zacaria Dolfin argued that the military reversals the Republic was suffering were an indication of divine displeasure at its toleration of the Jews. Dolfin, who was a senior member of the *Collegio*, proposed that they all be sent to live on the site of a former copper foundry at the margins of the city, to the area known as the *Ghetto Nuovo*. Surrounded by canals it would keep them confined and could be further sealed off with a drawbridge and gates. He recommended that guards should be stationed at the gates to stop anyone entering or leaving at night. The *Collegio* should determine the guards' salary and the Jews of the ghetto would be responsible for paying it.

There is quite a disagreement over the etymology of the word 'ghetto'. In 1934 the British historian Cecil Roth published an article entitled 'The Origin of Ghetto: A Final Word', in which he outlined ten possible derivations of the term. Since then there have been dozens of papers and at least one book written about the origin of the name, all proving at the very least that it is never a good idea to call anything a final word. The majority consensus, the one which Roth also plumps for, is that ghetto derives from the Venetian word *geto* meaning foundry, because of the former use of the site.[3]

Whatever the derivation of the name, Marin Sanudo records that when the Doge and members of the *Collegio* heard Zacaria Dolfin's proposal, they sent for the Christian occupants of the houses in the *Ghetto Nuovo* and told them they had to move out. Some objected, saying they had spent considerable sums maintaining their properties and did not want to leave. Sanudo does not tell us how the *Collegio* responded, but they clearly got their way because they next summoned Anselmo del Banco and two of his colleagues and told them that the Jewish community was to move into the *Ghetto Nuovo*. And that, by the way, they were forbidden to build a synagogue.[4]

THE GHETTO

On 29 March 1516 the Senate issued its decree. In the preamble they declared that the main purpose of permitting the Jews to enter the city during the war had been to 'preserve the property of Christians which was in their hands. But no God-fearing subject of our state would have wished them, after their arrival, to disperse throughout the city, sharing houses with Christians, and going wherever they chose by day and night, perpetrating all those misdemeanours and detestable and abominable acts which are generally known and shameful to describe, with grave offence to the Majesty of God.'[5]

Consequently, the Senate's decree continued, all Jews living in the city, and any who may arrive subsequently, were obliged to live in the ghetto. Any Jews found by officials or public servants outside the ghetto during prohibited hours were to be arrested.

Furthermore, the Senate declared, the rent the Jews in the ghetto were to pay to their landlords was to be one-third more than the departing Christians were paying. To incentivize the presumably reluctant landlords to rent their houses to Jews, they waived the property tax that should have been paid on the additional third. They gave the Jews permission to keep an inn in the ghetto, but, as they had already told Anselmo, there were to be no synagogues. The Jews were probably less bothered than the Venetians imagined by the last restriction, they could pray anywhere, they didn't need a formal synagogue. When, some years later, they did receive permission to build synagogues they concealed them within the existing buildings so that they could not be seen from the street. No one could guarantee that the permission to have a synagogue might not one day be revoked.

Anselmo del Banco was once again at the head of the protests. He reminded the Senate that the previous year, after the proposal to relocate the Jews to the Giudecca had been rejected, he had been assured that no further measures would be taken against them. Furthermore, the idea of moving them out to the edge of the island city raised questions of public safety. At present the Jews lived close to the guards at the Rialto in the centre of the city, yet they were still regularly attacked and assaulted. If they were shunted out to the city fringe they would be even more vulnerable than now. There was also an economic question: the Jewish merchants had invested considerable amounts of money renting and improving their pawnshops on the Rialto. Were they now to be forbidden to use them?

Finally, Anselmo pointed out that sending Jews to live in the ghetto would cause a major financial loss to the Serenissima. It had been agreed that it was his responsibility to collect and hand over the taxes that the Jewish residents were obliged to pay. If they were exiled to the ghetto, it was very likely that a good number of Jews would decide to leave Venice altogether and consequently there would be fewer of them for him to collect taxes from. All in all, he surmised, in what sounded more like a threat than a question, might it not be better for the Jews to move back to Mestre? The city would of course lose the tax revenues from the Jewish community as well as their banking and pawnshop facilities, but at least the Venetian citizenry wouldn't have to encounter Jews in the streets.

Anselmo, though, was losing his touch. This time his protests were of no avail. Anti-Jewish feeling in the city had reached the point at which the Senate felt obliged to take action. His implied threat of moving back to Mestre may even have backfired. The thought of the Jewish pawnbrokers moving out of the city, still holding on to the household objects and clothing that the Venetians had given them as collateral for their loans, may have strengthened the government's resolve to keep them close at hand. Albeit out of sight.

Two days later an edict was proclaimed at the Rialto advising the Jews of Venice that they had ten days in which to relocate to the *Ghetto Nuovo*. After some procrastination the ten days turned into three months, but by the end of July all the Jews, including the two del Banco brothers, Anselmo and Vita, were living with their families in the ghetto. Every Christian who had previously lived there had moved out.

As Dolfin had suggested, the government furnished the ghetto with two gates, which were closed from dusk to dawn. They hired four Christian sentries to make sure nobody sneaked in or out. The sentries were ordered to live at the gates, away from their families. The responsibility of keeping the Jews confined was so great that the Senate could not brook the possibility of the sentries being distracted by family matters.

The Collegio made the Jews pay the sentries' wages and for additional security they engaged two boats to patrol the canals surrounding the ghetto. Dolfin's idea for a drawbridge was not taken up, and although the two high walls were planned, they were never built. But every canal-side building had the doors to its landing jetty sealed, and its loading bays shut up. For most of the ghetto's history its residents and the city authorities conducted an ongoing battle whereby the Jews managed to reopen the doors to the canal, allowing them to leave by boat at night. Then the city workmen would come by and seal them up again. Eventually, many years later, the city authorities gave up trying.

The only Jews allowed to pass through the gates at night were doctors, and even they were only permitted to leave for a good reason. The Venetians may have felt it necessary to confine the Jews, but they weren't prepared to risk their own health in doing so.

Venice was not the first city to confine its Jews to one area; that honour had gone to Prague about 250 years earlier. But Venice gave the world the name 'ghetto'.

COINCIDENCE AND CONVERSION

When we read of the wealthy banker Anselmo del Banco, who was unafraid to stand up to the powerful Venetian government and whose economic utility seems to have earned him their grudging respect, we might consider whether he, or someone like him, was Shakespeare's real-life model for Shylock, the Jewish moneylender in *The Merchant of Venice*.

It is unlikely that Shakespeare had heard of Anselmo specifically. For all his prominence in Venice, Anselmo del Banco was little more than a local personality, his name and fame are unlikely to have carried abroad. The only reason that we know about him is because the Venetians were remarkable record-keepers. The Venetian State Archive, one of the most comprehensive and valuable collections of historical records in the world, dates back to 1030. It cites Anselmo as being responsible for collecting the taxes payable by the Jewish community. Marin Sanudo, another valuable historical source, wrote about him in his extensive diary. So did Eliyahu Capsali. None of these resources would have been as freely available in Shakespeare's day as they are in ours and we can be pretty sure he didn't have access to any of them.

Shakespeare read voraciously and picked up stories wherever he went. He may not have been able to place himself into the mind of a Venetian Jew, but he is likely to have heard anecdotes. This may explain a couple of similarities between events in Anselmo's life and the portrayal of Shylock in *The Merchant of Venice*. Both similarities concern their children: Shylock's daughter Jessica and Anselmo's son Jacob.

In *The Merchant of Venice*, when Jessica eloped with Lorenzo she stole a casket of jewels from her father. Among the jewels was a diamond which, Shylock declared in great distress, had cost him 2,000 ducats. In the real world, Jacob Meshullam was twice accused of stealing jewels. The first time he was said to have made off with a sapphire that had been deposited in his father's bank. Jacob denied the charge, claiming that he had won it from a nobleman at a game of cards. The second occasion was when he was convicted of stealing a diamond belonging to the Count Palatine of Krakow. The court sentenced him to be blinded, but he managed to avoid the punishment, by paying the sum of 2,000 ducats as a fine for stealing the diamond.

That Shylock's daughter and Anselmo's son both stole diamonds estimated at 2,000 ducats can easily be dismissed as coincidence. Less of a coincidence, but not necessarily any more indicative of a connection between the two, is that both Jacob and Jessica converted to Christianity.

Conversion to Christianity had been a concern in Jewish life for centuries. Not just forcible conversion at the point of the sword, as was notoriously threatened in Rhineland Jewish communities during the Crusades, nor as happened in fifteenth-century Spain and Portugal, as the only way to avoid persecution. Such conversions were common enough. Yet untold numbers of Jews during the medieval and early modern periods converted to Christianity voluntarily.

Some did so out of penury, a few of the more *chutzpadik* ones apparently putting themselves forward for baptism regularly, in different places, so as to scrape together a few coins each time from missionary funds. Others converted to rid themselves of the stigma of being a Jew, the social leprosy of being an outcast in a Christian world. Of course, there would have been some who did convert for genuine religious reasons. But the most common cause of conversion was for social advancement, to marry into a Christian family, to follow a trade, or to accept a position forbidden to Jews.

This seems to have been Anselmo's son Jacob Meshullam's motivation after his scrapes with the law. He was baptized along with his own son Salamon at the Festival of the Madonna on 15 July 1533. His entry into the upper echelons of Venetian society and no doubt his personal sense of vindication was complete when the Doge created him a *Cavaliere di San Marco*, a member of the order of the Knights of St Mark. He took the name Marco Paradiso.

Marin Sanudo was outraged when the Doge honoured Jacob Meshullam in this way. He declared that it was without precedent. Five years earlier, when another of Jacob's sons had been baptized in a lavish ceremony, surrounded by bishops and ambassadors and with a wind ensemble playing, Sanudo had reported on the event with glee. He must have imagined such a sumptuous ceremony breaking the hearts of his father and grandfather. To witness Jacob not only accepting the fact of his son's conversion but following in his footsteps, while being treated with such distinction, clearly caused Sanudo quite some discomfort.

Jessica's willing conversion in *The Merchant of Venice*, her statement that 'I shall be saved by my husband; he hath made me a Christian', would not have been considered remarkable in Shakespeare's England. The religious environment in the country was chaotic. Henry VIII's Protestant Reformation had caused havoc among the faithful and destabilized the beliefs of the masses. His son Edward VI made matters worse by accelerating the pace of reforms. Then everything went haywire when the next monarch, Queen Mary, attempted to reverse the changes and re-introduce Catholicism. Five years later when Queen Elizabeth ascended to the throne she proscribed Catholicism once more and reinstated Protestantism.

The religious chaos and the confusion in the minds of ordinary people paved the way for a new brand of preacher, visionary millenarians who proclaimed the imminent return of Christ and a forthcoming utopian age. Christ would return, they said, once the Jews had all converted to Christianity, as had been foretold in the books of Revelation and Daniel and promised by St Paul in Romans.

One could ask why the conversion of Jews mattered so much to these preachers; and indeed why Shakespeare saw fit to include Jessica's conversion in *The Merchant of Venice*. James Shapiro, in his scholarly book *Shakespeare and the Jews* offers two interconnected reasons. The first stems from the identity crisis experienced by many English Christians in the wake of the Reformation. The succession of religious upheavals that the country went through in the space of a decade had left many people uncertain of what made a Protestant different from a Catholic and indeed what the fundamental beliefs of Christianity were. There was no better way to persuade unsettled minds of the promise held by Christianity than to assure them that the conversion of the Jews was about to begin. As Jews began to recognize the correctness of Christianity, to accept its teachings, any uncertainties harboured in Christian minds would vanish.

The second reason why the conversion of the Jews mattered in Shakespearean England stems from the period's fascination with the accusation that Jews ritually murdered Christian children, a charge rooted deep in early Christianity but one with a particularly English origin.

There had been tensions between Christians and Jews since the earliest days of Christianity. It was inevitable. Christianity saw itself as having superseded Judaism, certain that the old covenant between God and the Jews had been replaced by a new covenant through Christ. Indeed, this had been predicted, they argued, by the prophet Jeremiah. He had declared that because of their unfaithfulness God had rejected the covenant that he had made with the ancestors of the Jews, in favour of a new covenant that he would make in days to come.[6] Those days had arrived with the advent of Jesus, anyone thereafter who held firm to the old Jewish ways was in error. The charge that the Jews were obdurate was given extra heft when Christianity was adopted as the official religion of the Roman Empire. It proved, said Christian preachers, that the Jewish faith was stubborn and rebellious, refusing to accept the truth.

The most damning charge that the early Church laid against the Jews was the accusation that they had killed Christ. It cast the Jews into a satanic role, and sparked off a series of fantasies, each more bizarre than the one before. Conforming to the archetype we discussed earlier of the outsider as monster, it was whispered among the fearful that Jews had horns and tails, that they poisoned wells, were responsible for the Black Death and, most enduringly of all, that they murdered Christian children at Easter to use their blood to make unleavened bread for Passover. When, on Easter Saturday in 1144, a Christian child was found stabbed to death in the woods of Norwich, the Jews were blamed for his murder.

The Benedictine monk, Thomas of Monmouth fantasized a biography of the murdered boy's life, proclaiming him a martyr and attributing miraculous powers to him:

> The Jews of Norwich bought a Christian child before Easter and tortured him with all the torture that our Lord was tortured with and on Good Friday hanged him on a cross on account of our Lord and then buried him. They expected it would be concealed, but our Lord made it plain that he was a holy martyr, and the monks took him and buried him with ceremony in the monastery, and through our Lord he works wonderful and varied miracles, and he is called St William.[7]

William of Norwich's death is the earliest documented case of what became known as the blood libel. It proved to be a hugely influential way of accounting for unexplained deaths, particularly around Easter time. William of Norwich's alleged martyrdom was followed by that of Harold of Gloucester in 1168, Robert of Bury St Edmunds in 1181, and unknown children in Bristol in 1183 and Winchester in 1192. The first accusations of ritual child murder all originated in England; it was a particularly English manifestation of antisemitism.

These charges of ritual murder had been laid four centuries before Shakespeare wrote, but they had continued to circulate in folk memory, in written chronicles and church art. A painting in a church in Norwich, which survived the wholesale destruction of religious imagery during the Reformation, shows William of Norwich stretched out on two wooden uprights, surrounded by Jews who are drawing off his blood. The painting probably dates from the early fifteenth century, long after the blood libel calumnies started to circulate.[8]

The conversion of the Jews hastening the return of Christ was a hot topic in Elizabethan England. With their conversion the terrible crimes that Jews were accused of would come to an end. Nevertheless, the obsession with Jews and the weight given in England to their impending conversion does seem odd, since officially there were no Jews in England at the time. They had been expelled by Edward I in 1290 and would not be allowed to return until 1656.

But Jews can't be shunted out of sight so easily. James Shapiro estimates that there may have been around 200 Jews in England in the Elizabethan period. Perhaps the most famous, certainly the most notorious, was Roderigo Lopez, Queen Elizabeth's physician. He was executed in 1594 after being accused of trying to poison her. Lopez had been baptized, but one of the anomalies of the time was that while baptism admitted Jews into Christianity, in the public mind (and indeed in Jewish law) converts were still regarded as Jews. The sixteenth-century poet Gabriel Harvey described Lopez as 'descended from Jews but is himself a Christian and from Portugal'. Francis Bacon wrote that Lopez was suspected of secretly being a Jew, while the calumnious *Leicester's Commonwealth*, written to denigrate the Queen's friend Robert Dudley, Earl of Leicester, had no compunction about reviling 'Lopez the Jew . . . for the art of destroying children in women's bellies'.[9] In a world where baptism scarcely seems to have washed away the scourge of being Jewish, the fact that the English queen could employ Lopez shows just how lightly the ban against Jews in England was applied in practice.

Around 25 years before Shakespeare wrote *The Merchant of Venice* a ceremony was held in London to convert the Jewish Yehuda Menda to Christianity. It was a high-profile event and John Foxe, author of the *Book of Martyrs* and one of the most influential churchmen of the age, preached a sermon at the ceremony. He had his conversionary sermon translated into Latin so that it could be disseminated in Europe.

Following his baptism, Menda, who was now christened Nathanael, went to live in the Domus Conversorum, the House of Converts, in Chancery Lane. He was likely to have been one of several former Jews living there; the House of Converts was established by Henry III in 1232 and had been in use ever since. Shakespeare lived nearby; it is more than likely that he would have encountered Jews or former Jews, even if not socially, then at least in the street.

Having Jessica convert to Christianity would have endeared her to Shakespeare's audiences. Shylock's conversion, hinted at in Act 4, may have made them think more kindly on him too. But the coincidence of their conversions with that of Jacob Meshullam tells us no more about whether Shylock was modelled on Anselmo del Banco than does the coincidence of Jacob and Jessica each stealing diamonds worth 2,000 ducats. The correspondences do not give us enough to prove that Shakespeare modelled Shylock on Anselmo. Nevertheless, the possibility exists. Shakespeare was known to be a literary magpie, he gathered ideas constantly and wrote them into his plays. He might have heard about Anselmo from a traveller or in the ale house. Scholars believe that *The Merchant of Venice* relied on several different sources which were woven together. Maybe the story of Anselmo del Banco was one. Perhaps he was one of the role models for Shylock, after all.

MOVING TO THE GHETTO

We can only imagine how it felt for Jewish families as they packed up their lives and moved into the ghetto. It had been barely seven years since their last upheaval, when they had been forced by war to flee from their homes on the *terraferma* into Venice. On their arrival they had at first enjoyed an unprecedented freedom of movement. Preachers may have railed at them in sermons and they were obliged to wear the humiliating yellow hats demanded by Venetian law, but they were at liberty to move around the city more or less at will. Provided of course that they did not offend Christian sensibilities in doing so.

Seven years is enough time to become settled in a new life, it is rarely enough to make a further change; particularly when that change is enforced and results in dislocation from the heart of a vibrant city to its watery margins.

Seeing the ghetto for the first time was unlikely to have lifted their spirits. Four rows of houses, built in a square around a large, enclosed space or *campo*, 'a field surrounded by buildings',[10] in the words of one Venetian writer, made it feel more like a fortress than a city space. The narrow brick houses were too few to accommodate everyone comfortably. Although the Jews of Venice at the time numbered only a few hundred, the population density of the ghetto was at least twice that of the rest of the city. Several Jewish families left Venice and its new ghetto during that first summer, either hoping to return to their former homes on the *terraferma* or try their luck elsewhere. Their departure made little difference to the overcrowding.

Almost as soon as they moved in, families started to divide and subdivide their tiny apartments to give themselves as much privacy as possible. They used timber partitions rather than brick, so as to minimize the load on the uncertain watery subsoil. In time, unable to extend their properties outwards due to lack of space they would build upwards, into towering, tottering terraces seven or eight storeys high. But for now, squeezing as many people as they could into the available accommodation had to suffice. The overcrowding was such that the increase in rents collected by the landlords far exceeded the one-third that the Senate had permitted; the number of additional units that had been created by subdividing houses and rooms brought the landlords a rental income significantly higher than they had originally anticipated.

The overcrowding made living conditions even more unsanitary than the poor quality of the housing alone could account for. Small apartments accommodated ten or more people, many dwellings had no latrines or fireplaces. The *campo* itself was unpaved; there was mud, dirt and excrement everywhere, the stench was described as unbearable. The owners admitted that should the Jews leave the ghetto the properties would be worth very little; Christians would need to spend a fortune to live comfortably there.[11]

The ghetto was a place of work as well as a prison town. Pawnshops and second-hand stores occupied the bottom storeys of the houses, open fronted they looked out onto the square. Butchers, a baker and a tavern managed to squeeze in, as did spaces for prayer, despite the prohibition on building a synagogue. The landlords, who were doing far better out of the ghetto than the inhabitants themselves, let out some of the ground-floor units that should have been set aside for shops to the very poor, to those who could not afford to rent the so-called residential space above.

Dark, quiet and confined during the night, the ghetto came to life in the mornings, when the bells of St Mark's Basilica rang and the gates were opened. The path between the ghetto and the city turned into a bustling thoroughfare, with Jews going out and Christians coming in to pawn or redeem items, negotiate with moneylenders, or buy *strazzaria*, a word which means rags but came to encompass a wide range of second-hand goods, clothing and furniture. The trade in *strazzaria* thrived in the pre-industrial age when everything was made by hand and few people could afford new goods. Everyone, other than the most wealthy, bought used goods and in Venice it was the second-hand merchants in the ghetto who allied with the pawnbrokers to dominate the trade. Furniture might be sold and resold until it was no longer usable, clothes were recycled until they literally were rags, hence the name *strazzaria*.

The Jews organized their life in the ghetto as best they could. When the weather was right the *campo* functioned as a community centre, it was the only place where space was not at a premium. Schoolteachers held classes, the judges of the Jewish court would adjudicate in disputes, barbers gave haircuts, pedlars hawked their goods, a busker might play hoping to earn enough for a meal, beggars were ubiquitous. Despite the restrictions on the jobs they were officially permitted to work at, stall holders in the ghetto square provided most of the necessities a family might need for their daily life. There were fruit and vegetable stalls, wine, cheese and pasta merchants, a tailor, a hatter, even a bookshop. It could have been idyllic. If only the ghetto hadn't been so crowded, full of desperate people trying to make the best of a life they hadn't chosen.

Throughout their history Jews have learned to adapt to restrictions imposed upon them by others. The Venice Ghetto was no different, its residents soon began to settle into a new pattern of life. It lasted just three years. Then all the old political problems started up again.

In 1519 the *Condotta*, the residency licence negotiated by Anselmo del Banco six years earlier, expired. The question of whether there should be a Jewish presence on the island became a hot topic once more. The war against the League of Cambrai was over, Venice had regained her mainland territories, the arguments for sending the Jews out of the city and back to their original homes seemed compelling.

Anticipating an exodus of the Jews, the government issued an order closing their second-hand shops. The stores had always been contentious with Christian second-hand dealers complaining that the Jews were muscling in on their trade. Reluctantly accepting the decree, Anselmo del Banco and his banking colleague Abram di Friceli gave notice that they would close their banks within six months, giving their clients time to repay their loans and redeem their pledges. For the best part of a year the Senate debated the merits and disadvantages of expelling the Jewish community. In the ghetto the Jews went about their lives in a state of anxiety and uncertainty.

The discussion in the Senate was dominated by fear of divine displeasure. One speaker argued that they risked God's wrath by keeping the Jews in Venice. The proof of this, another senator declared, was that the kingdom of Naples had fallen because they welcomed Jewish refugees from Spain and that Ludovico Sforza, Duke of Milan, was expelled from his territory because he favoured Jews. Both claims were nonsense; the fall of Naples had nothing to do with the welcome they extended to Jews, and Ludovico Sforza had been expelled by the French king Louis XII, who claimed that the Duchy of Milan was his. The Venetian Republic had allied with Louis to drive out Sforza, gaining Cremona as the price for their support.

Warming to the theme, another senator argued that expelling the Jews would not only avoid divine wrath, it would actually invite heavenly favour. He reminded the Senate that after the King of Portugal threw out his Jewish subjects he was divinely rewarded by Vasco da Gama's discovery of a sea route around the Cape of Good Hope to India. On the contrary, declared another, God wanted the Jews to stay. He pointed out that when the Jews left Spain they brought great benefit to those countries who took them in. Indeed, he said, after Sultan Selim allowed the Jews to settle in Constantinople, he conquered Syria and Egypt. If the debate proved anything at all it was that the rulers of Venice were no closer to understanding the mind of God than any other government, anywhere in the world, before or since.

Divided on what God might think, the Senate turned to the practical consequences of expelling or retaining the Jews. Many Italian cities had overcome their reliance on Jewish moneylenders by establishing Monti di Pietà, charitable institutions that loaned money to the poor, subject to stringent moral criteria. The money they lent came from deposits made by those who were not concerned about earning interest on their funds, as they were prepared to wait for the afterlife to receive their reward. Although the question of establishing a Monte di Pietà in Venice had often been raised, the idea had never come to fruition. Since Christians were prohibited from lending money to each other on interest (though many did), Jewish moneylenders and bankers were essential for the welfare of the poor and the smooth running of the economy. In the absence of a Monte di Pietà it seemed expedient to allow the Jewish pawnbroking moneylenders to stay.

At the end of the debate, the proposal to renew the licence for Jews to lend money was put to a vote. It was defeated by the narrow margin of 66 votes to 64. The ghetto was indeed to be closed and its Jewish population sent away.

Or so it seemed. The debate over the future of the Jews took place in November 1519. Four months later the Senate discussed the finances of the Republic's Arsenal. Several ships were in the process of construction, but funding for them had run out and unless the government stepped in they would never be finished. It was suggested that an emergency property tax be imposed on the landed nobility, but that didn't go down well with the many senators who owned property themselves. Then it was suggested that the required funds be raised from the Jews. Rather than expelling them, their *condotto* could be renewed and the rate increased, to 10,000 ducats per year instead of the present sum of 6,500. When the proposal was put to the vote it was passed by 93 votes to 65, a substantial majority in favour of revoking the previous decision to expel the Jews.

As ever the Senate's offer for renewal of the licence came with conditions. The rate of interest that Jews were allowed to charge was fixed at 15 per cent. The figure sounds high to us, but it was significantly lower than the 60–80 per cent that had been charged by Christians in Brescia a century earlier (presumably to compensate them for committing a mortal sin) and the 20–25 per cent charged by Jewish moneylenders in Padua. The Senate also forbade the moneylenders of the ghetto from lending against a written promise to pay without putting up a pledge. If a Christian wanted to borrow against an IOU they would have to go to a moneylender in Mestre and pay a rate of 20 per cent. If they chose to borrow in the ghetto, debtors were obliged by the Senate to deposit objects as collateral against the loans they were receiving.

The one positive concession that the Senate made was that they allowed the reopening of the second-hand shops. The extra charge which the Jewish community had previously paid to operate these stores was waived; it was now included in the 10,000-ducat licence fee.[12]

The ghetto was saved. But the perilousness of Jewish life in the city remained. The new charter would come up for renewal once again, in just three years.

Neither the Venetian government nor the Jewish leadership had foreseen it, but the fact that the ghetto was a separate, geographically defined Jewish space radically reshaped the way Jews thought about themselves and their relationship with their Christian neighbours. They were constrained and their lives closely regulated, but they had a greater degree of autonomy and self-governance than they could possibly have had if they were living cheek by jowl with the Venetian citizenry. Counter-intuitively, confining the Jews to their own area, setting them apart from their Christian neighbours yet able to engage and trade with them, at least during daylight hours, opened up new opportunities for cultural interaction between Christians and Jews. Each group recognized the other as a distinct religious, cultural and ethnic entity, not just as inconvenient strangers who they were forced to mingle with in the street.

Physically the ghetto was a miserable place, unsanitary and crowded. But despite, or perhaps because of the hardships, it slowly began to flourish intellectually and creatively. The Venice Ghetto was on its way to becoming the centre of European Jewish civilization during the late Renaissance; the Hebrew equivalent of Florence in terms of its cultural significance. It is often said that the roots of the Jewish enlightenment lay in mid-eighteenth-century Berlin. Arguably they lay in Venice 250 years earlier. Had the Jews of the Serenissima not been corralled into a ghetto, the stirrings of the Jewish enlightenment in Venice would never have occurred.

3

Crossing Boundaries

With the exception of the del Banco family the first inhabitants of the ghetto appear to have been an unremarkable lot. They got on with their lives quietly, accepting their status as outsiders and refraining from anything that might undermine their precarious security.

Beyond its watery boundaries, however, the Venice Ghetto was beginning to attract interest. There was something magnetic about a self-contained community of Jews living in their own space, where ideas could be discussed freely without too much in the way of outside interference, in one of Europe's most powerful and prosperous states.

For Jewish intellectuals, Venice held a further attraction. The city was growing into a renowned centre of printing and the Belgian printer Daniel Bomberg had recently obtained an exclusive, ten-year licence from the Venetian government to print Hebrew books. At around the same time as the Jews of Venice were moving into the ghetto, Bomberg and Friar Felice da Prato, a converted Jew, the son of a rabbi, were working on their first landmark Hebrew publication. It was the first Hebrew Bible with the major medieval rabbinic commentaries on the same page as the biblical text. Bomberg's layout, and da Prato's selection of commentaries, was a radical departure from the way the Hebrew Bible had been

presented before. It led to a new method of Hebrew Bible study
that is still in vogue today.

Bomberg was not a Jew, but the presence of his printshop in
Venice helped transform the ghetto from a rather miserable colony
of small-time, Jewish second-hand dealers and pawnbrokers into a
vibrant intellectual hub. A lodestone for scholars and intellectuals
that became the centre of Jewish scholarship in late Renaissance
Europe. Technically and commercially, Bomberg was the printer,
but it was the succession of scholarly Jews he employed in his
printshop which brought to fruition the 250 or more Hebrew titles
he produced in his thirty-year career.[1]

Bomberg could not have succeeded as a printer of Hebrew
books had Felice da Prato not worked alongside him, had he not
drawn his attention to the different sensitivities of Jewish and
Christian readers of the Bible. It was their printing of Psalm 22
that flagged the issue for the two men. Christians, who see the
psalm as foreshadowing the Crucifixion, read verse 17 as 'they have
pierced my hands and my feet', a clear allusion to the Cross. Jewish
tradition reads the same phrase differently, as '(they have mauled)
like a lion my hands and feet'. The difference in readings hinges
on the printing of one Hebrew vowel. It is apparently a minor
variation but it is one which, if presented incorrectly to the wrong
audience, would have stopped them from buying the book.[2]

Da Prato's advice helped the entrepreneurial Bomberg to develop
a keen eye for the market. He printed a Hebrew grammar by
Abraham de Balmes in two versions; one with a Latin translation
for his Christian readers, the other in Hebrew alone for Jewish
customers. He did something similar with a grammar written by
the twelfth-century Provençal scholar David Kimhi. On the title
page of the version aimed at Christians he printed the date as '1544
since our redemption', but he used the Hebrew year of 5305 in the
version intended for Jews.

Da Prato showed Bomberg how to make his books acceptable
to a Jewish readership, but he was a problem himself. His
conversion to Christianity meant that Jewish readers would
always be somewhat suspicious of the texts he produced, fearing

he may have doctored them in some way to support Christian beliefs. In 1518 Bomberg decided it was time that he and da Prato parted ways. In his place he brought in two Jewish scholars from the newly established ghetto; Cornelius Adelkind, who took over as Bomberg's master printer, and Rabbi Hiyya Meir ben David. Adelkind had worked with Bomberg off and on since the printshop was first established, and apart for a few periods when he worked with other printers, he would stay there until Bomberg retired from printing. He was such a fan of Bomberg that he added the name of the printer's father, Cornelius, to his own given name of Israel Adelkind.

Adelkind's colleague, Hiyya Meir ben David, was a scholar of Jewish law, one of the three judges who presided over the Jewish court in the ghetto. His role in the printshop was to examine and correct Hebrew texts, both in manuscript before they were printed and again afterwards, when they came off the presses. He worked on Bomberg's seminal and much-admired 1520 edition of the Talmud, checking and correcting the million-word text. Only fourteen copies of Bomberg's and Hiyya Meir ben David's Talmud still survive; immaculately laid out and beautifully designed, they epitomize the art of Hebrew printing in Renaissance Venice. It seems self-evident to us but Bomberg was the first printer to include page numbers in his volumes of the Talmud. The edition that he produced is instantly recognizable to anyone with even the sketchiest knowledge of the Talmud, because it became the template for nearly all future printings of the work, everywhere in the world. Nearly every copy printed today uses the same page layout and numbering that Bomberg instituted in 1520. It makes cross-referencing between editions extremely easy.

Adelkind and Hiyya Meir ben David were Bomberg's principal Hebrew scholars, but he brought in others, all 'well-educated' Jews from the ghetto, to cut type, lay out pages, revise copy, and check the authenticity of manuscripts. He started with just four ghetto Jews alongside Adelkind and ben David; the number grew steadily as demand for his output increased and more scholars brought him their works to print.

Bomberg treated his Jewish staff well, asking the authorities to allow them to wear black caps in the street, rather than the obligatory yellow variety. He was a businessman from a wealthy Belgian family, and his concern for the welfare of his staff may have been as much for commercial reasons as anything else. But it wasn't his only display of concern for Jews. We will see that he played a critical role in the charitable networks that helped smuggle forcibly converted Portuguese Jews away from the clutches of the Inquisition. He led the way too in showing how Jews and Christians could coexist in the workplace, the atmosphere in his printshop being one of ecumenical harmony. The religious identities which so divided Christians and Jews elsewhere vanished in the pursuit of learning and scholarship.

The presence in Venice of Bomberg's printshop drew a steady stream of Jewish scholars into the ghetto from afar. They brought him their monographs for printing or sought patronage from Christian Hebrew scholars to underwrite the production of classic Hebrew texts that until then had only existed in manuscript. At least 14 books have survived which indicate on their title pages or in their colophons that they were printed by Bomberg from manuscripts brought to him by Jews from around the world. Congregations in Syria and the Crimea sent emissaries asking him to print their prayer books. But whoever they were and from wherever they came, all visiting Jews were obliged to lodge in the ghetto during their sojourn. They could leave the ghetto during the day to visit Bomberg's printing press, but when night fell they had to return to the ghetto.[3]

A MAN OF MANY TONGUES

Among those visiting Bomberg's press was a man approaching middle age. He was returning to Venice after spending ten years as a scholar in the home of the renowned Cardinal Egidio da Viterbo, a seemingly extraordinary amount of time for a Jewish wanderer and a senior Christian cleric to live together. The middle-aged man was named Elia Levita, though he was known to his Yiddish-speaking companions as Elye Bokher. The Yiddish name means Elijah the youth or Elijah the bachelor, though he was neither young nor a bachelor when he returned to Venice.

Elia Levita was born near Nuremberg in Germany around 1469. He travelled to Italy in his early twenties, living in the university town of Padua where he worked as a copyist and teacher. Unusually for an early sixteenth-century Jew, he was also working on a novel, though not a novel in our sense of the word. The book, *Bovo d'Antona* or, as it was called in later editions, *Bovo-Bukh*, is a reworking in Yiddish of a well-known Italian chivalric poem, a courtly romance about the legendary Buovo of Antona. In the English version of the same story he is known as Bevis of Hampton.

The story is simple. As a child Bovo had run away from his wicked mother who had killed his father and was trying to murder him. He escaped to a faraway kingdom where he found employment in the service of the king. He fell in love with the king's daughter, Princess Drusiana, and she with him, but despite performing many mighty deeds to save the kingdom from its enemies he was wrested away from his beloved and forced to flee again. Like all good knightly stories he had many adventures and mishaps, but in the end he was reunited with the princess, and they lived happily ever after.

It is not an original tale, but the story's enduring appeal and the fact that it is one of the earliest popular literary works in Yiddish made *Bovo d'Antona* a classic among its Jewish readers.

It used to be thought that the 'Old Yiddish' in which *Bovo d'Antona* was written was nothing more than a Hebrew–German patois, a folk language spoken by small groups of Jews in Germany, long before the language became established as the mother tongue of Ashkenazi Jews. Recent research, however, has shown that as early as the end of the fourteenth century, Yiddish was already established as a language with a literary tradition. The Tedeschi, the Jews of German background who were the first to be corralled into the ghetto, most probably spoke Yiddish as their first language. It remained their native language until the beginning of the seventeenth century, by which time Italian had taken over as the principal ghetto tongue.[4]

Bovo d'Antona was reprinted over and again during the following centuries. Like the King Arthur legends, other writers expanded and developed it, incorporating new characters and adventures. An English translation was published in 2003 and a critical edition with commentary in 2015.

Elia Levita wrote other Yiddish works, few of which have survived. Some, like *Paris un'Wien*, need further research before they can be definitively credited to him. Nobody has managed to compile a definitive bibliography of his writing because there is a scholarly tendency to declare Elia Levita the author of books that were probably not his at all. Claudia Rosenzweig, who published the recent critical edition of *Bovo d'Antona*, wrote that 'it is a commonplace that, whenever an important Yiddish work from Italy has no stated author, it is attributed to Elye Bokher'.[5]

Like Leone Ebreo, Elia Levita was one of those Renaissance Jews who were inquisitive enough to step outside their native culture, crossing boundaries to share ideas with the Christians among whom they lived. Jews in Muslim countries had long been doing so; Don Isaac Abarbanel was an heir to a shared Jewish–Islamic tradition which stretched back for centuries. But Jews in Christian Europe had to wait until the early modern period for a similar process to begin.

Despite what is likely to have been a considerable literary output, Elia Levita's reputation does not rest on the Italian legends that he rewrote for Yiddish readers, nor indeed on his skills as a secular storyteller. In the same year that he published *Bovo d'Antona* he wrote a commentary on a twelfth-century book of Hebrew grammar. Grammar would become the field in which he made his name. And where he would experience a not-inconsiderable amount of aggravation.

In 1509, as the forces of the League of Cambrai approached Padua, Levita fled into Venice along with all the other Jews in the town. We don't know how long he stayed for, certainly no more than seven years because the next time we hear about him is in 1516 when he and his family were living in Rome with Cardinal da Viterbo. He may well have been one of those who, as Anselmo del

Banco had predicted, left the city when the ghetto was established. Levita returned to Venice, and the ghetto, after he left the Cardinal's employ.

Cardinal Egidio (or Giles) da Viterbo was the Prior General of the Augustinian order and one of the most popular preachers in Italy. His reputation was such that Pope Julius II reserved the right to decide where he would preach. A deeply learned man, with one of the largest and most comprehensive libraries in Europe, the Cardinal was one of a small circle of scholars known today as Christian Hebraists. Based predominantly in Italy and Germany, Christian Hebraists recognized that an understanding of Hebrew and its sister language Aramaic would offer them greater insights into the origins and beliefs of Christianity. They took a particular interest in the translations of the Bible into the Aramaic language that Jesus spoke, and in the Kabbalah, the mystical tradition of Judaism. A reforming theologian, Cardinal Egidio was of the opinion that an understanding of Kabbalah would lead to a renewal of the Catholic Church and to a transformation of human history. He scoured the world for kabbalistic manuscripts, even importing a copy of the Zohar, the principal text of Kabbalah, from Damascus. He engaged Elia Levita to help him source Hebrew documents and translate them into Latin for him. Levita enthusiastically wrote that the Cardinal spent 'an enormous amount of money' on Hebrew books, 'and his hand is still stretched out to spend it until he is possessed of all the books which we have'.[6]

Levita had written his first book on Hebrew grammar while in Padua, but it was during the time that he lived with Cardinal da Viterbo that his reputation as a Hebrew grammarian started to flourish. Grammar may not be a field that we consider to be particularly academic; for most of us it is little more than a system of rules that determine how a language is constructed. But the development of those rules has a long history, particularly so when it comes to Judaism and the language of the Bible.

In common with Arabic and other Semitic languages, literary Hebrew is written without vowels. The spoken language has vowels but they are not written down.[7] To pronounce a word correctly the reader has to know which vowels go where, because they change depending on the conjugation of a verb or a particular part of speech. The same happens occasionally in English; 'I sit' and 'I speak' are present tense, 'I sat' and 'I spoke' are past. The consonants are the same, the vowels have changed.

It is the vowels that help determine the meaning of a Hebrew word.[8] Getting them right is critically important in understanding the intended sense of the Bible text. As is knowing which syllables to stress in a word because meanings can change depending upon pronunciation. During the seventh and eighth centuries teams of scholars worked tirelessly at producing an immaculate version of the Hebrew Bible where everything was spelt correctly, punctuation was accurately applied, and words were pronounced properly.

Classical Hebrew grammar and philology became a much-studied science in the medieval and early modern periods. Inspired by Arabic grammarians, who delighted in extolling the perfection of their language through beautifully written poetry and clearly defined grammatical rules, Jewish scholars progressed from the study of the Bible text to the production of a formalized Hebrew that could be used in liturgy, verse and prose. Studying their works and becoming acquainted with verb and sentence structure led those Christian scholars who studied Hebrew to realize that the Latin Bible they used did not always translate the original text accurately. The Vulgate, the fourth-century standard Latin text principally composed by Saint Jerome, was full of errors. The Christian scholars, the Hebraists of whom the Cardinal was one, aspired to recover the original meaning of the text. To do this meant not only learning the Hebrew language and its grammar, but also studying the works of the medieval Jewish Bible interpreters, people like Rashi, David Kimhi and Abraham Ibn Ezra, who had devoted their lives to the explication of the text.

Christian Hebraists often engaged Jews, or converts from Judaism, as their teachers. They looked to them for instruction both in grammar and in understanding the more esoteric aspects of Kabbalah. But in Elia Levita's case, although the Cardinal paid him a wage and provided him with food and accommodation, the two men shared a reciprocal intellectual relationship. Levita taught the Cardinal Hebrew and Aramaic, the Cardinal instructed him in Latin and Greek.

In the introduction to his most important work, *Masoret Hamasoret*, Levita told his readers that he was criticized for his relationship with the Cardinal. The Talmud frowned on the teaching of Torah to non-Jews and although many rabbis dismissed the prohibition, arguing that it only applied to teaching idolaters, some adhered to it heartily. We don't know the specifics of the attacks on Levita but he felt obliged to justify his actions:

> I swear by my creator that one Christian man encouraged me and brought me thus far, by being my student for ten years continually. I stayed in his house and studied with him, for which a great cry was raised against me . . . I fully acknowledge, as one acknowledges before a solemn court, that I have taught non-Jews . . . But Heaven forfend that I am evil; I am innocent without sin because the sages only forbid transmitting the esoteric secrets of the Torah, they do not say one should not teach it.[9]

Anyway, Levita stressed, he had no alternative to teaching Hebrew to Christians. His flight from Padua had reduced him to penury, he couldn't afford not to work:

> What am I? A low and subjugated man trapped in the snares of my iniquity, burdened with sons and daughters, with nothing in my possession . . . not a penny was left to me. There were no clothes for the cold and in my home there was no bread and no wood . . . What can a man touched by all these things do?[10]

He did confess, though, that there was some substance to the criticisms that had been levelled at him. Spending so long in proximity to the Cardinal had helped him to appreciate the appeal of Christianity. Running together quotes from Proverbs and Psalms he said, 'I opened my mouth and I ate "good knowledge and taste; the comb of honey, pleasant words", which dripped from their lips, drop by drop.'[11] He made no apology, or at least not much of one. He had only sampled some of the ideas of Christianity, he hadn't accepted its creed: 'I ate the centre and I threw away the shell. I did not eat the tasteless egg white. If I tasted a little of this honey, should I die?'[12]

It could not have been easy for Levita as a Jew in the Cardinal's palace. Whatever their personal relationship, which we can assume from Levita's writings was fairly good, he was under continual pressure, not just from the rabbis who wanted him to cease his activities but also from Christian clerics pressurizing him to convert. He seems to have enjoyed Christian teachings, tasting from the honeycomb as he expressed it, even if he was not persuaded into the faith. This must have led those Christians with whom he conversed to encourage him to be baptized, just as many other Jewish teachers of Hebrew to Christians had done. He doesn't seem to have been a particularly religious man, and it has been suggested that because his scholarship shows a lack of interest in matters of faith it was easier for him to avoid the pressure from both sides.[13]

Levita wrote several works of Hebrew grammar while living with the Cardinal. He dedicated the first to Egidio noting in the introduction that in 1517 the Cardinal had asked him to write a book that would improve on the many inadequate Hebrew grammars that he had read. A year later he delivered another treatise to the Cardinal, which, in the spirit of the age, he had deliberately structured with a quasi-cosmic elegance. He divided the book into four parts, corresponding to the seasons, and subdivided each part into thirteen sections, symbolizing the traditional attributes of God in Judaic thought. The total of 52 segments equalled the number of weeks in the year and the numerical value of his own Hebrew name, Elijah.

When not working on his books, Levita published pamphlets containing paradigms of verb forms and different parts of speech. Eventually he amalgamated his pamphlets into another book that was published in 1520. The German Hebraist and cosmographer Sebastian Münster, professor of Hebrew at the university of Basel, translated Levita's works into Latin.[14]

Elia Levita's scholarly interlude in Cardinal Egidio's palace came to a sudden and dramatic end in 1527 when the army of the Holy Roman Empire burst into Rome, looting the city, terrorizing and slaughtering its inhabitants. The Cardinal's palace was vandalized, his extensive library and Elia Levita's comprehensive collection of Hebrew manuscripts were set on fire. Both men lost the valuable collections they had spent years building up. The Cardinal was forced to run for his life; he crossed the country to settle for a year in Padua before returning to Rome. Elia Levita found himself isolated in Rome without the protection of his patron, vulnerable and impoverished. For the second time in his life he gathered together his few possessions and fled. He and his family headed once again for Venice and moved into the ghetto.

Life for the Jews in Venice was as perilous as it ever had been. A few weeks before the Levita family arrived the Senate had passed yet another resolution expelling the Jews from the city. A senator by the name of Gabriele Moro had proposed that the Jews should be returned to Mestre, that their pawnshops be closed, and that henceforth they could not remain in the city for more than 15 days in the year. The Senate approved Moro's proposal by a narrow margin, but the decree was never implemented. Following through on resolutions was one of the weaker features of Venetian governance. The city was riven by a plague of typhus and food prices had soared, so senators must have had more on their minds than the perennial problem of dealing with the Jews. The aggravation of expelling them and dealing with the consequences was probably more than anyone in authority could face at that moment.[15]

Elia Levita was virtually unknown when he had first lived in Venice. Now, on his return, he carried with him a reputation as both an author and a grammarian. He was known as one of the small, select band of scholars consulted by those Christians who, puzzlingly as far as the Jews were concerned, were obsessed with Hebrew, Aramaic, Kabbalah and Jewish biblical interpretation. As one of the foremost authorities consulted by Christian Hebraists, Elia Levita was a curiosity among his people.

Levita found employment in Daniel Bomberg's printing workshop. The two men had probably never met before, but they knew about each other: Bomberg had even published a poem by Levita in his second edition of the rabbinic Bible.[16] Bomberg was probably relieved to take Levita on, as he hadn't had a lot of luck with some of his other Jewish employees. A few years earlier he had engaged Abraham de Balmes to write a Hebrew grammar to be used by Christians, but the project hadn't been straightforward. De Balmes died before the work could be finished and what he did complete was obscure in some places and difficult to follow elsewhere. Another of Bomberg's Jewish collaborators, Jacob ben Hayyim ibn Adonijah, who worked with him on the rabbinic Bible, had disappeared just as Levita arrived back in Venice. He may have died, converted to Christianity, or both. Levita thought the latter. Inverting a traditional Jewish eulogy for the dead he wrote: 'May his soul be bound up in a bag full of holes!'

Life became easier for Bomberg when Levita joined him. They collaborated on an edition of the *Arukh,* an eleventh-century Talmudic lexicon, and they printed an Aramaic–Hebrew dictionary that Levita had compiled. Bomberg encouraged Levita to resume work on a concordance of the Hebrew Bible. He had started it while living in Rome but most of his work had been consumed in the fire that destroyed his library. Levita had only managed to save a few fragments. They didn't amount to much, but the knowledge that he would be able to print the finished concordance, backed up by Bomberg's encouragement, was enough to motivate him to resume the task. He published the first edition in 1536, dedicating it to another of his patrons, Bishop George de Selve of Lavour, to whom he had also been teaching Hebrew. The bishop, who doubled as the French ambassador to Venice, sounds like the perfect pupil:

To his most exalted eminence, my lord, George de Selve, Bishop of Lavour, much peace! It is now some years since I began a work which appeared to me important and very useful to those who study the structure of the sacred language. The devastation of Rome, however, which took place shortly after it, was the cause of my not finishing it at that time and leaving it incomplete. And even the incomplete part was taken from me, and became a prey of spoil; it was torn and shattered so that nothing but a small portion was left to me, which I brought with me here to Venice, and I gave up all thought of finishing the work anymore. But God, who willed that I should complete it and that the book should be published, stirred up your spirit, and put it into your heart, to study the sacred language under me, which you learned from me with great ease and in a very short time. So that you are famed for your knowledge of the three classical languages – the sacred Hebrew, the rich Greek, and the elegant Latin tongues.[17]

Of all his works, Levita's *Masoret Hamasoret* is far and away the most important. Completed in Bomberg's workshop and published in 1538 the book is a voluminous compendium, listing the correct spelling and vowel notation of every word in the Hebrew Bible. Levita wrote rhyming allusions to signify the number of occurrences of every letter in the Bible, mnemonics to help identify where variant spellings occur, notes on irregular word forms, and much more. It is the sort of reference book that one approaches with trepidation only to still be absorbed in it hours later, if one is that way inclined. Today it might be called a book for grammar geeks.

Elia Levita represented a new type of Jewish Renaissance scholar, one who took advantage of the cultural freedoms offered by the independent space of the ghetto. Although they were physically confined to one small, dilapidated area, the ghetto residents were not intellectually constrained in the way that earlier generations had been. Taking their cues from people like Leone Ebreo and Abraham de Balmes, the more curious among them engaged with the new intellectual trends beginning to disseminate across Europe. They took an interest in science and philosophy, art, poetry, literature and medicine, exploring what they had to offer and making their own contribution to the development of human knowledge.

But culturally inquisitive intellectuals were not the only people to be found in the Venice Ghetto. Some very odd people passed through it too.

A CREDIBLE CHARLATAN

Towards the end of 1523 a small, dark, exotically dressed stranger turned up in the ghetto. 'He wore striped silk according to the customs of the Ishmaelites,[18] and on his head a white scarf with which he covered most of himself.'[19] He told a tall tale, announcing himself as David, the son of King Solomon from the wilderness of Havor. His brother, he said, was King Joseph, ruler of the Israelite tribes of Reuben, Gad and half the tribe of Manasseh. He claimed to be on his way to Rome, sent by the 70 elders of his nation to ask the Pope to negotiate peace between the King of France and the Holy Roman Emperor. He had been journeying for over a year and was hungry and broke. For the past six days he had been fasting and the first thing he did on entering the ghetto was to ask for seven ducats, which he said he needed for his sick servant.

The residents of the ghetto were less than enthusiastic about helping him, they'd heard stories like his before. Reuben, Gad and Menasseh, over whom he claimed his brother ruled, were three of the ten tribes exiled from the Northern Kingdom of Israel by the Assyrians in the seventh century BCE. The events are recounted in the biblical Book of Kings. Known as the Lost Tribes of Israel nothing had been heard of them since. Although there were always rumours floating around about people who had supposedly found the lost tribes, nobody had ever produced tangible proof of their existence. Jews tended to listen to the rumours because the re-emergence of the Ten Lost Tribes from wherever they had been hidden was believed to herald the return of Israel to its homeland and the speedy advent of the Messiah. But none of the previous rumours had ever proved to be true and after a fleeting wave of optimism the overriding reaction to each new report was one of scepticism. The new arrival may have been more exotically dressed than previous travellers who told similar stories, but that wasn't enough to encourage the ghetto residents to help him.

Eventually a Jewish artist named Moses dal Castellazzo came to the unhappy traveller's rescue. The traveller referred to him simply as 'a painter', but dal Castellazzo was no run-of-the-mill artist. In one of the earliest examples of the ghetto's porous cultural boundaries, of how there were always prominent Jews to whom the restrictions of the ghetto didn't fully apply, dal Castellazzo lived behind its walls but received commissions from Christian patrons throughout northern Italy. In 1521 he wrote to the Council of Ten asking for a licence to print a series of woodcuts illustrating the Five Books of Moses. He explained that having reached old age and needing to provide for his family, he had instructed his daughters to 'cut all the five books of Moses into wood, beginning with the creation of the world and proceeding chapter by chapter'. His intention was to illustrate the entire Hebrew Bible, making it intelligible to everybody.[20]

The Council of Ten granted permission but no copies of his wooden Bible have survived. However, when the Russian army liberated Warsaw after World War II they found an illuminated Bible in the cellars of the Gestapo's former headquarters. It was made up of 211 drawings illustrating the entire Pentateuch. Two of the drawings match a pair of woodcuts known to have been made in early sixteenth-century Venice. The scholarly consensus is that the pair of woodcuts from Venice are all that have survived from Castellazzo's original printing, but that the illuminated Bible in Warsaw was copied from his entire original series. The strangely dressed traveller was probably unaware that Moses dal Castellazzo was the leading Venetian Jewish artist of his generation.[21]

Moses dal Castellazzo took the traveller under his wing, invited him to stay in his house, and introduced him to Simon Meshullam, the son of Asher who we know as Anselmo del Banco. Simon Meshullam listened to the traveller's story and generously offered to pay all the expenses of his trip to Rome, even engaging two Jews to accompany him on his journey. All Simon wanted to know in return was why the 70 elders had sent him on his mission. The traveller fudged his reply, declaring that he could say no more than that he was going to Rome for the good of Israel. But if Simon would send two men with him to Rome, then he too would have a share in the deed and they would bring him back good tidings.[22]

This conversation is recorded in a remarkable chronicle written by the traveller, whom historians call David Reuveni. The chronicle, written in Hebrew, covers the years 1522 to 1525 and is one of the most incredible works of fiction or delusion, it is hard to know which, in early modern Jewish history.

The chronicle opens with David Reuveni setting off disguised as an Arab from his brother's kingdom in the Arabian wilderness of Havor. Havor is mentioned in the Bible as the place to which the Assyrian King Tiglat Pileser exiled the tribes of Reuven, Gad and the half-tribe of Manasseh, the very tribes allegedly ruled over by David's brother.[23] The chronicle describes Reuveni, his lengthy journeys, and the astonishing sights he saw. He travelled by boat from Jeddah across the Red Sea to Ethiopia, then overland by camel, through Cairo, Gaza, Hebron and Jerusalem, before returning to Alexandria and getting on a boat bound for Venice. He met people who ate elephants, wolves and leopards, kings who offered him whatever he desired, and young men who gave him lions as gifts. He dispensed blessings and money liberally and imperiously demanded assistance from whoever he could. Passing himself off as a holy Islamic sage he granted those he met a full title to paradise and through the force of his personality cowed an unruly young man into instant repentance. This opening part of David's chronicle is long, fantastic and almost completely unbelievable.

David Reuveni's chronicle lay undiscovered for 300 years, eventually surfacing at the beginning of the nineteenth century. It was placed in Oxford's Bodleian Library in 1848, but by 1867 it had vanished. The document's history is almost as bizarre as that of its author. It would have been forgotten today had the Bodleian librarians not made a facsimile copy of it during the brief period it was in their possession. It has been published in modern editions several times. The only English translation was made by the author Elkan Adler, who included it in his book *Jewish Travellers*, published in 1930.

David Reuveni left Venice for Rome in March 1524. He arrived in style, according to his chronicle, riding on horseback to the Pope's palace, where he was met by Cardinal Egidio da Viterbo, Elia

Levita's patron. Elia does not figure further in Reuveni's narrative, but he does make frequent reference to one of the Cardinal's teachers, a German Jew named Joseph. Given Reuveni's vagueness about facts it is possible that he meant Elia, who was also German. But it doesn't pay to speculate too closely about any alleged facts in his chronicle.

Reuveni met the Pope several times, with Cardinal Egidio acting as translator. He told the Pope about his peace mission and was disappointed to hear the Pope say he did not have the ability to help him. Instead, he suggested that Reuveni travel to Portugal to request assistance from King João III. It is difficult to understand why the Pope would have suggested this, and a different account of Reuveni's mission, which features in Marin Sanudo's Venetian diary, makes more sense. In this version Reuveni was not on a peace mission at all. Rather he approached the Pope asking for his help in procuring cannons and flamethrowers from the Portuguese king.

Just what he intended to do with these weapons is uncertain, but there is a letter from the Pope to the King of Portugal in which he asks him to send his fleet to accompany Reuveni and the weapons he hoped to procure.[24] Other accounts written at the time suggest that Reuveni was hoping to sail back to Jeddah in order to launch an attack on the city of Mecca. The existence of these accounts suggests that Reuveni only claimed in his chronicle to have been travelling on a peace mission in order to save face, once he had failed in his original purpose of procuring weapons.[25]

Things started to go wrong for Reuveni while he was still in Rome. He fell ill and it took him a full year before he could leave. When he did leave his departure was as flamboyant as his arrival, his servants riding ahead of him with streamers unfurled, with pride of place given to a banner made from fine silk, embroidered in gold with the words of the Ten Commandments. It had been made for him by one of his many prominent acolytes, Benvenida Abarbanel, the wife of Don Isaac's youngest son Samuel.

He travelled north to Pisa where he was welcomed by Asher Meshullam's daughter Diamante and her husband. They offered him lodging in their home. Oddball he may have been, but Reuveni knew how to court the wealthy. He described with uncharacteristic frankness in his chronicle how Diamante would play the harp and the other women of the household would dance in the room where he was. They asked him if he enjoyed the music, to which he replied: 'You are very kind.' However, he confessed to his chronicle, 'God knows my thoughts that I did not wish to listen to the sound of the harp and the flute and rejoicings.'

When David Reuveni finally reached Lisbon, the Portuguese king received him but did not jump at the opportunity of offering his assistance. But his appearance in Portugal did generate huge excitement among the *conversos*, those Jews who had converted to Christianity so as to be allowed to continue living in the country rather than being expelled with the rest of the Jewish population. The devastating expulsion from Spain and Portugal only 30 years earlier had set off a flurry of messianic expectation based on the long-established belief that the ultimate redemption would only occur in the wake of an apocalyptic catastrophe. Many regarded the expulsion, the greatest upheaval in Jewish life for nearly 1,500 years, to be the predicted catastrophe that would lead to the Messiah's arrival. These messianic yearnings were particularly strong within the *converso* community, who longed for the day when they could return to their native faith.

The pomp and ceremony with which David Reuveni entered Lisbon led the *conversos* to imagine him as a harbinger of the expected messianic redemption. It was a role he was only too happy to play. He started preaching messianic fantasies, attracting large crowds and followers. One young man in particular, a young *converso* named Diego Pires, fell thoroughly under his spell. Pires asked Reuveni to convert him back to Judaism, a dangerous and foolish request in Inquisition Portugal. When Reuveni was smart enough to refuse, Pires took matters into his own hands. He circumcised himself, changed his name to Solomon Molcho, and declared himself to be the Messiah.

Solomon Molcho proved to be a persuasive orator. His mystical sermons drew a large following of Portuguese *conversos* to him, all believing that he was the Messiah whose arrival had been heralded by David Reuveni.

The King of Portugal did not think Molcho was the Messiah. He blamed Reuveni for stirring up dangerous ideas, considered him a dangerous religious provocateur, and ordered him to leave the country. Reuveni boarded a boat bound for Livorno in Tuscany, from where he intended to make his way overland back to Venice. But he was blown by the wind onto the Spanish shore, where he was arrested by the local magistrate on the grounds that Jews were forbidden to enter Spain. He was released, according to his chronicle, only through the personal intervention of the Holy Roman Emperor, and he carried on with his journey, surviving a shipwreck and enduring two years of imprisonment in France. Finally, the leaders of the Jewish community in France raised a ransom to liberate him and get him off their hands. He travelled back through Italy, arriving in the Venice Ghetto to no great acclaim in 1530. By this time his reputation was shot, he was regarded increasingly as a political nuisance by the Christian authorities and a liability by the Jews.

Back in the ghetto Reuveni met up once again with Solomon Molcho, who had been forging his own course across Europe, burnishing his messianic credentials as he went. He had spent time in Salonika and Ancona, writing treatises, preaching to large crowds and building up a substantial following of those who believed, as he did himself, that he was the Messiah. When he reached Venice he won the influential support of Rabbi Elijah Menahem Halfon, the scion of a well-known rabbinic family and one of the ghetto's foremost intellectuals, a kabbalist, Talmudist and expert in Jewish law.

Halfon had already heard of Molcho by reputation and had read his writings.[26] When he heard him preach in Venice he was convinced that the man who history has condemned as a deluded messianic pretender was in fact the real thing; either the Messiah or at very least his herald.

In those days there were no such things as rabbinic salaries; scholars, even of Halfon's status, could not make a living through their religious knowledge or intellectual ability. Like many rabbinic scholars, Elijah Halfon was also a physician, earning his livelihood as a doctor to the Venetian elite. Among his patients was Caterina Sandella, the wife of a controversial poet named Pietro Aretino. Aretino by all accounts was not a pleasant individual, indeed one of his biographers candidly described him as a monster.[27] But he did not treat Halfon monstrously. When Halfon saved Caterina's life, Aretino praised him effusively. It was a rare testament from a Venetian to a Jew:

> From you who are a Jew all can learn how to be a Christian. For the fear of God and the love of your fellow man are inborn to the kindness of your nature. I have never met a man who equalled you in the love for their relatives . . . I should like anyone who has a family to see the tenderness and the purity of the way you honour your wife and bring up your children in the dignity of your customs.[28]

Unfortunately, Halfon's support for Molcho did not serve him well. It drew him into a row with another Venetian scholar, Jacob Mantino, also a physician to the great and the good among the Venetian nobility. The two men were professional rivals, but whereas Halfon supported Molcho, Mantino did his best to condemn him.

Like Halfon, Mantino was an accomplished scholar. His translations of Hebrew scientific and philosophical works into Latin had won him the admiration of the Pope. Many of his patients were members of the Venetian Senate. They showed him their respect by exempting him from wearing the yellow cap obligatory on all other Jews. Repression was not always doled out uniformly in the Venice Ghetto.

It is not clear why Mantino took such exception to Molcho, but it drew him and Halfon into an intense personal quarrel which only grew worse when the messianic pretender fled Venice for Rome. Mantino followed him, denouncing him to the Pope and sending him scuttling back to Venice.

When he returned to Venice the messianic pretender renewed his acquaintance with David Reuveni. Whether their meeting in Venice was planned or accidental is uncertain, the historical records are vague and confusing, but the upshot was that the two men decided to seek an audience with the Holy Roman Emperor. Again it is not certain what their purpose was; it must have either been to convince the Emperor of Molcho's messiahship or perhaps to convert him to Judaism. They sent letters of introduction to the Emperor, purportedly from King Joseph, Reuveni's imaginary brother who ruled over the non-existent tribes in Havor. Confident that the letters would guarantee them an audience, they set off from Venice. They got as far as Mantua, 90 miles from Venice, where they were arrested for forgery.

It was the end for both of them. Molcho was burnt at the stake in Mantua and Reuveni transported in chains to Spain, where he was imprisoned by the Spanish Inquisition, until his death in 1535.

4

Concord and Dispute

A CULTURAL NOVELTY

According to the Senate's decree of 1516 the ghetto was established to confine the Jews to one area and prevent them from going wherever they chose around the city. It was an impossible aim; to achieve it the gates of the ghetto would have had to be permanently sealed and the Jews effectively incarcerated. But the pawnbrokers and second-hand dealers of the ghetto were too economically useful to shut them away and the balance between confining them in the ghetto and taking advantage of their economic utility was a tricky one to get right. The Senate had always intended to keep the ghetto open from sunrise to sunset each day, allowing both Jews and Christians to come and go as they please. As it turned out, they did not come and go for economic reasons alone. For many Christians the ghetto was an intriguing place, offering them a cultural or social experience very different from their own lives.

In March 1531 Marin Sanudo recorded in his diary that the Jews had put on a 'very nice' comedy in the ghetto, which lasted until eight hours after sunset. The Council of Ten had announced that Christians were forbidden to attend. The fact that the Council found it necessary to prohibit Christians from attending suggests that they often went to events of this nature. Sanudo does not say whether he was in the audience that night, but he probably was; he knew enough about the performance to eulogize it as *bellissima*.

The March date suggests that it was the Jewish festival of Purim, a carnival-like occasion often marked by plays and entertainments.[1]

There are few documented social encounters between Jews and Christians in the early days of the ghetto. But there are many more records after the Inquisition was set up in Venice in 1540.

The Venetian Inquisition was never as all-powerful as it had been in Spain and Portugal. The Senate had always jealously guarded the Republic's temporal independence from Rome; unlike its hegemony over the Papal States, when it came to secular matters Rome could not tell the Venetians what to do. When the Church demanded that the Inquisition be established in Venice, the Council of Ten flexed its muscles and insisted on circumscribing its powers. They demanded that the Inquisition could not arrest anyone without the permission of the Council of Ten and that three Venetian noblemen, known as the *Savii*, or Sages, for Heresy, should sit as part of the tribunal. The unique, lay presence at inquisitional proceedings of the three *Savii* acted as a brake on the enthusiasm of the Inquisitor, who found his potency further tempered in 1551 when the Council of Ten reduced the number of the crimes that the Inquisition could investigate.

Generally, the Inquisition was not interested in what Jews did, as long as they remained within their own society. They did come after them, though, if they were suspected of Judaizing, of encouraging Christians to become Jews. They banished two Jewish physicians for life after they were found guilty of secretly circumcising Christians, probably members of the large *converso* community whose families had converted from Judaism to Christianity in Spain or Portugal and who now lived as Christians in Venice.

The Inquisition also had acute concerns about Christian intimacy with Jews. One of the favourite judicial penalties in Venice was to condemn convicted criminals to forced labour, to rowing on the galleys. They called it sending them to the oars. Francesco Oliver, a Jew from the ghetto, was sent to the oars for having sexual relations with a Christian woman. A young Christian sailor, Giorgio Moretto, received a similar punishment for being caught in the ghetto after nightfall where he was having an affair with a Jewish woman named Rachel. At first the Inquisition tried to deal with him leniently, forbidding him from approaching the ghetto, warning him that they would sentence him to three years at the oars if he did. But he couldn't keep away, he kept turning up in the Jewish quarter, attending Jewish weddings and circumcision celebrations, even eating unleavened bread with his Jewish friends at Passover. He was once seen walking around the ghetto wearing a yellow Jewish hat, an accusation he dismissed as a prank. Despite earnestly expressing his love for Rachel and his desire to convert her to Christianity, the Inquisition carried out their threat and sentenced him to three years at the oars. We don't know whether Rachel was still waiting for him when his sentence came to an end.[2]

Foreign travellers passed through the ghetto too. Dennis Possot, a Frenchman, mentioned the ghetto in a book published in 1532, but said nothing of interest about it. Then in 1545 the English William Thomas waxed lyrical about the liberal nature of Venetian society and its treatment of the Jews:

> He that dwells in Venice may reckon himself exempt from subjection. For no man there marks another's doings, or meddles with another man living. If you are a papist, there shall you want no kind of superstition to feed upon. If you are a gospeller, no man shall ask why you come not to church. If you are a Jew, a Turk, or believe in the devil (so you spread not your opinions abroad) you are free from all control. To live married or unmarried, no man shall ask you why.[3]

The Jews of the ghetto may have taken exception to this description of liberal Venetian society, had they read it. It is true that Venice was a liberal society, but the Jews were hardly free of all control. Though it may have appeared so to someone unfamiliar with the conditions of their residency.

HENRY VIII'S DILEMMA

For some foreign Christians the ghetto was more than just a cultural novelty. A consequence of confining the Jews of Venice into one small area was that it became so much easier for like-minded people to meet, debate and share ideas. The few rabbis and scholars in the ghetto took full intellectual advantage of their proximity to each other and it didn't take long for Venice to become known as a hub for Jewish scholarship. Within a few years of its establishment the ghetto had developed into one of Europe's most important rabbinic centres. For those who had questions about religious belief, about the Bible, Talmud or Jewish Law, the Venice Ghetto was where an answer was likely to be obtained. The ghetto became a magnet for inquisitive Jews. And sometimes also for Christians seeking a Jewish perspective on an issue they were grappling with.

One such Christian was an Englishman named Richard Croke. He arrived in 1530, having been sent by the man who was soon to be Archbishop of Canterbury, Thomas Cranmer. Cranmer at the time was advising King Henry VIII in his 'Great Matter'; his quest to find a way of ending his marriage to Catherine of Aragon after the Pope had refused to grant him a divorce.

Henry was fairly confident that he could find a way out of the marriage. He had been advised by John Stokesley, the future Bishop of London, that his marriage to Catherine should never have taken place. She was the widow of Henry's brother Arthur and the Bible was clear that one cannot marry a former sister-in-law.[4] Henry didn't need a divorce, Stokesley said, because his marriage to Catherine had been invalid and should be annulled.

But Henry had also been told that there was one biblical exception to the prohibition on marrying a brother's widow. If his brother had died childless then he was not only *allowed* to marry his widow, he was *obliged* to.[5] It was his duty to have children with the widow and raise them in his brother's name. And his brother Arthur had died childless; it was even said that his marriage with Catherine had never been consummated.

John Stokesley had batted this objection away, saying that the obligation to marry a childless widow only applied to Jews. To confirm this he suggested that Henry should seek an opinion from learned Christian theologians and Jewish legal scholars. Officially there were no Jews in England and even the few who were there

were not competent to rule in a matter like this. So Richard Croke
had been despatched to Venice, by now the most important centre
of Jewish scholarship in Europe, to obtain an opinion from the
rabbis there. Stokesley, who was now Bishop of London, had gone
with him.

Arriving in Venice, Croke consulted the renowned Franciscan
friar Francesco Giorgi, or Zorzi as he is sometimes known.
Giorgi was Venice's leading theologian. Like Cardinal Egidio da
Viterbo, he was a Christian Hebraist and Cabbalist,[6] one of those
who studied the language of the Hebrew Bible and the mystical
Jewish Kabbalah, believing it would help them draw closer to a
true understanding of Christianity. Their interest was not only
theological: the challenge of the Protestant revolution had made
Catholic intellectuals acutely aware that the Roman Church was
in desperate need of reform. Christian Hebraists believed that a
deeper understanding of the origins of their faith was essential in
setting the Church back on the right track.

Unlike Cardinal Egidio, Giorgi did not need to employ a personal
Hebrew tutor. He had the great advantage of living in Venice where
a growing number of Jewish scholars were congregating, bringing
their Talmudic, kabbalistic and philosophical manuscripts to
Daniel Bomberg's prolific Hebrew printing press.[7] The centre of
Jewish scholarship in Europe was also the city most devoted to
the study and practice of Kabbalah. Venice had everything that a
Christian Hebraist could need.

For a man like Giorgi the benefits of living in such an
environment were huge. Far more than just another member
of the Christian Cabbalist fraternity, Francesco Giorgi was the
author of the hugely influential and important *De Harmonia
Mundi*, a treatise on the mathematical symmetry of the universe.
De Harmonia Mundi proved to be one of the most significant
products of Renaissance thought, paving the way for genuine
mathematical thinking about the universe.[8]

In yet another example of just how porous the boundaries of
the ghetto were, how its walls and boundary canals were unable to
prevent information from flowing freely and relationships forming,

Giorgi took Croke into the ghetto and introduced him to his friend and fellow kabbalist, the rabbi Elijah Menaham Halfon, the man who in supporting Solomon Molcho had attracted the wrath of his professional rival Jacob Mantino.

Elijah Halfon listened to Richard Croke's arguments and gave a favourable answer to his query, telling him that in his view Henry VIII's marriage to Catherine of Aragon was invalid because she had been married to his brother, and that since Henry was not a Jew he had not been obliged to marry Arthur's widow.

It is no surprise therefore that when the Pope asked Jacob Mantino for his opinion he came down on the opposite side. He knew that the Pope held him in high regard, it would have been foolish to cross him, and in any event his enmity for Halfon almost obliged him to take the contrary view. Mantino had no hesitation in telling the Pope that that there was nothing in Jewish law invalidating Henry's marriage to Catherine; the king and queen were legally married, and if the Pope was not prepared to allow a divorce, that is how they should stay.

Croke's efforts to obtain an opinion on Henry's marital situation, and the contrary opinions expressed by the ghetto rabbis, caused a diplomatic row between Venice and England. Once again it was Marin Sanudo's diary which gives us the background. Croke and Stokesley had told the *Signoria*, the six councillors who advised the Doge, that they wanted to consult the scholars of theology at the university in Padua about Henry's proposal to have his marriage annulled. Stokesley asked the *Signoria* to confirm that they had no objection. When they refused to give their consent, Bishop Stokesley 'used violent language, reviling the *Signoria* . . .bursting forth into expressions which they are convinced were very remote from the King's good disposition towards them and their affairs'. The *Signoria* responded by threatening Stokesley with a trade boycott, telling him that if this was the English attitude, once the Venetian merchants heard of it they would stop shipping their goods to England.[9]

The matter was raised three days later in the Senate, with the additional information that Henry VIII had written to say that

Giorgi, 'a most able theologian', had written a book supporting him, but that a bishop had seized the book and burnt it. He was probably referring to a transcript of the opinion that Giorgi had obtained in the ghetto from Elijah Halfon. Henry had asked the *Signoria* to have the book remade but they had declined, not wishing to oppose the Pope.

The diplomatic spat eventually fizzled out. A few weeks later the Senate noted that Bishop Stokesley was about to depart from Venice. They approved a motion giving him a parting gift of 130 ducats. It concluded the Venetian involvement in Henry VIII's Great Matter.[10]

Of course it was only the beginning in England; Henry even ordered a copy of Daniel Bomberg's new edition of the Talmud, and Richard Croke brought Marco Raphael, a Jew who Francesco Giorgi had converted to Christianity, back home with him to interpret it for Henry. Raphael was enthusiastic in Henry's support but he could not provide him with the evidence he needed to have the marriage annulled. Henry gave up hope of getting a Talmudic ruling; but the copy of Bomberg's Talmud that he purchased remained in Westminster Abbey until the late twentieth century.[11]

UNIVERSAL HARMONY

We might ask how much Shakespeare knew of Richard Croke's mission to the Jews of the ghetto. Henry's divorce from Catherine of Aragon, which took place in the generation before Shakespeare's birth, was a defining event in sixteenth-century England: it led directly to the religious convulsions that dominated life throughout that century and the conception and birth of Elizabeth (later Elizabeth I) to the king's second wife, Anne Boleyn.

Shakespeare would no doubt have known of Henry's many and complex machinations to procure a divorce. Yet even if Henry had not sought a divorce, even if Croke had not travelled to Venice and met Francesco Giorgi, Shakespeare would have been familiar with the friar's name and his treatise *De Harmonia Mundi*.

In her remarkable book *The Occult Philosophy in the Elizabethan Age*, the late Dame Frances Yates shows just how influential Francesco Giorgi's work was in Elizabethan England. She argues that *The Merchant of Venice* was profoundly influenced by Giorgi's book; that the harmony which the friar regards as underpinning the structure of the universe is allegorized in the play through the reconciliation of Christian and Jew.

Yates develops her argument by quoting two speeches from *The Merchant of Venice*. In the trial scene, where Shylock is demanding a pound of Antonio's flesh, the two disputants appear as irreconcilable polar opposites, irresolvably opposed to each other. Between them Portia, disguised as a lawyer, seeks to harmonize them.

The harmonization of two opposing principles by a third is a classic kabbalistic construction and Portia's speech at the trial is full of kabbalistic motifs:

> The quality of mercy is not strained;
> It droppeth as the gentle rain from heaven
> Upon the place beneath . . .
> It is an attribute to God himself;
> And earthly power doth then show likest God's
> When mercy seasons justice.[12]

Mercy's seasoning of Justice is based on the idea that God's ten mystical potencies, known in Kabbalah as Sephirot, are arranged in couplets, each standing in opposition to the other, with the pair harmonized by a third. In the Tree of Life, the schematic diagram used to describe the kabbalistic system, two of the opposing attributes are Justice and Love. The principle which harmonizes them is Mercy. Mercy in its turn distils upon the earth, dropping 'as the gentle rain from heaven upon the place beneath'. Yates argues that Shylock, who is demanding that his contract with Antonio be fulfilled and that he receive his pound of flesh, is the epitome of strict, unyielding Justice. As a Christian, Antonio represents Justice's opposing potency of Love. Between Justice and Love sits Portia, symbolizing Mercy, seeking to harmonize the pair. In her speech Portia is trying to persuade Shylock to abandon Justice and side with Mercy.[13]

The second speech that Frances Yates quotes is where Lorenzo and Jessica, Shylock's daughter, sit gazing at the night sky:

> Sit, Jessica. Look how the floor of heaven
> Is thick inlaid with patines of bright gold:
> There's not the smallest orb which thou behold'st
> But in his motion like an angel sings,
> Still quiring to the young-eyed cherubins;
> Such harmony is in immortal souls;
> But whilst this muddy vesture of decay
> Doth grossly close it in, we cannot hear it.

Lorenzo is talking to Jessica about the harmony of the universe, the theory expounded by Francesco Giorgi in his book *De Harmonia Mundi*. In the Christian interpretation of Cabbala the ethereal angels and the gross, material world are connected together through the harmonizing medium of the planets. Knowledge of Cabbala allows humankind to transcend beyond its earthly limitations, its 'muddy vesture of decay', to ascend through the heavens to the angels.

Musicians enter at this point in Lorenzo's speech and he proclaims the 'sweet power of music'. In Giorgi's system this is the music of the spheres; the music of the heavens heard when all is in harmony. Heard in Shakespeare's play when Jew and Christian are reconciled through the marriage of the Christian Lorenzo to the formerly Jewish but now converted Jessica. When they sit together beneath the heavens.

Frances Yates's analysis, on which we have only touched, leaves us in no doubt that Shakespeare was familiar with Giorgi's universal harmony and that he harnessed it when composing *The Merchant of Venice*. It helps build her argument, to which we will return a little later, that far from this being an antisemitic play, it is arguably philosemitic. But as for the question of whether Shylock was based on, or intended to represent, a historical character, the answer from this analysis is no. In Shakespeare's interpretation of Friar Francesco Giorgi's universal harmony, Shylock is allegorical. He represents the harsh quality of Justice that needs to be mediated by Mercy. Or if we prefer, he represents the Law, which to the early modern mind was the defining feature of Judaism, as opposed to Christian Love.

THE GHETTO GROWS

In 1528, shortly after the devastating typhus plague which probably thwarted Gabriel Moro's attempt to expel the Jews, the Senate renewed their charter. The conditions attached to this renewal were marginally more liberal than in the past. The tax was reduced to 5,000 ducats a year, of which 10,000 ducats were to be paid in advance and offset against future annual payments. The restrictions on the trades that Jews could perform were eased slightly; as well as selling second-hand goods they could now make coifs and veils. Most significantly, for the first time the charter stated that the Jews could live according to their rites and customs. It was this that led to the opening of the first official synagogue in Venice. Known as the Scuola Tedesca, or German Synagogue, it was sited on the fourth and fifth floors of a building on the south-east side of the *campo*.

The Scuola Tedesca is still there today, undergoing a major restoration at the time of writing. Throughout its history the synagogue has been unrecognizable from the outside, its only distinguishing external features being five tall arched windows that are noticeably different from the square and rectangular casements on the rest of the façade. Always elaborately decorated, the building has been through various refurbishments over the years and very little of the original gold leaf and red wooden interior remains. Noticeable, though, is the creative use that the original architect made of the limited and unusual space. The main prayer area on the fourth floor is an odd shape, an irregular trapezoid in which the length of every wall is different. It feels strange but has been cleverly balanced out by an overhanging, elliptical women's gallery. The overall effect is of a spacious and airy construction. It is still possible to see markings on the floor where the original furnishings were placed, compared to which some of the reconstructions in previous centuries feel a little clumsy. In its current siting the *bimah*, the reading desk from where prayer services are conducted, obscures two of the windows and covers up part of the Ten Commandments inscribed on a gold band running across the top of the wall.

Four years later another synagogue was constructed just a few doors away, on the third storey of a building in the corner of the *campo*. Known as the Scuola Canton there is some uncertainty about the name Canton. One opinion is that it was so called because the synagogue is in the corner of the square; canton carrying the meaning of corner. Another view is that Canton was the name of the family for whom the synagogue was built. Again, the synagogue is virtually unrecognizable from the outside, but in this case its distinguishing mark is a funny-looking construction; a wooden box on the roof of the building, above which sits a tall octagonal window crowned by a shallow cupola.[14]

The original prohibition against synagogues had never prevented small gatherings of Jews from praying together discreetly in private dwellings. But with the building of the first two synagogues in the ghetto, they prayed openly for the first time, in buildings that they adorned magnificently.

On 2 June 1541 the Senate announced that they had been petitioned by a group of travelling Jewish merchants whose business was the importation of goods into Venice from the Balkans. These merchants were not Venetian residents; they came from Turkey and the Ottoman territories in the Eastern Mediterranean. The Senate referred to them as Levantines. They told the Senate that if they were to continue to sail into Venice in order to trade they would need to be provided with accommodation. They could never find anywhere to stay in the ghetto; it was too cramped and crowded.

Until then the Venetians had refused to allow merchants from the Levant to trade in the city. Their trade policy was unapologetically protectionist; only Venetian citizens were allowed to sail from the Republic's ports to ply the lucrative trade routes to the East. But Venice's status as a mercantile seafaring power had declined badly in recent years. They were still suffering from Vasco da Gama's discovery of the sea route to India on behalf of Portugal, nearly half a century earlier. As the Venetians had feared back in Don Isaac Abarbanel's day, the Portuguese had succeeded in diverting much of the trade away from the Mediterranean, severely impairing the Republic's dominance of the waters. More recently, Venetian merchants had begun facing challenges from British, French and Dutch fleets who were competing for what remained of the Mediterranean shipping trade. The Serenissima's economic woes were compounded by the humiliation it had suffered in a disastrous war against the Ottoman Empire. The Venetian fleet had been seriously depleted and the Republic had lost control of several colonies. To top it all, Venice's rival cities, Ferrara, Ancona and Ragusa, were actively inviting foreign traders to come and join them, causing further damage to the Republic's economic standing. Most of these foreign traders were former Jews who had fled the Inquisition in Portugal: well-connected individuals with trading networks across the Mediterranean. Exactly the sort of people who Venice should have been attracting if they were to have any chance of reversing their fortunes.

The Venetians were feeling hemmed in, fearing they were on the brink of losing their status as the Mediterranean's premier mercantile power. Their solution was to backtrack on their previous protectionist policy that had excluded Jewish merchants from the East from trading openly with the Republic. In a full-blown reversal they invited the Levantine Jews into the city, even exempting them from customs duties on key merchandise for the next two years.

The Republic was willing to make the Jewish Levantine merchants welcome provided, of course, that they resided in the ghetto. However, the Levantine merchants quickly discovered there was not enough room for them to live comfortably. Hence their petition to the Senate.[15]

The obvious solution to the problem of space in the ghetto was to expand the area in which Jews were allowed to live. The Senate went about the task with alacrity. They instructed the *Cinque Savi alla Mercanzia*, the 'five sages' who oversaw the regulation of trade, to research the land surrounding the ghetto so as to find a place in which the Levantines could live. The *Savi* identified an almost empty area between two canals, with nothing more in it than a few gardens, orchards and old wooden huts. It looked ideal. A wall could be erected around it with just a single gate, and a bridge over the canal would connect it to the existing ghetto. Best of all, most of the land belonged to just one owner, allowing a relatively simple negotiation to take place. When all was settled the Levantines moved in and the ghetto doubled in size. They called the new area the *ghetto vecchio*, the old ghetto. The original area was referred to as the *ghetto nuovo*, the new ghetto. It sounds perverse, but it was not. The names relate to the original, pre-ghetto use of the sites: the old foundry and the new foundry.

The Venetians were never altruistic. They wanted the Levantine Jewish merchants to import their goods into the city, but they did not need to make it easy for them. They did not allow them to live permanently in the ghetto; the Levantines were considered to be visitors to the city and they were told they could only remain for four months at any one time, a limit that was soon raised to two years. They were told they could not bring their families with them, that they had to pay rents that were one-third higher than those paid by the former tenants of the area, and they could not engage in moneylending or deal in second-hand goods. Those trades were reserved for the original inhabitants of the ghetto, the German and Italian Jews.

One of the notable features of the expanded ghetto was that although its inhabitants were all Jews, they were segregated and regulated according to nationality. The Tedeschi, the original German and Italian Jews of Venice, who had fled into the city during the war with the League of Cambrai, lived in the *ghetto nuovo*; the Levantine Jews lived in the *ghetto vecchio*. Each was considered, both by the Venetians and to a large extent by the Jews themselves, to be a separate nation or *università*. Not only did they live separately; the Levantines and Tedeschi worshipped in different synagogues, kept more or less to their own social circles, and by and large married people from the same national background. The Senate negotiated different charters with each nation and subjected them to different levels of taxation. In due course there would be a further wave of Jewish immigrants from western Europe; they too would live in their own, newly demarcated, designated area.

There was nothing particularly sinister about dividing the Tedeschi and Levantine Jews into separate nations – no more sinister than shunting them into a ghetto in the first place. Dividing them into nations was not an attempt by the authorities to divide and rule; segregation, by trade, nationality and religion was part of the corporate nature of early modern life. Foreign merchants and craftsmen came to Venice from all over the world and were regulated by the Venetian authorities according to their origin or trade. Some communities were granted privileges such as reduced tariffs, others were restricted in their activities to avoid competition with Venetian citizens. Many communities had both privileges and restrictions imposed upon them. Social intercourse between Venetians and outsiders was often regulated for the better protection of the dominant Catholic faith. Opportunities for interaction between Venetians and Protestants or Jews were particularly constrained.

NEITHER JEW NOR CHRISTIAN BE

The new arrivals to the ghetto were called Levantine Jews but they were not all natives of the Levant, the area of the Mediterranean that stretches from Constantinople southwards towards Egypt. Many had travelled from Spain and Portugal after the expulsions of the 1490s and rebuilt their lives in the Ottoman Empire. Others came from Iberian families that had converted to Christianity as an alternative to expulsion. Then they found that the Inquisition was taking an interest in them, either because they were secretly living underground lives as Jews or because they were suspected of an insincere conversion. They had fled Portugal, ending up in Constantinople, Alexandria or elsewhere in the Ottoman Empire. Those who had converted to Christianity to avoid expulsion were known as *conversos*, New Christians or *Marranos*, the latter being a Spanish term of abuse. It means pig.

Not all New Christians went to the Ottoman Empire. Some made their way to Italy. There were many New Christians in Venice, who had no connection with the Levantine merchants in the ghetto. Those who had integrated fully into Christianity found Venice a tolerant city in which to live. Some New Christians took the opportunity of their new life in Venice to return to Judaism; they moved into the ghetto and rejoined the Jewish community. But several straddled a line between Judaism and Christianity, still secretly retaining some of the practices of their former faith, whilst not obliged to enter the ghetto because they were living as Christians. The Venetian authorities took particular exception to this latter group, referring to them by the abusive term *Marranos*. In July 1550 the Senate resolved to banish them from Venice. A letter from the Duke of Ferrara's ambassador explained the thinking behind the Venetian decree:

> There are several motives for this act, and the first is that the lords of Venice have been advised that the Marranos are worse than Jews, because they are neither Christians nor Jews. All the Jews live together in the ghetto, separated from Christians, but the Marranos have to do with Christians and live in several parts of the city . . . they are malevolent, faithless people up to no good and they might suffice to infect not only the souls of Christians but also their bodies with some pestilential disease . . . The lords of Venice [have] issued this ban at the exhortation of the [Holy Roman] Emperor, who had asked how this Christian dominion, which professed to be Catholic, could allow a people so wicked, perverted and filthy to live in Venice and its territories.[16]

There was another reason behind the proposed expulsion of the Marranos, one which the ambassador's letter failed to mention. It had to do with a bad miscalculation on the part of the Venetian authorities, who had been unable to get their heads around the complexities of Jewish family networks and had allowed their attraction to money to cloud their judgement.

One of the routes that the New Christian refugees used to escape the Inquisition in Portugal was to travel to Flanders where there was an underground network that would smuggle them to Turkey. The network was the brainchild of Diego Mendes, a fabulously wealthy, New Christian spice merchant who was based in Antwerp. The printer Daniel Bomberg, who had originally hailed from Antwerp, ran the Venetian branch of the operation.

When Mendes died, his widow Brianda Nasi inherited his substantial fortune. Brianda's elder sister Beatrice Nasi, who had married Diego's brother, had also been widowed a few years earlier. Between them, the two sisters controlled a phenomenal amount of money, but the way in which the two husbands' wills had been structured drove a wedge between the women. The quarrel between them was aggravated when the authorities in Antwerp accused both women of secretly reverting to their Jewish roots, a none too subtle device which, if proved, would have allowed the royal court to get their hands on the widows' fortunes.

The two women fled to Venice, leaving Beatrice's son João to negotiate the release of the family fortune. After he had managed to reclaim as much as he realistically could, he too left Antwerp for Venice. The Venetian authorities, hearing that the Mendes fortune was now in their city, rubbed their greedy hands with glee. They told themselves that the arrival of this phenomenally wealthy, emotionally vulnerable, New Christian family proved how astute they had been in allowing Marranos to settle in Venice. When the two sisters fell out once more, with Brianda now accusing her sister of being a secret Jew, the Venetian government moved to confiscate their fortune.

It was then that the Turkish Sultan, Suleiman, stepped in. It was apparent, at least to him, that the Mendes family were only passing through Venice. They were on their way to Turkey, taking advantage of the underground network that Diego Mendes had set up. The Sultan demanded that the Venetians leave the widows and their money alone. A diplomatic row broke out between Venice and Turkey and, unwilling to enter into yet another war with their perennial Ottoman enemy, the Venetians backed off.[17] They had overreached themselves; they now realized that the Marranos in Venice and the New Christian networks with whom they were allied were too powerful to be exploited. Yet if they couldn't exploit them, there was little point in allowing them to remain in Venice. They might as well expel them all.

Once again the Venetians failed to follow through on their decision. The ban on the Marranos was never implemented. Not only did it prove too difficult to determine who was a Marrano and who wasn't; the Venetians realized that they were too commercially important to evict. The Marranos had links both to the Levantine merchants and to the Spanish and Portuguese trade networks from which they had once hailed.[18] The Venetians may have despised the Marranos, but they would not let a commercial advantage slip through their fingers.

As for the Mendes sisters, Brianda did move to Turkey, but she soon returned and settled with her sister Beatrice in Venice's rival city of Ferrara. They changed their names and lived as Jews, Beatrice being known as Doña Gracia Nasi, Brianda becoming Reyna. Doña Gracia eventually departed for Constantinople with her son João. The whole family could so easily have remained in Venice, with all their wealth, if the Venetians hadn't been quite so avaricious in dealing with them. As it was, the rift they had created with the Mendes–Nasi family would soon return to haunt them, in the person of Beatrice's son João, or Joseph, Nasi.

5

More Trouble

INTO THE FLAMES

By the middle of the sixteenth century the Jews of the ghetto were feeling relatively secure. They had lived in the compound continuously for 40 years; their charters had always eventually been renewed, usually for five years but in 1537 for ten. The dirty, crowded and unsanitary ghetto was not a particularly pleasant place to live, but in the context of early modern Europe, Venice remained a relatively tolerant city. Compared to how Jews lived elsewhere, life in the Jewish ghetto was not too bad.

But tolerance and security could not be taken for granted. From 1547 there was a marked deterioration in the relationship between the Venetian government and the Jewish moneylenders. Several cities in the Venetian territories banned Jews from pawnbroking or otherwise lending money in their territories. In Venice itself the government decreased the rates of interest at which Jews were permitted to lend and increased their tax burden. This policy may not have been a deliberate attempt to encourage Jews to leave but the consequence was that many did.[1]

It's no coincidence that the toughening of attitudes towards the Jews coincided with the beginning of the Counter-Reformation; the Catholic Church's assertive response to the new Protestantism. When the Pope urged the Venetians to take a stronger line against

Protestant heresy in their own city, they obliged by stoking the flames of a religious environment that was growing heated.

The dispute tearing at the heart of the Christian faith should not have had anything to do with the Jews in the ghetto. As far as they were concerned the Counter-Reformation was purely a Christian affair. Statistics seem to bear this out: of the nearly 3,000 cases of religious misdemeanour that the Venetian Inquisition dealt with between 1541 and 1600, only 73 concerned Jews or Christians suspected of Jewish affiliation. But statistics do not necessarily reflect mood. When religious fundamentalism is in the ascendant, Jews serve as the whipping boy against whom all can unite. Nothing illustrated this better than a dispute between two Christian printers that ended up as a disaster for the Jews of the Venice Ghetto.

Although Venice had become the world's leading centre for printing Hebrew books, Jews were still not allowed to own printshops. Daniel Bomberg had closed his in 1548 and Hebrew printing in the city was now the exclusive domain of Marco Antonio Giustiniani, a no-frills, bargain-basement printer. Some scholars believe that it was his cut-price, often plagiarized products that had forced Bomberg out of business.

The printers' dispute started when Giustiniani was asked by Rabbi Meir Katzenellenbogen of Padua, one of Italy's most eminent rabbis, to print copies of his commentary on the *Mishneh Torah*, the code of law compiled by the great Jewish philosopher Maimonides. Giustiniani was willing but the two men could not agree a deal and the rabbi turned instead to another Christian printer, Alvise Bragadin. Bragadin, who had not yet printed any Hebrew books, agreed to take on the commission and in 1550 he produced the first copies of the *Mishneh Torah* complete with Katzenellenbogen's commentary. Giustiniani, peeved at losing the commission, retaliated by producing a cheaper, plagiarized version of the same book. To add insult to injury, and apparently oblivious to the impact it was bound to have on sales, he printed a negative review of Katzenellenbogen's commentary and placed it inside the book itself. (Fortunately, publishers don't do this today.) It is thought that the bad review may have been written by Cornelius Adelkind, who had been Bomberg's master printer.

Claiming that Giustiniani had plagiarized his work and undermined his market, Katzenellenbogen appealed to Europe's leading authority on Jewish law, Rabbi Moshe Isserles in Krakow. Isserles ruled in Katzenellenbogen's favour and forbade Jews from purchasing Giustiniani's edition. Giustiniani countered by appealing to the Pope. The Pope referred the dispute to the Congregation of the Inquisition, a commission of six cardinals in Rome, headed by the future Pope Paul IV.[2]

This is where events become a little cloudy. Rather than concentrating on the commercial dispute between the two printers, the Congregation of the Inquisition diverted their inquiry into an attack on the Talmud. It came about because of a complaint made to the Venetian ambassador by Cardinal Verallo, the Inquisitor in Rome. He was perturbed that a print run of 800 copies of the Talmud was being produced in Giustiniani's printshop in Venice and was already half finished. The Cardinal told the ambassador that the Talmud contained 'the most pestilential attacks on the Christian religion that could ever be found'. Previously, he said, only six or seven copies had existed anywhere in the world, but now so many were being printed that Jews were likely to give them to their children as soon as they had been born.[3] The Congregation of the Inquisition in Rome took note of Cardinal Verallo's accusation. They appended it to their inquiry into the printers' dispute while the *Collegio* in Venice conducted a separate investigation into the Talmud.

Three years after the Congregation of the Inquisition first sat to consider the printers' dispute, the Pope issued an order condemning the Talmud to be burnt. Burnings were to take place across Italy beginning in Rome, on 12 September 1553.[4]

In the febrile religious environment of the Counter-Reformation any incident could be marshalled into an attack on the Jews. Although the original dispute had been between two Christian printers, the incident concerned a Jewish book, and according to the hostile logic of the times it was legitimate to add the Cardinal's complaint against Giustiniani's printing of the Talmud to the charge sheet. After all, in Christian minds throughout the Middle Ages the Talmud was the book that, more than any other, had come to epitomize the heresy of Judaism.[5]

On 18 October 1553 the Council of Ten made arrangements for Venice to participate in the nationwide burning of the Talmud. The conflagration took place on the Piazza San Marco, the bustling concourse leading to the Basilica and Doge's Palace that serves as a magnet to tourists today and which, according to the early seventeenth-century traveller Thomas Coryate, thronged no less when he visited.[6]

One of the editors in Bragadin's workshop, Rabbi Abraham Menahem Rapaport, a former pupil of Elia Levita, was present when the pyre was laid and the volumes of the Talmud were set aflame. Years later Rapaport composed a commentary on the Torah. When he reached the words in Deuteronomy 'in his right hand a fiery law',[7] he wrote:

> The Torah is compared to fire, when a man comes too close, he is burned . . . this alludes to the great destruction our eyes have witnessed, for our many sins, in all the regions of Italy . . . The hand of God was against us when the decree went out from the city of Rome that [the Talmud] should be consumed by fire. In the city of Venice, woe to the eyes that saw this on the 13th and 14th of Marcheshvan 5314,[8] a continual fire which was not extinguished. I fixed these days for myself, each year, to fast, weep, and mourn, for this day was as bitter for me as the burning of the House of our God.[9]

According to Rapaport's account, the fire in St Mark's Square burned continuously for two days; an indication of how many books and manuscripts had been set ablaze. If Giustiniani was halfway through printing his 800 multi-volume copies of the Talmud, the number of pages in his workshop would have been in the tens of thousands. But to set alight a conflagration that burned for two days, there must have been far more on the pyre than just Giustiniani's pages. The church officers who were ordered to collect the offending books must have searched far and wide; it is unlikely that the Jews in the ghetto had many books, in those days even the wealthiest book collectors owned very small libraries by contemporary standards.

Apart from ordering the burning of the Talmud, the papal decree also forbade the printing of any new copies. As a result Hebrew printing in Venice ground to a halt, there was no point in printers producing material that ran the risk of being seized and destroyed. The only Jewish books which had not been proscribed by the papal order were those dealing with the Jewish mystical tradition of Kabbalah, and kabbalistic works soon became the only Hebrew books printed in Italy. In the Venice Ghetto itself the study of Kabbalah became almost the sole topic of Jewish enquiry. Kabbalah is not an easy subject to study; it requires a mind attuned to mystical speculation, it can be easily misunderstood, and in the most extreme cases it may prove psychologically harmful to those who allow themselves to be carried away. There had always been kabbalists in Venice, but they had been learned individuals who tempered their esoteric studies with the down-to-earth legalism of the Talmud. Now Kabbalah had the field to itself – and it didn't please everybody.

Abraham Menahem Rapaport, who had mourned the burning of the Talmud, was one of those few who tried to dampen down the occult fervour. He told the readers of his commentary on the Torah that he had written it for those who no longer had access to the Talmud but who wanted straightforward interpretations of the Bible rather than esoteric, kabbalistic allusions.[10]

'SINCE IT IS ABSURD . . .'

Two years after the Talmud was burnt in Venice the newly elected Pope Paul IV issued a bull restricting Jewish life in the Papal States. The bull was one of several measures taken during the Counter-Reformation ostensibly to defend the Catholic Church from the challenge of Protestantism. But this bull was not directed at Protestants or Catholics. Its target was Jews. It was not a coincidence that before being elected as Pope, Paul IV had headed the investigation into the printers' dispute. He was the man responsible for the decision to burn the Talmud.

The bull is known by its first three words, *Cum nimis absurdum*, 'Since it is absurd . . .'. The absurdity, the bull goes on to state, is the possibility that even though Jews have been condemned by their own guilt to permanent slavery, they may nevertheless become dominant over Christians. To prevent this absurdity from occurring the bull instituted fifteen measures to constrain Jewish lifestyles. They included the requirement for Jews to live in their own segregated area and to wear a special head-covering identifying them as Jews. They were only to have one synagogue, were forbidden from owning property, and were not to work on Sundays or Christian holidays.

The bull was only effective within the Papal States, the territories controlled by Rome. It didn't affect Venice which was an independent republic. But interestingly, with the exception of the limitations on synagogues, nearly every restriction imposed by the bull had already been instituted in Venice long before. Despite its tolerance, when it came to oppressing the Jewish population, Venice was years ahead of Rome.

There were a couple of respects in which the Venetian legislation was more lenient than the bull. According to *Cum nimis absurdum*, Jewish doctors were forbidden to treat Christian patients. This had never been the case in Venice, where, as we have seen, not only were Jewish doctors allowed to leave the ghetto at night to treat Christian patients, but they counted members of the Venetian nobility among them. And the Venetians had never forbidden Christians from calling Jews 'master', as the papal bull demanded. This leniency probably just reflects a more realistic attitude among the Venetians; why prohibit something that is clearly so difficult to enforce?

The only significant impact that *Cum nimis absurdum* had on the life of Venetian Jews was when their charter was renewed in 1566. For the first time it included a clause forbidding them to employ Christian servants. But like so many other enactments of the Senate that restriction was never fully enforced.[11]

The impression we get from comparing the reality of Venetian Jewish life with the provisions enacted in *Cum nimis absurdum* is that, at least since the establishment of the ghetto in 1516, Jews in Venice had been regulated more severely than elsewhere in Italy. The papal bull was doing little more than catching up with Venice; some of its provisions may even have been influenced by those of the island state. Yet Jews in Venice did not suffer the same indignities as in Rome or elsewhere. For example, they were never forced to congregate to listen to sermons denigrating their faith, telling them that they were in error and urging them to convert to Christianity.

To Venice's credit, its government doesn't seem to have taken some of its own restrictions too seriously. The Venetians were prepared to bend the rules when it suited them. In the sumptuary laws of 1548, designed to restrain extravagances in dress, we read that 'the daughter of Messer Israel Klemperer must also consider herself subject to the ordinances with respect to all the provisions as regards luxury issued by the Gentile authorities. But when she goes outside the ghetto it is not our intent either to prohibit or permit them.' In other words, Israel Klemperer's nameless daughter could dress like any member of the Venetian nobility when she went into town. Despite having to live crammed into the ghetto, the families of wealthy merchants and bankers could appear in Venetian high society looking just as elegant as their Christian counterparts. We don't find anything like this in *Cum nimis absurdum*.[12]

THE FIRE REKINDLED

Most Venetian Jews were not wealthy; they did not enjoy the same privileges as Israel Klemperer's daughter or her social equals in the ghetto. *Cum nimis absurdum* didn't affect them directly but hostility towards Jews remained virulent in Venice and they were now obliged to contend with a new aggravation, one that was a direct consequence of the burning of the Talmud fifteen years earlier.

In the wake of the burning of the Talmud, the Council of Trent, the ecumenical body of the Catholic Church, decreed that henceforth Jewish books were to be subject to censorship. They could be published but they had to pass through the hands of a censor first and any passages that were considered derogatory to the Church or Christianity were to be expunged. The *Esecutori contro la bestemmia*, the magistracy in Venice charged with the prevention of blasphemy, threatened fines, imprisonment, or forced labour in the galleys for anyone found in possession of an unexpurgated Hebrew book.

The magistracy's threats coincided with a period of extreme Venetian political paranoia about the Jews. Rumours were circulating that there was a cell of Jewish agents in the ghetto working on behalf of Turkey. The Turks were believed, correctly as it turned out, to be planning an invasion of the Venetian colony of Cyprus and the alleged Jewish cell was said to be spying for the enemy. In 1567 the government claimed they had intercepted coded messages giving details of a plot by Jews in Venice and Constantinople to bribe a Venetian ambassador. The next year the Venetian ambassador to Constantinople was nearly killed in a fire. The Venetians blamed the Jews.

It was against this background of paranoia that the *Esecutori* opened their campaign against uncensored books. In September 1568 they declared that Levantine and foreign Jews in Venice were in possession of hundreds of unexpurgated Hebrew books, many of which had been printed without a government licence. Declaring that 'the perfidy of many Jews is such that they seek with diverse means to subvert our true and holy Christian faith, and in order to castigate those who have committed these errors and to frighten others', the *Esecutori* imposed a wave of fines on the publishers and owners of the condemned volumes, ordered a large quantity to be exported and the remainder, numbering thousands, to be burned in the Piazza San Marco.[13]

Whether the burnings were fully carried out may never be known. Writing in 1978 one scholar noted that many of the books listed as being condemned to the flames were now in the British

Museum. It is not at all beyond the bounds of possibility that, as they had done so many times before, the Venetian authorities backtracked on their decision. The fines they had imposed were substantial enough, there were good commercial reasons for not overdoing their oppression of the Jews.[14]

ROOTLESS PHYSICIAN

When *Cum nimis absurdum* forbade Jewish doctors from treating Christian patients, David de Pomis feared that his promising new career as a young doctor had come to an abrupt end. It wouldn't have been the first time that his life had been turned upside down.

David de Pomis was 45 years old when he first settled in the Venice Ghetto, well into middle age for those days. His life before reaching Venice had been dogged by misfortune, but without those setbacks he would have neither settled in the city nor embarked on a literary career. His first book was entitled *A Discourse on Human Suffering and How to Escape it.*

David de Pomis was born around 1524 in the Umbrian city of Spoleto. He began his career by following his father into moneylending but it didn't work out for him; the family had never fully recovered from the theft of all their possessions when David was still a young child and his father had not managed to re-establish himself properly as a pawnbroker. In his early twenties David de Pomis decided to study medicine and enrolled as a student at the University of Perugia. He qualified in 1551 and obtained a job as both doctor and rabbi in the ancient settlement of Magliano Sabina, a town in the Papal States. He hadn't been working there long when *Cum nimis absurdum* was proclaimed and the decree against Jewish doctors treating Christian patients came into force. His embryonic career in Magliano Sabina came to an abrupt end.

Setback soon turned to tragedy. When he left Magliano Sabina, de Pomis managed to find a position as physician to Count Niccolò Orsini, whose Tuscan lands lay outside the Papal States. But de Pomis's wife fell ill and died, followed shortly afterwards by two of their sons. Devastated, he continued working in Tuscany, now for the powerful Sforza family, until he was eventually offered a more prestigious job as a doctor in Chiusi.

Chiusi was back in the papal territories but by now Pope Paul IV, the architect of *Cum nimis absurdum*, was dead and his successor Pius IV took a much more lenient attitude towards Jews. When the Bishop of Chiusi opposed his appointment, David de Pomis travelled to Rome where he petitioned the Pope and cardinals. His request was successful and de Pomis was granted permission to practise medicine among Christians once more.

But misfortune continued to dog him. Five days after granting de Pomis permission, Pope Pius IV died. The new Pope, Pius V, was less accommodating than his predecessor. He revoked the permission for de Pomis to practise in Chiusi and the unfortunate doctor found himself rootless yet again. Following a period of wandering he reached Venice in 1569 where, finally, things started to go right for him.

History has not granted David de Pomis the recognition he deserves. Like Leone Ebreo, de Pomis wrote for both Jews and Christians, putting a particular emphasis on the Jewish contribution to the European intellectual tradition. Writing nearly half a century later de Pomis was able to be more adventurous than Ebreo. Leone Ebreo had stressed the place of Jewish thought in the *prisca sapentia*, the Renaissance idea of a chain of divine teachings first revealed to Adam and handed down through the ages. De Pomis went further, actively advocating the universal value of Jewish teachings and their relevance in the contemporary world. These days, thinkers who draw on Jewish ideas and values are accorded as much respect as theorists from any other culture. But up until the late sixteenth century, even though Christianity had historic roots in Judaism and notwithstanding the study of Cabbala by a small Christian elite, Jewish thought was disregarded by European intellectuals. Jews, it was believed, had nothing to contribute to the intellectual discourse of Christian Europe. David de Pomis was arguably the very first actively to disabuse that notion.

David de Pomis's first book, written in 1571, was a translation of Ecclesiastes into Italian, accompanied by his own commentary.

He presented the ideas in Ecclesiastes as an antidote to sceptical, pessimistic thinking and expanded on his theories in *A Discourse on Human Suffering and How to Escape it* published the following year.[15] The book was his first attempt at universalizing Jewish thought and it doesn't seem to have made a great impact. Whatever reception it may have had was soon overtaken by events.

The year 1571 was one in which the Jews of the Venice suddenly realized that their life in the ghetto was not as secure as they had imagined. The Venetians, fighting alongside Spain and Rome, had won a pivotal sea battle against Turkey at Lepanto, in the Gulf of Patras on the west coast of Greece. But this success had come hard on the heels of a humiliating Turkish victory over the Venetian colony of Cyprus. The entire Catholic world shared Venice's outrage at the vicious torture and murder by the Turks of the Venetian commander Marcantonio Bragadin, who was slain as he sought to surrender.

Some blamed the disaster on Joseph Nasi. Formerly known as João, he was the son of the wealthy Gracia Mendes Nasi, one of the two widowed sisters who had caused diplomatic ructions when they fled Antwerp for Venice twenty years before.[16] After his mother had settled in Ferrara, Joseph Nasi had travelled to Constantinople where he became a close friend and ally of the Sultan, Selim I. The Sultan brought him into his inner circle, entrusted him with considerable power, and enthroned him as the Duke of Naxos. Joseph Nasi had no love for Venice, he still remembered how the Venetians had tried to seize his mother's fortune and had nearly expelled his fellow Marranos. Some in Venice said that the savage campaign in Cyprus was the result of his wish to take revenge on the Republic. They said he had persuaded the Sultan to launch the attack.

Whatever the truth of Joseph Nasi's involvement, the fall of Cyprus had been a humiliating loss for Venice, condemning the city to a dark and anxious mood. When a few weeks later the news came through about the victory at Lepanto, jubilation was unconstrained. 'Never before,' wrote one diplomat, had 'such a battle and victory at sea been seen or heard of.'[17]

The Venetian Senate agreed that a celebration was in order. They passed a resolution thanking God for the glorious victory and declaring it appropriate to 'show some sign of gratitude towards Jesus Christ by making a demonstration against those who are enemies of his holy faith, as are the Jews . . .'[18] Referring back to the old arguments that allowing Jews to live in Venice invited divine displeasure, they declared that they would thank God for the victory at Lepanto by expelling the Jews from the ghetto. We will never know whether the proposed expulsion really was a sincere, if perverse, act of thanksgiving or whether it was just a cynical way of taking revenge on Joseph Nasi for the defeat they believed he had inflicted upon them in Cyprus. In either case, the resolution left the Jews of the ghetto distraught, and gave David de Pomis an opportunity to write one of his hardest-hitting theses.

A DIVINE CONSTITUTION

De Pomis's response to the Senate's insinuation that the presence of Jews in Venice caused divine displeasure was to publish a tract, translated as *A Short Discourse Showing the Divine Origins of the Venetian Republic*. He argued that the Republic's divine origins were reflected in its perfect constitution, which was indisputably Jewish in nature. He based his argument on two passages from the Hebrew Bible. There was nothing original in citing these passages, several other medieval and early modern political thinkers had also used them to support similar arguments, but de Pomis insisted that they applied perfectly to the Venetian constitution. The first passage was the prophet Samuel's speech to the Israelites in which he warned them not to appoint a king, telling them that if they did they were likely to find themselves living under a tyrant.[19] The other passage was Jethro's advice to Moses to commission wise counsellors who would share his judicial and administrative burden. Jethro had urged Moses to appoint a hierarchy of magistrates, 'chiefs of thousands, chiefs of hundreds, chiefs of fifties and chiefs of tens'.[20]

De Pomis pointed out that Samuel's warning to the Israelites demonstrated that God's preferred system of government was a republic, free of any monarch who might tyrannize the people. Similarly, Jethro's speech to Moses indicated that the Republic should be governed by four levels of authority, each more senior than the next. The Venetian constitution fitted that model exactly. The chiefs of thousands corresponded to the Grand Council, made up of the men of the nobility. The chiefs of hundreds were the 120 members of the Senate. The rulers of fifty were the *Quarantia*, the three judicial councils of 40 judges each, and the Council of Ten corresponded to the chiefs of tens. Therefore, he argued, the Republic of Venice was constituted precisely according to divine prescription. Following the advice of the Hebrew Bible, it was Jewishly inspired.[21]

De Pomis wasn't original in applying this argument to Venice. In his commentary on the Book of Exodus, Don Isaac Abarbanel had done the same. Intriguingly though, both Abarbanel and de Pomis inverted Jethro's advice. In Jethro's model the rulers of tens sat at the bottom of the hierarchy and the rulers of thousands at the top. Abarbanel and de Pomis had it the other way round, the Council of Ten sat at the top of the tree. And neither man drew the obvious conclusion that the Doge corresponded to Moses. Perhaps that was taking the already imperfect analogy just a bit too far.

Demonstrating that the Venetian constitution was designed according to a Jewish model was just part of a greater argument that David de Pomis was trying to construct. His underlying thesis was that Jews were not inferior to Christians, their common origin meant they should be able to live alongside each other in a spirit of brotherhood. He set out the argument in full in his work *De Medico Hebraeo*, a defence of the role of Jewish doctors in Christian society. He wrote it in reaction to yet another set of restrictions that had been imposed on Jewish doctors, this time by Pope Gregory XIII. De Pomis repeated his theory of the divine origins of the Venetian constitution, before embarking on a discussion of contemporary medicine, a plea to Jews that they should study science, and an impassioned defence of Jewish doctors. He pointed out that Jewish doctors had a religious obligation to treat all patients, stressed the similarities between Judaism and Christianity, and explained their common brotherhood.

This brotherhood, he insisted, was an accepted idea. He quoted the Venetian friar Sixtus Medices, 'who proves in his treatise on the moneylending of Jews that the Jews could not think of the Christians as stranger'.

De Pomis's reference to Sixtus Medices' treatise on moneylending led him into a defence of Jews who loaned money to Christians. This too had to be seen in the context of brotherhood and meant, he insisted, that the lending of money on interest by Jews to Christians could not constitute a sin of usury:

> The moneylending of the Jews does not come under the name of usury, but rather of a contract agreed upon between an assembly of Christians and the Jew, publicly, and after mature consideration . . . Things which are allowed to spread by public consent must have been instituted to suit the convenience of all. Thus the Jew does not practise usury upon the Christian as upon a stranger, but he does this under the cloak of some contract.[22]

De Pomis wrote at a time when attitudes were changing on the question of charging interest. Economies were growing more sophisticated, merchants and traders were seeking capital more frequently and, despite the biblical prohibition, the charging of interest was a fact of economic life. In 1571 the English Parliament passed the Usury Bill, agreeing that an outright ban on interest was detrimental to trade. Although usury in the sense of excessive credit charges was still prohibited, the new Bill permitted loans to be made bearing up to 10 per cent interest. The Bill's proponents made their case by invoking the precise wording of the Bible. The Hebrew word for interest used in Deuteronomy can be translated as 'biting'. Loans at low rates, they averred, could not be construed as biting.[23]

David de Pomis used almost exactly the same argument. 'Thou shalt not lend upon interest to thy brother . . . is to be understood that the Jew must by no means "bite" with usury either the Jew or the Christian.'[24]

Although low rates of interest were becoming acceptable, in *The Merchant of Venice*, written 25 years or so after the Usury Bill, Shylock changed his mind about charging interest to Antonio. 'I will be friends with you and have your love . . . and take no doit of usance for my moneys.'[25] To this Antonio responds, 'The Hebrew will turn Christian; he grows kind',[26] implying that by lending at nil interest Shylock is acting as a Christian would. But Antonio has already agreed to forfeit a pound of his own flesh if he defaults on the loan; Shylock's demand for such a penalty hardly seems the sort of thing that would render him kind in Antonio's eyes. Perhaps the kindness was Shylock's recognition of the changing attitude to interest across the Christian world; that a loan between Christian and Jew is to be made, not on interest but 'under the cloak of some contract', in this case a pound of flesh.

The idea that Shylock did not charge Antonio interest because Christians and Jews were brothers who could lend to each other gratis is unlikely to have attracted much sympathy in Shakespeare's England. Despite changing attitudes to the charging of interest and the recent enactment of the Usury Bill allowing low-interest loans, the default position in England was for people to vilify and condemn Jewish moneylenders (of whom they knew none) as usurious. But there was another English point of view, of which Shakespeare was undoubtedly aware, which apparently turned the tables. We see it in a play written by Robert Wilson in 1584, a few years before *The Merchant of Venice*. In this play the Christian borrower was presented as the culprit and the Jewish moneylender as his victim.

Wilson was an actor, a member of the Lord Chamberlain's Men, a group to which Shakespeare also belonged. Wilson's play, *A Right Excellent and Famous Comedy Called the Three Ladies of London*, includes an exchange between a Jewish moneylender, Gerontus, and an Italian merchant, Mercadorus. The scene is a Turkish court where Mercadorus, who has defaulted on loans made to him by the Jew, is up for sentencing. The only way Mercadorus can avoid the consequences is to become a Turk and convert to Islam. In such a case, the judge assures him, his debts will be forgiven. Mercadorus is prepared to do this but he is clearly conflicted and the Jewish moneylender takes pity on him. Not wishing to be seen as the cause of Mercadorus forsaking his Christian faith, Gerontus forgives him the debt. The scene ends with Mercadorus gloating that he has succeeded in cheating the Jew.

Wilson did not write his play to express sympathy with Jewish moneylenders. His intention was to write an anti-alien polemic, an assault on the perceived greed of Italian merchants who were undercutting the English traders with whom they competed. Any sympathy that the play seems to have for Jews is coincidental, just a consequence of the trick that Mercadorus plays on Gerontus.

David de Pomis had never been to England but he would not have been surprised by negative English attitudes towards Jews. He comes across as a proud and self-confident man who was frustrated by the conditions under which Jews lived in Italy. His defence of Jewish doctors and moneylenders coupled with his praise of the Venetian constitution suggest that he expected more from a society that could be so competent that it could devise a perfect political system yet so self-regarding that it would treat those upon whom it depended with such contempt. His writings demonstrate a passion for lifting Jews out of the underclass, affording them dignity and social parity with their Christian brothers. As a man who had himself experienced more than enough of life's tragedies, he saw no reason to accept a second-class status for himself or his people.

De Medico Hebraeo was written a few years after a controversy broke out over a book published in nearby Mantua. The book, *Meor Einayim*, or 'Light of the Eyes', by the physician and scholar Azariah dei Rossi, was the first serious use by a Jewish scholar of the tools of critical historical scholarship. In a series of essays dei Rossi used a scientific approach to resolve some of the chronologies and historical contradictions in the Bible and Talmud. He critiqued rabbinic legends, explored some of the lesser-known texts that lay outside the rabbinic corpus, and generally re-evaluated many of the assumptions and orthodoxies held by the rabbis of his time. His purpose was religious, he sought Truth, using a method of argumentation that differed from rabbinic convention. Unlike many rabbis, dei Rossi was widely read, he knew Latin and Greek, was familiar with early Jewish thinkers, like Philo, whose works had fallen into disuse, he'd read the writings of the early church fathers, and was up to speed with the philosophical and scientific developments of his age. In the spirit of the times he subjected the reasoning and historicity of Judaism to critical analysis. De Pomis wrote in the same spirit, though his field was science rather than religion.

Both de Pomis and dei Rossi traced their family's presence in Italy back to Roman times. Their pride derived from their ancestry, from an inherited sense of self-worth. They had each been born into venerable Italian Jewish families that traced their presence on Italian soil back to the year 70 CE. That was when the future Roman Emperor Titus destroyed Jerusalem and shipped many of its population to Rome as slaves. Perhaps it was this personal sense of history that gave them the courage to think further and deeper.

In time their families must have bought themselves out of slavery and prospered in Roman society. They declared themselves to be among the four original Italian Jewish families and were thought of almost as aristocracy by other Jews. This wasn't an official status but it did garner them some respect.

David de Pomis wanted some of that respect. He needed recognition. He was an intelligent man, deeply learned, a rabbi and a physician. Yet as a Jew, a member of a pariah race, he was never permitted to fulfil his potential, to become the man he knew he should be. De Pomis knew he was better than he was given credit for, and he knew that to obtain that credit he would need to set about correcting the injustices that Jews suffered in Christian society.

He failed. In 1589, when he was in his mid-sixties, he was obliged once again to seek papal permission to treat Christian patients.

Four years later he wrote to Ferdinando I de Medici, the Duke of Tuscany, offering his services in Pisa as a teacher of medicine or Hebrew, as the need required. As far as we know no reply was ever received and he died in Venice the following year. And for all his attempts to usher Jews into mainstream society, and despite his interest in the study of medicine and science, his legacy rests in neither of these fields. Instead, it rests on his scholarship in another field altogether, the trilingual Hebrew–Italian–Latin dictionary *Tzemach David* that he published in 1587.

Stability and Friction

As David de Pomis was writing his *Short Discourse Showing the Divine Origins of the Venetian Republic*, the Jews of the ghetto were worrying about their future. At any moment the Senate might carry out their threat to expel them in thanksgiving for the Venetian victory at the Battle of Lepanto. But as with other threats made by the Senate against their city's Jewish population, it was never carried out. Events overtook it and the threat faded into history. In a dazzling volte-face, the Senate decided that instead of throwing the ghetto residents out, they should rather encourage more Jews to settle in the city. It goes without saying that there was nothing altruistic about the decision. It was taken on purely commercial grounds, to put right a mistake made over twenty years earlier.

After Venice's unsuccessful attempt to expel the Marranos in 1550, they found themselves at something of a disadvantage. While they'd been vacillating over the wisdom of the expulsion, other Italian cities were actively tapping into the international Marrano networks, the scattered New Christian families who still retained trade and diplomatic links to the powerful Spanish and Portuguese empires. As early as 1538 Venice's southern rival Ferrara had invited the Marranos to come and settle, guaranteeing them protection against religious persecution. They repeated their invitation several times during the 1550s. Tuscany, Urbino and Savoy all followed Ferrara's example.

Venice had signed a peace treaty with Turkey in 1573 and renounced all claims to Cyprus. The years of on-and-off war had done considerable damage to their already declining economy. The Republic could no longer remain aloof to the advantages that welcoming the Marrano merchants into Venice would bring. And so in 1573 the Council of Ten offered safe conduct to all Jews of Spanish and Portuguese descent, provided only that they declared they were Jewish and lived in the ghetto.

The timing was fortuitous. In 1576 the Spanish attacked Antwerp, driving out the large *converso* community living there. Five years later Ferrara broke up its Marrano community, giving in to pressure from the Inquisition who had claimed they were living as Jews. The *conversos* from Antwerp and the Marranos from Ferrara both headed for Venice. The Senate had not yet confirmed the Council of Ten's invitation, so the new arrivals had no formal charter permitting them to live in the city, but nobody made any attempt to throw them out. Provided they complied with the condition that they live in the ghetto, they were treated as de facto residents.[1]

Meanwhile Daniel Rodriga, a Jewish merchant of Iberian origin, was working on a new commercial opportunity that he intended to present to the Venetian government. His plan was to establish a new trade route to shorten the journey across the Adriatic from Dalmatia and divert trade away from Venice's rival city of Ancona. He'd do this by building a free port at Spalato, a Venetian possession on the Dalmatian coast (today's Split, in Croatia).[2] The port at Spalato, Rodriga told the Venetians, would snatch trade away from the nearby port of Ragusa (today's Dubrovnik), from where goods were regularly shipped to Ancona. He offered to fund the construction of the free port himself. In return Rodriga asked for permanent residency privileges in both Spalato and Venice for foreign merchants, by whom he meant Jews.

He submitted a proposal to the Senate in 1577, who passed it on to the *Cinque Savi alla Mercanzia*, the Board of Trade who customarily dealt with all petitions from Jewish merchants. They approved the building of the port but rebuffed the request for residency privileges for Jewish merchants. The Venetians were still holding onto the vestiges of their exclusivist trade policy. It was one thing to allow visiting Levantine Jews to trade through Venice's ports and reside temporarily in the ghetto. However, permanent residency was out of the question.

Rodriga was not the sort of man to be put off. In 1579 he sought permission to bring 50 Jewish merchant families to settle in the city. They would pay 100 ducats annually and live in the ghetto. In return they would be given the same privileges as the moneylenders in the ghetto and the visiting Levantine merchants, and they would have the same security of property and life as Venetian citizens. He pointed out that they would be far more valuable to the Venetian economy than the resident Tedeschi moneylenders in the *ghetto nuovo*. The Board of Trade considered his proposal and decided it was too complex for them to rule on. They deferred their decision.

Rodriga still didn't give up. Four years later he tried again. This time he specifically asked for privileges for both Levantine and Ponentine, or western, Jews. Ponentine is a word that crops up frequently in academic discussions of the Venetian merchants. It is used to describe *conversos* from the Iberian Peninsula. The scholar Bernard Dov Cooperman calls it a legal euphemism developed to allow the Iberian *conversos* the same privileges as Levantine Jews, without actually calling them Levantine.[3] The point about including Ponentines in his request was that Rodriga was not just asking for privileges for *conversos* who had returned to Judaism like the Levantines, but also for those who up to now had lived as Christians in Spain and Portugal. Once again he was turned down. The Board of Trade said that granting Rodriga his petition would allow the Jews to dominate commerce in the city. That, they declared, would be an undesirable turn of events.

In 1584 Rodriga tried once more. Once again he was unsuccessful. The Board of Trade replied, noting that for all this time the Jewish merchants had tacitly been allowed to continue living in the city and that they had made a great contribution to trade and customs revenues. The Board also pointed out that they had assisted the merchants by reducing customs duties. But the Board was not prepared to grant them the security and safe conduct that Rodriga requested. The status quo could continue. But the Board would not give the Jewish merchants the peace of mind of a formal charter.[4]

Doggedly, Daniel Rodriga persisted. In 1589 he submitted a detailed petition to the Doge, 'in the name of the Levantine, Spanish and other Jewish merchants living in Venice with their families'. In the preamble he noted that he had been able to bring his brother and ten other families of friends and relatives to the city, and that he planned to bring more, 'in order to increase your customs and excise duties both in Venice and Spalato'.

He attached five requests to his petition. Most importantly, the merchants and their families should be allowed to live securely, safely and with freedom of worship. This applied equally to those who may elsewhere 'have worn some other dress or followed some other religion'. Rodriga was thinking of the Marranos and New Christians. He was making sure that they were not to be subjected to the Inquisition.

Additionally, he asked that the merchant families were to be regarded as a community in their own right, allowed to participate in any sort of trade, with the right to tax themselves and to take action against those who did not pay. They would not be obligated to contribute to the expenses the state imposed on the Tedeschi moneylenders. In order to keep out fraudsters and wrongdoers all newcomers would need a certificate issued by the Board of Trade. These, and the other regulations that Rodriga requested, were to apply equally to the merchants in Spalato who, 'for fear of evildoers' would be allowed to wear black hats, instead of the statutory yellow ones, when they were outside the town.

Finally, Daniel Rodriga took care of himself. All those who would benefit from the privileges he was requesting would be obliged to pay him, as their consul, 'such sums as shall be allocated to him by the heads of the Congregation of Venice and Spalato as a reward for his many merits and for his trouble and expense'.[5]

This time the Board of Trade were sympathetic. They accepted his arguments. Just one month later the *condotto* that Daniel Rodriga had spent over a decade agitating for was finally granted. The only substantive change to his request was that the charter would come up for renewal in ten years. It doesn't seem to have troubled Daniel Rodriga too much, the Venetians had a habit of renewing their charters, even if they made a fuss at first.

Almost single-handedly Daniel Rodriga had brought about a dramatic change in the Venetian government's attitude towards those of Jewish background. In 1550 the Venetians had been considering expelling the Marranos. Forty years later they were admitting anyone of Jewish origin, no matter what their conversionary status, granting them privileges and benefiting economically from their presence. As they put it themselves: 'The inclusion of the Spanish [Jews] . . . causes no greater detriment or harm than that which now results from their freedom to pass into Turkish lands and from there to this city to enjoy, as they do now, the benefits of the law under the name of Levantine Turkish subjects.'[6]

By obtaining residency permission for the Ponentines, the converted Spanish and Portuguese Jews, Daniel Rodriga changed the demography of the ghetto. But it is the free port in Spalato for which he was most remembered. In 1638 Simone Luzzatto, who we will meet shortly, wrote: 'Venice will never forget the memory of this man . . . who . . . succeeded in attracting to [Spalato] the trade of most eastern countries, so that its port is now considered the strongest foundation of [Venice's] trade.'[7]

INQUISITION BLUES

The records of the Venetian Inquisition contain details of various Jewish characters and events from their lives in the ghetto. Obviously these accounts relate to the more dastardly and disreputable residents of the ghetto, they wouldn't have been of interest to the Inquisition otherwise. Among the records is the story of a certain Giuseppe from Mantua, a Jewish teacher of dance who earned his livelihood teaching Christian children, apparently with the tacit approval of the Venetian authorities. Giuseppe was reported as getting on particularly well with one of his pupils, a six-year-old boy named Paulin. He took him into the ghetto to dance and on one occasion the boy's parents asked Giuseppe to take him to Mantua. These days we would be concerned that Giuseppe might be an abuser, a paedophile, that he might be grooming or otherwise harming the boy. This doesn't seem to have worried the Inquisition. If it did, they didn't say so. Their sole concern was the unsavoury influence that regular contact with a Jew might have on a Christian child. Should their contact continue for too long, the child may start to take an unhealthy interest in Judaism. He might even decide to convert to being a Jew.

The Inquisition treated Giuseppe fairly leniently, by Inquisitorial standards. They ordered him to stop teaching Christian children under the age of 12 and, in a rebuke to us moderns who might have feared that Giuseppe's sexual preference was for children, they told him to keep away not only from the boy but also from the child's young, good-looking mother. Maybe his interest in the child was merely to get into her good books. In any event, the Inquisition told Giuseppe, if he disobeyed their orders he would be sentenced to three years at the galleys.

Giuseppe's case had been a fairly simple one for the Inquisition to resolve. The trial of the wealthy merchant Gaspare Ribiera proved to be more complicated. Beginning in 1569 and not concluding until 1586, it ended up as one of the longest trials to be heard by an Inquisition anywhere in the world.

Gaspare Ribiera was a Christian, or at least that is what he claimed to be. He only came to the attention of the Inquisition because his son Giovanni married Alumbra, a Jewish woman from the ghetto. They had married on the island of Murano, famous for its glass workshops, in a ceremony attended by both Jews and Christians. After the wedding the bride and groom lived separately; Giovanni continued to live outside the ghetto, Alumbra, as before, residing behind its walls. Giovanni would visit her regularly, he celebrated Jewish festivals with her, and declared his intention to become Jewish and take her to Constantinople.

None of this was known until Giovanni died and Alumbra asked her father-in-law to return her dowry, as was customary under Jewish law. When he refused to pay her, she turned to the authorities. The Inquisition looked into Giovanni's background and activities and took the testimony of a maidservant who claimed that after attending communion services he and his family would slip outside and spit out the sacrament. Another witness described him as a ship 'who sails with two rudders, because he is neither Jew nor Christian'.[8]

Eventually Gaspare Ribiera was found guilty of judaizing, of being a Christian who behaved in ways that were Jewish. He was dead by this time but it made little difference, they condemned his memory as 'judaizing and impenitent' and had his corpse reburied in unsanctified ground. It then turned out that this wasn't the first time the family had been caught out; years earlier Giovanni had been condemned by the Inquisition in Lisbon, also for judaizing.[9]

The crime of judaizing, behaving Jewishly or persuading others to do so, crops up frequently in the Inquisitional records. Behaving Jewishly was a charge that only a born or converted Christian could be guilty of. So the obvious defence to anyone accused of it was to claim that they were Jewish. When Abraham Righetto was charged with the offence he defended himself by saying he had been born in Ferrara as a Jew, the son of Jewish parents. Righetto, who also went under the names of Enriques Nuñes and Abraham Benvenisti, knew that he was taking a risk; Pope Paul IV had ruled that anyone born in Spain or Portugal after the expulsion or forced conversions would automatically be regarded as a baptized Christian. Righetto knew that if his story of being born as a Jew in Ferrara was shown to be a lie, if it could be shown that he had actually been born in Portugal, he would have no way of escaping his sentence.

Righetto's trial became a cause célèbre. The Pope requested a full account, the Bishop of Vicenza gave a deposition, six witnesses came forward from Ferrara, nine parties sent affidavits from Lisbon and one from Rome. They all testified that Righetto was a wealthy, Portuguese, New Christian, a member of the Nuñes family. Having been born in Lisbon, he had set off on his travels, living a playboy life, gambling and losing heavily in the salons of Cosimo I de Medici of Florence. It sounded true, it was well known in Venice that Righetto was a cousin of the fabulously wealthy Joseph Nasi, Duke of Naxos, the friend of the Turkish Sultan who the Venetian establishment believed was the Republic's sworn enemy. The Inquisition kept Righetto in gaol for nearly two years, only examining him every few months, wearing him down through boredom.

Throughout his ordeal Righetto stuck to his story, but the Inquisition knew full well that early on in his incarceration he had foolishly admitted to the Council of Ten that he had been born in Portugal. Nothing they'd heard from the witnesses since then had disabused them of that fact.

In 1573 Righetto, suffering from ill health, was transferred to a prison at San Marco, where he was able to roam freely through the rooms and corridors. A public hanging in the Piazza caught the attention of his gaolers; they went to watch and Righetto seized his opportunity. The last time he was seen in Venice he was heading down the Calle dei Albenesi.[10]

Abraham Righetto found his way to Constantinople where he joined his powerful cousin Joseph Nasi. At heart he was still a playboy, happy to take risks. Ignoring the warrant that was out for his arrest, he eventually set off again and returned to Europe. This time he was arrested by the Portuguese Inquisition, a far more fearsome tribunal than their Venetian counterparts.

Righetto gave up any attempt at dissimulation. He confessed to having been born in Portugal, to parents who had been forcibly converted to Christianity.[11] His fate was sealed.

Variety was never in short supply at the Inquisition. On one occasion a visitor from Spain reported seeing a black teenager aged about fourteen in the ghetto. The boy was wearing the yellow Jewish cap. The visitor said he had remonstrated with the boy, telling him that as he was black he clearly could not be Jewish. But then he had been told by a bystander that there were Jews who bought slaves in the Istanbul market, circumcised them, and converted them to Judaism. This boy had probably been converted in a similar way.

This straightforward, believable explanation worried the Inquisition on two counts. They didn't know whether or not the boy had been a Christian before he was converted. If he had not been, those who converted him would still have committed a crime because heathens were potential Christians. They could not be allowed to become Jews. Furthermore, Jews were not allowed to own slaves.

The Inquisition made inquiries and arrested a couple of people on suspicion of having converted the boy, but their investigation soon reached a dead end because they could not find the young man. They decided he must have been the dark-skinned Samuel Maestro, the son of a woman from Ferrera whom they described as neither white nor black. But they had to let Samuel go when it turned out that his mother was Jewish herself, as was Samuel's father. The boy was never found and no further progress was made in the case.[12]

Similarly inconclusive was an inquiry by the Holy Office into two Jews who were accused of exorcizing a spirit which had possessed a Christian child. Their offence, it appeared, was to command the spirit to leave by appealing to both Christian and Jewish saints. They compelled the spirit to swear by the Gospels that it would depart through the child's left foot. When it did leave, the child suffered convulsions and was left stunned and exhausted. As the exorcists were only investigated but not arrested it appears that the Inquisition did not regard their activities as particularly venal.

A Fractious Divorce

By the second half of the sixteenth century the residents of the ghetto had settled into a pattern of life similar to anywhere in the world. They had their share of joys and tragedies, crises and successes, romances and confrontations. The only difference was that in addition to the law of the Republic where they lived they were also subject to Jewish law. Unlike the law of the Republic, however, Jewish law was not underpinned by the authority of government;

rulings of the Jewish court could not always be enforced effectively and were easily ignored or challenged.

In 1560, Moses HaCohen Tamari, a Jewish physician in Venice, announced that his daughter Tamar had become engaged. She was to marry Samuel Moses Ventura, commonly known as Venturozzo. The physician Tamari agreed to write a generous dowry into the marriage contract.

Three months later it had all fallen apart. Tamari and Venturozzo fell out over money, and Tamar fell out of love. The wedding was off. Even though they were only betrothed and not married, Jewish law still required a formal divorce, one that could only be granted by the man. But Venturozzo refused. He had fled Venice after Tamari had reported him to the authorities for living outside the ghetto and for owning books that the physician asserted were kabbalistic but were in fact works of magic. Venturozzo responded by lodging a claim against Tamari who had distrained his property. In these circumstances, there was no way he would grant a divorce.

Eventually Tamar appealed to the Venetian rabbis, asking them to implement a very rare, often unsuccessful process that would allow her to insist on a divorce. It marked the beginning of a long, drawn-out legal battle.

While the two parties traded legal blows in the Jewish courts, and contesting rabbis traded the opinions of medieval authorities, Venturozzo was writing books and pamphlets. He libelled the Tamaris, abused the rabbis of Venice and, inexplicably, made foolish and derogatory comments about Christianity. The Levantine community in the ghetto responded by excommunicating him and, unusually and controversially, gave Tamari permission to take his case to the secular authorities. On the basis of Venturozzo's comments about Christianity, Tamari reported him to the Inquisition. When the Inquisition summoned Venturozzo he ran away again, this time hiding in the house of the Florentine ambassador to Venice, who must have had his own reasons for sheltering him. Eventually Venturozzo escaped the city, fleeing to Mantua. Once he had left Venice, the Council of Ten pointlessly banished him.

It was only then that the controversy really took off. Hostilities broke out between the rabbis who had been supporting the opposing sides. One rabbi was excommunicated by his opponents on the eve of the Sabbath. The next morning he went to see the bishop's deputy to get the decree postponed, asking him to threaten or sanction his opponents. The idea that a bishop had the right to intervene in a religious dispute between rabbis shows just how bizarre the situation had become. Learned rabbis argued over the legal issues involved, less learned Jews quarrelled in the streets. Things didn't settle down until the secular authorities became involved.

The Tamari–Venturozzo affair, as it has become known, puts to rest any conception that the ghetto in Venice was isolated from the rest of Venetian society; or that Italians paid no attention to issues involving Jews.[13]

HOW TO CONVERT A JEW

No matter how difficult it was to be a Jew in the sixteenth century, even in Venice, a more tolerant place than most, there was always a means of escape. No matter how unsanitary, overcrowded, filthy and malodorous the living conditions, restrictive the civic regulations, irrelevant or baffling the cultural environment was to ordinary Jews, they could put it all behind them. All they had to do was convert to Christianity and everything would change.

The Counter-Reformation had placed conversion at the centre of the Church's policies towards Jews. *Cum nimis absurdum* had made it clear that the Church tolerated Jews only for the sake of their eventual conversion. In common with other cities Venice had built a House for Catechumens, where Christian doctrine was taught to recent and aspiring converts. Some were already blessed with valuable skills and knowledge. In the case of Giovanni Battista Eliano, a grandson of Elia Levita and the first Jewish Jesuit, these included a familiarity with Jewish life, an understanding of how to encourage Jews to convert, and the ability to speak six languages.[14]

The records of the Inquisition preserve accounts of several Venetian Jews who converted to Christianity. One account concerns a certain Isaac Pugliese who was converted twice, once forcibly and once out of choice. He'd grown up in the Piedmontese town of Alessandria and as a boy had fallen under the influence of a family of local gangsters. They forced him to be baptized, so the story goes, as part of a bizarre sexual ritual. Many years later, living in Venice, Pugliese was baptized again. He had been working for a local nobleman, Antonio Boldu, who had obtained a licence for him to leave the ghetto at night and work as a glass-blower on the island of Murano. When the Inquisition summoned him to discover why he had been baptized twice, Pugliese said that for months he and Boldu had argued about religion. Eventually the nobleman, frustrated that he could not convince Pugliese to convert, took him to hear a sermon at the church of Santi Giovanni e Paolo. Sitting in the row in front of them was the influential aristocrat Pietro di Lorenzo Loredan. While the preacher was delivering his address, Loredan would turn round periodically to Pugliese and tell him to take good note of what he had heard. At the conclusion of the church service Loredan invited Pugliese to visit him daily for instruction in Christianity. For his part, Boldu persuaded Pugliese to buy and study a polemical book aimed at potential converts, composed by the theologian Pietro Colonna who wrote under the pen name of Galatino.

Galatino's polemic, *De Arcanis Catholicae Veritatis*, is an attempt to persuade Jews of the truths of Christianity by presenting them with kabbalistic and Talmudic texts that had been interpreted in in a Christian fashion. Isaac told the Inquisition that whenever he came across a difficult passage in Galatino's book he would take it to the ghetto and ask learned Jews to explain it to him. He said that on one occasion he asked some Levantine Jews whether it was true that Jesus was the Messiah. To satisfy the Inquisition he claimed that they agreed 'but that one cannot see it'.

Isaac Pugliese was a serious and committed convert. He studied and discussed Christianity for over a year, fasting and praying that he would be granted the grace to understand the theological difficulties that eluded him. He said in his testimony to the Inquisition that he was baptized 'for no other purpose than the saving of my soul . . . I will accept death for the faith as readily as any other good Christian and I hope to be the means of bringing other Jews to the light of the holy Christian faith.' Following his baptism Pugliese took the name Marc'Antonio degli Elletti.[15]

Although conversion to Christianity removed the stigma for Jews of belonging to a despised faith, it could equally saddle them with disadvantages. Any Jews who owed money to recent converts were unlikely to pay it. Converts struggled to receive inheritances, rents, wages, or anything else that they were owed by Jews. The Jews were not just being bloody minded, though there was probably some of that as well. More importantly, making it financially difficult to become Christian was as good a method as any of discouraging their fellow Jews from conversion. In 1610 the convert Paolo Gradenigo complained that his life continued to be a succession of legal disputes and quarrels with those Jews among whom he had formerly lived. He had converted to Christianity 36 years earlier.

THE CONTROVERSY THAT DIDN'T TAKE OFF

The ghetto's rabbis, whether of German, Spanish or Levantine origin, had one characteristic in common. They were conservative in their adherence to tradition. Even if the brightest among them were willing to open their minds to the cultural renaissance taking place, the less imaginative resisted new ideas vigorously. In 1573, when Azariah dei Rossi's book *Meor Einayim* made use of the new tools of scientific criticism to challenge some of the chronologies and beliefs of traditional Judaism, the backlash was vigorous.

The reaction to *Meor Einayim* was led from Venice, by an up-and-coming young rabbi, Samuel Judah Katzenellenbogen. He had seen a letter sent by his father-in-law to the distinguished kabbalist Rabbi Menahem Azariah da Fano. The letter expressed horror at dei Rossi's conclusions and the threat they posed to traditional belief.

Samuel Judah was the son of Meir Katzenellenbogen, the rabbi whose book had been plagiarized by Marco Antonio Giustiniani, setting off the dispute that culminated in the burning of the Talmud. Samuel Judah Katzenellenbogen had first come to public attention just a year earlier when he delivered a eulogy on the death of the renowned Polish rabbi, Moses Isserles. Isserles had supported Samuel Judah's father during the printers' dispute by threatening to excommunicate anyone who bought Giustiniani's cheaper, plagiarized edition of Katzenellenbogen's book. Samuel Judah decided to repay the debt his family owed to Isserles by delivering a tribute to him in the synagogues of Venice.

The young rabbi eulogized Isserles's stature as a legal codifier and his tremendous reputation throughout the Ashkenazi communities of northern Europe. However, he failed to mention the personal support that Isserles had given him a little while earlier, when he controversially insisted that the women of the ghetto should visit the ritual bath each month at night, as was the Ashkenazi practice, rather than following the Sephardi custom of going during the day.[16] Most of the women in the ghetto were of Sephardi origin and the young rabbi's ruling had not gone down well. That he didn't mention the incident when delivering the eulogy in front of many of the people he had upset might suggest that Samuel Judah had learnt the value of discretion. If so, he forgot the lesson when it came to Azariah dei Rossi's book.

Samuel Judah Katzenellenbogen had a long and distinguished career ahead of him, but at this point in his life he was still young. Apparently without bothering to read *Meor Einayim*, the impetuous rabbi leapt into action. He sent a circular letter to all the Jewish communities in Italy, summarizing objections to *Meor Einayim* and enclosing a manifesto that he wanted everyone to sign. Unfortunately, the manifesto was vague and uncertain. It did not spell out in any detail what was wrong with dei Rossi's book, probably because Katzenellenbogen hadn't read it. 'There were some chapters,' he wrote, 'full of new issues never dreamed of by our fathers.'[17]

The manifesto, which he hoped would be signed by 'the very excellent scholars of each and every city', condemned dei Rossi's book but was as mild as it was vague. He hoped that every Jew who wanted to read it would obtain permission from the rabbi of his city. Other than offering an opportunity to any rabbi who wanted to be obstructive, it didn't seem a particularly onerous demand.

Most rabbis in Venice paid little or no attention to Katzenellenbogen's manifesto. Few bothered to sign it. Those who did tended to be recent arrivals from the Levantine community, probably because they had not yet fully imbibed the changing intellectual climate of the ghetto. Rabbi Abraham Menahem Rapaport, who had witnessed the burning of the Talmud in the Piazza San Marco, wrote from his new home in Cremona to Rabbi Menahem Azariah da Fano, who had received the original complaint about dei Rossi's book.

Rapaport told da Fano he had received a letter enclosing a 'decree of the excellent scholars and leaders of the holy community of Venice', but although he hadn't read the book he had heard good and positive reports of it. He had known dei Rossi when they both lived in Mantua and he was sure that he would be able to defend himself against any criticisms. He didn't know whether he should sign the manifesto or not. In the end he posted a copy of the manifesto on the wall of his synagogue, without signing it, and hedged his bets by delivering a sermon warning against the dangers of accepting dei Rossi's conclusions.

Katzenellenbogen's manifesto did not fail completely. Some rabbis elsewhere in Italy did sign it, although few of them were of the stature that Katzenellenbogen was hoping for. It is thought that a counter-manifesto was circulated, supporting dei Rossi's book and signed by rabbis of greater reputation, but if this document did exist it has not survived. For his part dei Rossi travelled to the ghetto to agree certain amendments to his book, although none of the passages he changed were particularly contentious. He also agreed that the next edition of the book would include a critique by the rabbi of Mantua, and his own response.

These days dei Rossi's *Meor Einayim* is regarded as a pioneering book, the first time that any rabbinic scholar had used the tools of literary criticism to challenge aspects of Jewish belief. But it didn't have much impact in the ghetto or indeed in the wider world at the time. The intellectual climate was certainly changing, but that change was slow. There was still a contingent of people in the ghetto, of whom Rabbi Katzenellenbogen was one, who were not ready to deal with the threat of new ideas. It would be another half century or so before Venice's Jewish renaissance would really take off, and even then it was only due to a handful of people. Most notably the rabbis and controversialists, Leon Modena and Simone Luzzatto.

The Lion Who Roared

UBIQUITOUS KABBALAH

The destruction of the Talmud and the subsequent ban on Hebrew printing had a devastating impact on the ghetto. The standards of literacy among ghetto residents were high, more so probably than any other Jewish settlement in Europe, and the dearth of Hebrew books, both religious and secular, was keenly felt.

After a while the Inquisition noticed that Hebrew books were beginning to find their way onto the market again. Suspicion fell on Marco Antonio Giustiniani, the printer whose plagiarizing had led to the Talmud's burning in 1553. Obviously an enterprising character, it was rumoured that he had established a clandestine printing press on the Ionian island of Cephalonia and was smuggling Hebrew books into Venice. But the Inquisition could find no evidence; when the authorities boarded his ship and seized a chest they believed was full of contraband books all they found were furs and sponges. But everyone could see that books were appearing on the market from somewhere and, despite the lack of evidence, so many fingers were pointing at Giustiniani that there could be little doubt about his involvement. Either he was printing secretly in Cephalonia, as the rumours suggested, or he was reimporting books he had smuggled out when the decree against the Talmud was first proclaimed.[1]

By 1574, as fury at the fall of Cyprus began to fade and hostilities towards the Jews started to ease, two printshops did open in the city. They flourished only briefly as an unprecedented plague of colossal proportions broke out the following year, putting an end to most commercial activity. The pestilence destroyed 51,000 Venetian lives, nearly one-third of the population. It lasted for the best part of three years, devastating the economy and destroying families. It wasn't until 1577, when the plague had subsided, that Hebrew printing in the city really resumed in earnest. But the market had changed. There was still some demand for prayer books, copies of the Talmud and legal texts, but outstripping them all was the market for kabbalistic works. For want of any alternative, Jews had turned to the study of Kabbalah when the ban on the Talmud was imposed, but this latest surge in demand was something different. Kabbalah, the near-impenetrable, mystical aspect of Judaism, had become the dominant topic of religious study. Rabbis, poets, intellectuals, even the student doctors at the nearby University of Padua were obsessed by it; they could think of little else.

The burgeoning interest in Kabbalah had been given impetus by events on the other side of the Mediterranean, in the small Galilean town of Safed. Galilee was the fabled setting for many of the legends occupying the pages of the Zohar, the primary text of Kabbalah. When the Ottomans captured the Holy Land in 1517 and the Sultan permitted Jews to settle there, the Galilean hills became the destination of choice for those mystically minded Jews who were still rootless after the expulsion from Spain. They built homes and gathered together in devotional cabals in the small town of Safed.

Over the years Safed grew into the Jewish world's focal point for mystical scholarship. And when Isaac Luria, the most famous and important kabbalist of all, settled there in 1570 the small hillside town became the heart of a rapidly expanding global, kabbalistic universe. Safed became the nucleus for Jewish mystical ideas, from where the teachings, rituals and literature of Kabbalah radiated.

New works were being written almost daily. Their authors wanted them published. And where better to bring them for publication than Venice. In the sixteenth century Venice was Italy's preeminent centre of printing, producing over half of all books printed in the region. Ever since Daniel Bomberg had set up shop in 1516 the city had been the dominant centre of Hebrew printing throughout the world. For scholars travelling from the Holy Land or the Jewish communities of Egypt and Turkey, the island city on the shores of the Mediterranean was the easiest printing centre to reach. If a kabbalist wanted his new book of mystical insights printed or had an urge to share his intuitions with the Jews of Christian Europe, Venice was the obvious place to go.

Towards the end of the sixteenth century a kabbalist named Israel Sarug travelled from Safed to Venice. He had been one of Isaac Luria's first pupils in Safed and now, following the kabbalistic master's untimely death at the age of 37, Sarug took it upon himself to disseminate his teachings.

Sarug visited Venice several times between 1592 and 1598. He found a community thirsting to hear his words. The inhabitants of the ghetto were entranced by his magical personality and by his ability to identify souls, to tell his awed listeners who they had been in previous lives. But greater than his own personal charisma were the insights he gave them into the radical mysticism of Rabbi Isaac Luria. Luria had taught a Kabbalah of exile; a mystical system that explained how the sufferings and displacements of this world were the result of a primordial cosmic upheaval. It was a balm to Venetian Jews living excluded lives on the fringes of society, only too familiar with the adversity of exile and the pain of separation. Kabbalah flourished in Venice, not because it was all that was available after the Talmud was banned but because, in Isaac Luria's rendition, it brought comfort and understanding to those whose own experience was one of dislocation and misery.

By most accounts Israel Sarug was a sincere and devoted disciple of Isaac Luria, sitting at his feet in Safed when the master first arrived from Egypt. Sarug taught the mysticism of Safed to some of Italy's leading kabbalists, among them Rabbi Menahem Azariah da Fano who had received the letter that kicked off the *Meor Einayim* controversy. Sarug's charisma endeared him to nearly everyone with whom he came into contact. With just one exception.

One man, possibly the most erudite scholar ever to live in the ghetto, thought that Sarug was a charlatan, that he used his knowledge of Kabbalah to ingratiate himself with the wealthy and powerful. He developed a personal antipathy towards Sarug and what he considered to be his showmanship. But Sarug's behaviour was of little account, compared to the subject for which he was an apostle; the topic that concerned this man most deeply. He was profoundly disturbed by the proliferation of Kabbalah in his city of Venice, by its ubiquity, and the hold that kabbalistic magic and superstition had over the residents of the ghetto. He criticized its irrationality, disputed the claims made about Kabbalah's ancient origins and strongly objected to the cult of personality surrounding its leading proponents. He challenged the identification of Kabbalah with philosophy, and the belief that kabbalistic thought was an integral part of the sacred tradition of Judaism. He disapproved of those scholars who regarded the pursuit of Kabbalah as a serious endeavour. Most of all he regretted that his own favourite student had abandoned his medical studies and sacrificed his future career to immerse himself more deeply in Kabbalah.

This man's name was Leon Modena. He was a rabbi, teacher, musician, singer, polemicist, acclaimed preacher, scholar and gambler. He wrote prolifically on an astonishing range of subjects: the Bible, rabbinic literature, Hebrew grammar, Jewish rites and rituals, alchemy, music and, once again, gambling, to name just a few. He edited ancient texts, proof-read and authorized new printed works, wrote more than 400 poems and penned dozens of responsa, legal answers to questions sent by correspondents across the world. He was the most learned Jew of his generation, a polymath whose fame extended far beyond the walls of the ghetto. The autobiography that he wrote, and indeed his many other books, have taught us far more than we might otherwise have expected to learn about life for the Jews of Venice at the close of the sixteenth century and well into the seventeenth.[2]

A SEVENTEENTH-CENTURY AUTOBIOGRAPHY

Leon Modena's autobiography doesn't conform to our understanding of how a life story or memoir should be written. He started the book when he was 47 years old, spurred on to begin it by the death of his oldest son two months earlier, a tragedy that he never got over. He wrote it almost as a diary. When he began it he said that he intended to update it every six months, a commitment he rarely managed to keep. He begins the book by telling us that he was writing it because it may be of value to his children, their descendants and his students. Indeed, much of the work is little more than a chronicle of his family life. He often offers very little detail other than dates and places, and throughout the autobiography there is hardly any mention of his many achievements. Even so, the incidental material he throws in is enough to help us understand just how difficult life was in the ghetto, even for somebody who for many years was its most eminent resident.

Leon Modena was born in Venice in 1571. Modena, best known today for its balsamic vinegar and Ferraris, was the duchy south east of Milan where Leon's ancestors settled when they first came to Italy in the fourteenth century. Although he is known as Leon of Modena or Leon Modena in English and similarly in Hebrew, in Italian he signed his name as Leon Modena *da Venezia*.

Reading Leon Modena's life story we are reminded of the frailties of times past, of incurable disease, occluded lifespans and high levels of infant mortality. At the age of eighteen he was betrothed to his mother's niece Esther, a young woman he had not yet met but whose image he saw clearly in a dream. He relates that while he was contemplating the image in his mind her face changed so that he could not make it out. He told his parents, but they did not believe him.

As the day of the wedding approached his bride fell ill. She grew worse day by day until it was evident she was about to die. She summoned him to her bed: 'I know this is bold behaviour,' she said, 'but during the year of our engagement we did not touch each other even with our little fingers. Now at the time of my death the

rights of the dying are mine.'³ She embraced him and kissed him.
It was their first physical contact. Piety was so taken for granted
among the Jews of Venice that even engaged couples did not touch.

Just two weeks after Esther's funeral Leon surrendered to the
urging of his mother and relatives and married her sister Rachel.
It was a marriage that lasted nearly 60 years, producing three sons,
two daughters, and several babies who died in infancy. It was,
however, a marriage marred by tragedy.

Leon's oldest son Mordecai took up the study of alchemy,
learning in the workshop of Joseph Grillo, a Catholic priest.
Eventually he struck out on his own, renting a space in the *Ghetto
Vecchio*. In his autobiography Leon testified that he twice saw
Mordecai transmute one ounce of silver and nine of lead into ten
ounces of silver. 'This I saw done by him twice and examined it and
sold the silver myself for six and a half lire per ounce.'⁴ According
to Leon's testimony Mordecai appeared to be on the threshold of
a prosperous career.

Several months later Mordecai began haemorrhaging blood
from his mouth. The doctors told him it was the result of vapours
he'd inhaled in his alchemical laboratory. Although he gave up
alchemy and struggled to regain his health he never recovered.
His father consulted eleven doctors, both Jewish and Christian,
to no avail. Finally, he yielded to his son's request and called for
the alchemist Grillo with whom Mordecai had studied. But his
remedies were useless, probably as harmful for the patient as the
alchemical poisons that had brought on his illness in the first place.
Mordecai got out of bed for the last time in October 1617, to hear
his father preach on repentance in the synagogue. His death came
a few weeks later. He had been sick for two years, dying at the age
of 26 and two months.

We know more about Leon Modena's life than anyone else in
the ghetto, largely due to his autobiography. He has given us far
more insight into ghetto life than could ever be gleaned if our
only sources had been formal documents and communal records.
Despite Leon's intellectual reputation there is no reason to assume
that his day-to-day life was very different from anybody else's, or

that his suffering was any greater. The likelihood is that misfortune and tragedy were endemic in the ghetto, and joy in scarce supply.

Of all the misfortunes that besieged Leon during his life, this was the one that he found hardest to take. He described his relationship with Mordecai as being that of two brothers. He claimed that he didn't know how to praise him adequately, but he left us with a fair impression. Like his father, Mordecai was a scholar and preacher, delivering sermons in Florence, Mantua, Ferrara and Venice. We are told that he was wise, always able to give good advice to those who asked him about divine matters, neither happy nor sad, that he got on well with people and was surpassed by none in his respect for his parents.

In contrast to the joy that Mordecai brought him, Leon's greatest disappointment was his second son Isaac. When we read about him now we may conclude that the young man's struggle to live up to expectations were as much the consequence of bad parenting as anything else. Despite his piety and eminence Leon Modena was addicted to gambling. He played at tables in the company of Christians and Jews on and off throughout his life. Until what started, in his eyes, as a temptation from Satan, ended up as a fully-fledged addiction, though of course he didn't describe it in those words. His son Isaac, perhaps trying to impress or emulate his father, followed in his footsteps, continually losing the little money he earned and perpetually broke.

Isaac eventually fell out with his father after he was discovered to be engaging in 'childish escapades': activities that Leon did not spell out in detail but which led to a quarrel so bad that his father sent him away from home, to the port of Morea in the Peloponnese. Leon told a friend that he had exiled his son to afflict him and straighten him out because his head was swollen. The young man stayed away for thirteen years, wandering around Greece and Turkey. When he returned home, the mariners he had travelled with would not allow him to leave the ship without a ransom. His father paid it, hoping that his son had learnt his lesson and would now settle down.

He didn't. He fell in with a bad crowd, spent his time drinking and betting until his father once again asked him to leave. He went on his way again, travelling and gambling, returning home from time to time for a short while and then departing again. He did marry and briefly managed to earn a living. It didn't last long, he started gambling again, and after three years of marriage he left his wife and children and set off from Venice once more, this time with the intention of travelling to Brazil.

Four years later his father received a letter from Isaac. It said that he had reached Brazil, where he had made his fortune and was now a rich merchant. He said he was coming home to his wife because he was now able to take care of the whole family.

That was the last that Leon heard from him. Sometime later he heard a report that Isaac had reverted to gambling while still in Brazil and had lost all the money he'd made.

Isaac Modena did not live the life that his father had hoped for. We can only assume that his mother shared her husband's distress; like many men in former times Leon only tells us about his wife if something noteworthy has happened or he has a complaint to make. He rarely writes about her feelings or thoughts, though he did write about her tenderly once, describing her as his other half, when he feared she was about to predecease him. But whatever emotional turmoil Leon and Rachel experienced over their son's behaviour, from our vantage point Isaac's story reminds us that Jews in the ghetto did not live uniform lives. They could have adventures like anybody else, they could travel to far-flung places, they could be disreputable, they could make and lose fortunes. The residents of the ghetto were as diverse as other people anywhere else in the world.

After the death of his oldest son and with Isaac already in exile, Leon invested all his hopes in Zebulun, his youngest. The blow he was dealt was to be the cruellest of all. Like his brother Isaac, Zebulun lived a discreditable life. He became involved in a feud with a Christian gang which led to the murder of a builder and to Zebulun being taken into protective custody. Three years earlier he had been called as a prosecution witness in the trial of two Jewish brothers accused of murder. They vowed revenge on him and for a while his life was in danger from both the Jewish brothers and the

Christian gang. On the night before the holiday of Passover, when most households were busy making festival preparations, the two brothers laid a trap for him. He heard a voice calling for help. He rushed downstairs, passing his father who was too slow to realize what was happening, and dashed into the street. There he was set upon by a gang of eight men. They beat him on the head and stabbed him in the throat. Zebulun called out for his father and the old man arrived to see his son lying in a pool of blood. He died four days later. He was twenty years old. Only now did Leon write about his wife's grief and her tears.

AN EMINENT MAN OF IGNOBLE CONTRADICTIONS

For those of us who equate religious leadership with impeccable personal virtue, it is a challenge to reconcile the ignoble elements of Leon Modena's life with his reputation as one of Europe's leading rabbinic authorities, the ghetto's most distinguished preacher and rabbi, the head of Venice's yeshiva.[5] His gambling habit and the delinquency he inspired in his sons were just the most egregious of his flaws. His autobiography is full of crime and violence. When he was young one of his teachers was killed by a highway robber. His uncle was defrauded and killed by a stranger who had offered to help him with his alchemical experiments. Leon himself pursued a friar who had stolen a book from him; when he and a friend caught up with the friar and took the book back, he was beaten up himself.

He fell foul of the law on at least two occasions. The first was when he asked his grandson, Isacco Levi, to print one of his books. He told Isacco that it was the treatise that he desired to have printed more than any other, as he was sure that it would earn him 'merit and honour and an everlasting reputation that would never be lost'.[6] He did know, of course, when he asked his grandson to print the book, that Jews were forbidden to work as printers. It was a restriction that was frequently ignored, but even so Leon was aware he was exposing his grandson to risk. Leon was not in the printshop when the authorities raided. Had he been there he may have ended up spending two weeks in the darkness of a dungeon alongside his grandson and the two friends arrested with him. Leon visited the prison daily, eventually persuading the gaolers to move the young men from the dungeon to a cell with a window. Sixty-six days later they were finally released from gaol.

Leon's other brush with the law may well have had nothing to do with him, but he did react as if he were a guilty man. In March 1636 four Christians entered a shop in the *Merceria*, the stalls close to the Rialto, and stole a valuable quantity of gold cloth and silk. They took the loot by barge to a canal where three Jews were waiting. The Jews hid the goods in various locations around the ghetto.

The Council of Ten quickly received information revealing the identity of the culprits. They conducted a house-to-house search of the ghetto, arrested the malefactors, and banished them from Venice forever. They warned them that should they return in the future they would be hanged in the Piazza San Marco. They instructed anyone with any further knowledge of the affair to come forward and disclose what they knew.

Some weeks later the Council of Ten instructed the Venetian rabbis to excommunicate three individuals in the ghetto who had failed to obey the order to disclose what they knew about the theft. Leon appeared before the Council with two other rabbis, Graziadio Saravel and Simone Luzzatto (of whom we will hear much more shortly). They explained that they could not excommunicate the individuals because two had already been banished and the third, Sabbadin Cattalan, was in gaol.

It may have been the threat of excommunication that encouraged Sabbadin Cattalan to cooperate with the Council of Ten. He gave them information that allowed them to solve another case, one with far more serious consequences than the robbery in the *Merceria*. The information Cattalan provided led to two Venetian judges being convicted of accepting bribes and the arrest of several Jews who had acted as intermediaries in the bribery of the judges. Among the accused was Leon's son-in-law. He managed to avoid arrest by fleeing with several others to Ferrara, but the Venetian authorities, outraged at the Jews' role in subverting the administration of justice in the Republic, threatened the entire community with expulsion. It was no idle threat, for several weeks the fate of the Jewish settlement once again hung in the balance. In the panic and paranoia that resulted, accusations of bribery and conspiracy were hurled around the ghetto. A rumour circulated that Leon had been involved; he said it was untrue, that he'd not been involved. But so many accusations were being made, and so many people arrested, that he decided to flee to Padua. He stayed there for ten days, 'like someone in hiding'.[7]

On a third occasion he was arrested together with seven other Venetian rabbis in a dispute with the government. The rabbis had tried to excommunicate a ghetto resident who Leon described as a complete sinner. The government decided the rabbis had exceeded the authority granted to them by the state. After a lengthy investigation by the court they were acquitted.[8]

Leon also got into trouble over gambling, several times. In 1624 he found himself denounced by an informer. He doesn't say what the charge was but he did declare his innocence. He went to the Office of the Censor and made a voluntary declaration. The informer was arrested and sentenced to three years in the galleys. Leon writes that he was in great danger all year as a result.

Nor were family relationships Leon's strongest suit. Apart from mishandling his son Isaac's youthful delinquency, he kept up a lengthy feud with the husband of his daughter Diana. The husband sounds like a nasty piece of work: he abused his wife and Leon confronted him about it more than once. But although he was in the right in that dispute, his lack of sensitivity towards his own wife when she became ill indicates a profound lack of empathy. As they approached the age of 70, with them both in ill health, Rachel fell into a deep depression. It lasted the best part of a year until, in Leon's words, she 'assumed a strange mood and she began to quarrel with me and make me angry . . . I cannot write about how foolish she was, or of how from day to day I was led astray by her wheedling . . . We quarrelled all day long . . . I would grow angry and shout and act foolishly. My blood would boil, my heart would flutter, and my insides would churn up. From time to time she would vow to keep still and to cease being boisterous, but a few days later she would resume her foolish behaviour.'

Reading his autobiography we get the impression that Leon's life was one of perpetual crisis. Much of it, like the gambling and the problems with Isaac, were of his own making. Many of his misfortunes, the death of Mordecai, Esther's illness, his own depression, and of course the oppressiveness of life in the ghetto were all matters beyond his control. Had he not written an autobiography we would know him only through his accomplishments and reputation, as we do with so many other historical characters. That Leon was not discouraged from publicizing his flaws and achieved so much in the face of his many crises is all the more impressive.

In August 1593 Leon Modena preached in the German or Great Synagogue in the ghetto. He was 22 years old and it was the first time he had delivered a sermon to such a large and distinguished crowd. There were, he says, so many great and venerable sages present that the synagogue could not hold them all. Even if we allow for exaggeration it was obviously an awe-inspiring event for him. For the next twenty years he preached regularly every sabbath, in three or four different synagogues each week. Not a man inclined to too much modesty, he wrote that during all that time his congregations had never tired of him, nor had their fill of his sermons.

There is no doubt that he was a popular preacher, the most popular in the ghetto. In another example of the porous boundaries between the inhabitants of the town and the ghetto, Christian nobility and clerics would regularly come to hear him preach. When he preached at the Sephardi synagogue in April 1629 the Duc d'Orléans, the brother of King Louis XIII, came to hear him accompanied by 'some French noblemen and five of the most important Christian preachers who gave sermons that Pentecost. God put such learned words into my mouth that all were pleased, including many other Christians who were present . . . People wrote to distant places all over Italy about how unique it was.'9

To the Jews of the ghetto Leon Modena was a tolerably good preacher whose sermons were somewhat better than most. To the nobility of Venice, and increasingly to the scholars and educated aristocracy across Christian Europe, he was a figure of interest, a Jew to be treated as an equal, a polymath whose oratory and scholarship were a refreshing experience, his sermons an indispensable feature on the itineraries of those enjoying the newly fashionable distraction of cultural tourism.

Leon Modena wrote prolifically: his autobiography lists dozens of books, pamphlets, poems, sermons, prayer anthologies, mystical remedies and commentaries. He wrote his first book at the age of 13, ironically enough on the virtues and vices of gambling. He did not attach his name to the book because, he said, he did not want to be associated with such an inconsequential work.

Round about 1616 he composed a treatise for an 'English nobleman' who wanted to present it to his king, James I. Leon does not say who the nobleman was but the historian Cecil Roth conjectured that it was Sir Henry Wotton, the learned and scholarly English ambassador to Venice who lived close to the ghetto, was familiar with the circumstances under which the Jews lived, and who Leon mentions by name in a letter that he sent to a correspondent in England.[10]

The treatise that the nobleman wanted to present to King James I was one of the earliest attempts to explain the practices and beliefs of Judaism to a non-Jewish readership, in this case specifically to Protestants. Entitled *Historia de gli Riti Hebraici* and usually known just as *Riti*, it has been described as one of the most important books ever published on Judaism, one that contributed to a new understanding of Jewish identity and of the place of Jews within Christian society. Leon Modena said that he wrote it to refute a polemical work by the German Hebraist Johannes Buxtorf which had tried to depict Jewish ritual as superstitious. In contrast, Leon's *Riti* is plainly intended to explain to its Christian readers the rationality and ethical foundation of the Jewish religion.[11]

Leon's *Riti* was designed to serve another purpose too. In a subtle and uncontroversial way Leon framed his discussion to show that, contrary to common prejudice, Jews were benevolent in nature and did not hate Christians. Some years earlier he had encouraged Jews to have a better understanding of Christianity by translating the popular ethical treatise *Fior di Virtù* into Hebrew. Now, in the *Riti* his intention was to make Christians more tolerant of Jews by opening a window into their lives and practices. He had many Christian contacts and correspondents; on a personal level he was hoping for an environment in which he could feel as comfortable in their company as they could in his. Leon Modena was just one of several early modern authors, both Christian and Jewish, who were arguing for religious toleration and a more open-minded environment. Living in the oppressive Venice Ghetto where he probably could not even conceive of a life in a fully open, tolerant society, he did the best he could, trying to rid both Jews and Christians of their prejudices towards each other.[12]

The *Riti* circulated widely for almost twenty years as a handwritten manuscript. Leon didn't print it for fear of the book being distributed too widely and falling into the hands of the Inquisition. Although the Inquisition paid little attention to what Jews did when it came to the practice of their religion, in normal times they drew the line at what they perceived as Jewish attempts to undermine or contradict Christianity. And these were not normal times; the Catholic Counter-Reformation was still vigorously pursuing any indication of religious dissent and the Inquisitors were assiduously scrutinizing anything that they suspected might carry the taint of heresy. Had the *Riti* been written for Jews, Leon may have had less reason to be concerned. But he had written it deliberately for a Christian readership; he had even gone so far as to say in his introduction that when writing the book he had put out of his mind the fact that he was a Jew. Leon's fear of how the Inquisition might respond was very real indeed.

When, in 1637, the French mystic Jacques Gaffarel printed the *Riti* in Paris, Leon Modena panicked. He had entrusted the manuscript to Gaffarel in order that he might publish it, but that had been two years earlier. Leon had assumed that he would be notified before the book was printed, that he would have the opportunity to remove passages to which he now realized the

Inquisition in Italy might take objection. But Gaffarel had gone ahead with the printing without telling him.

Leon wrote in his autobiography that when he heard the *Riti* had been printed he dug out his original draft and inspected it with a pounding heart. He found four or five passages that he was sure were bound to offend. Rattled, he yelled and tore at his beard until he nearly passed out. He was convinced that the wrath of the Inquisition would descend upon him and indeed upon all the Jews of the ghetto for his impudence in writing a book about Judaism in Italian, a book that anybody could read, that might tempt Christians into apostasy. Worse still, he now realized he had written some passages that may have been construed as critical of Christianity.

Terrified of what might happen Leon decided the best course of action would be for him to take the initiative and approach the Inquisition before they came looking for him. It turned out to be the right decision. He submitted a copy of his manuscript to the Inquisitor and awaited his decision. The verdict was not good, but it came as a relief to him. The Inquisitor ruled that Leon's reproduction of Maimonides's thirteen principles of faith was objectionable, as was his treatment of the subject of reincarnation. Apart from that he raised no objection. Leon was released without punishment, but the Inquisitor ordered the manuscript to be destroyed and warned him against publishing or circulating any further copies.

Leon had escaped punishment and the ban on publishing the book only applied where the Inquisition's authority was upheld. It didn't affect the copies printed in France, or any of the subsequent reprintings of the book in Europe. And as it turned out the manuscript that Leon submitted was not destroyed. It is still in the Inquisition archive in Venice.

THE ENGLISH CONNECTION

It was the English lawyer John Selden who helps us to see just how widely Leon Modena's fame had spread, and how ideas flowing out of the ghetto were coming under the scrutiny of Europe's leading thinkers. Some years before the *Riti* was printed Selden was given an autographed manuscript copy of the book by William Boswell. Boswell, who had studied with Leon in Venice in his youth, was a distinguished theologian and diplomat who had been a Member of Parliament and would go on to be the English ambassador to The Hague. He was one of England's few Christian Hebraists, a small band of Hebrew scholars of whom the most prominent and fascinating was John Selden, the man to whom he sent his copy of the *Riti*.

John Selden has gone down in history as an expert on ancient British law and constitution. During the constitutional crisis which led to the execution of King Charles I in January 1649 he was twice imprisoned for supporting Parliament against the king, before switching sides. He briefly became a royalist, then resumed his former republican stance, playing his part in Parliament's prosecution of the king. But the most fascinating aspect of Selden's life were his activities as a Hebrew scholar. His knowledge of Hebrew, the Talmud and the other rabbinical texts far exceeded that of most Jews, to the extent that, although being a Christian, he was addressed by one of his correspondents as Rabbi Selden. John Milton described him as the 'chief of learned men reputed in this land' and the Dutch jurist Hugo Grotius called him the 'glory of the English nation'.

During his period in prison Selden asked to borrow Westminster Abbey's copy of the Talmud; the same volumes that Henry VIII had imported from Venice. After his release Selden drew on his prison studies to write several tracts on Jewish law. One was an analysis of the rabbinic opinions that Henry VIII had sought when trying to divorce Catherine of Aragon. This led him into a discussion of Jewish marriage law, in which he twice quoted from 'the little book of R. Leo of Modena, head of a synagogue in Venice, on the customs of the Jews or *Historia de gli Riti Hebraici*.'[13] Selden had previously quoted Leon in an earlier work on the Jewish laws of inheritance. Leon was delighted. He wrote about it in his biography, 'so that it be known (although without merit) what fame I have'.[14]

Leon Modena had several English contacts and correspondents apart from John Selden and William Boswell.[15] But perhaps his most entertaining encounter with an Englishman was with a gentleman named Thomas Coryate on the streets of the Venice Ghetto. Coryate was a traveller who published an account of his travels in *Coryat's Crudities*, likely to have been the first ever English-language guidebook for travellers. In his account he described an encounter he'd had with a rabbi in the ghetto. We can't be certain who the rabbi was, but Coryate's description of his erudition and the fact that he spoke Latin has led many researchers to conclude that it must have been Leon Modena.

Coryate fell into conversation with the rabbi and the topic quickly turned to their religious differences. Coryate asked the rabbi whether he accepted that Christ was the Messiah. The rabbi's response was that he could accept that Jesus was a great prophet but he could not accept his divinity nor acknowledge him as the Messiah. Coryate pressed him on the matter and the conversation went back and forth with the Englishman growing more and more insistent that the rabbi was mistaken and urging him to reconsider his opinions. He seems to have forgotten that he was in the middle of a Jewish enclave and spoke down to the rabbi as if speaking to an inferior, with the boorishness of someone who could not possibly be wrong. Ultimately, he warned the rabbi that if he did not renounce his Jewish faith and accept Christianity he would be eternally damned. It was only then he realized that the rabbi 'seemed to be somewhat exasperated against me'.

As Coryate and the rabbi were speaking a few passers-by stopped to listen, the crowd gradually swelling as their exchange continued. Coryate described the scene to his readers:

> After there had passed many vehement speeches to and fro betwixt us, it happened that some forty or fifty Jews more flocked about me, and some of them began very insolently to swagger with me, because I durst reprehend their religion. Whereupon fearing least they would have offered me some violence, I withdrew myself by little and little towards the bridge at the

entrance into the ghetto, with an intent to flee from them, but by good fortune our noble ambassador Sir Henry Wotton passing under the bridge in his gondola at that very time, espied me somewhat earnestly bickering with them, and so incontinently sent unto me out of his boat one of his principal gentlemen, Master Belford his secretary, who conveyed me safely from the unchristian miscreants.[16]

It is a wonderful image. A pompous English sightseer trying to convince a foreign rabbi of the error of his ways and convert him to Christianity in front of an inquisitive, mildly hostile Jewish crowd. Fearing that the crowd might have set upon him he backed away, ready to flee, until all of a sudden he was saved by an English knight who just happened to be passing in a gondola. Life in the ghetto, one suspects, was rarely so entertaining.

We might wonder, given his English connections, whether Leon Modena had ever heard of Shakespeare or knew that he had written a play about a Jew set in the very same town in which Leon lived. It would not have been surprising if he had heard of Shakespeare. His contact Sir Henry Wotton, who had probably commissioned the *Riti*, was certainly familiar with the playwright; in 1613 he wrote to Sir Edmund Bacon telling him about the recent fire which destroyed Shakespeare's Globe Theatre during a performance of his play *All is True*.[17] Wotton's literary friends included John Donne and the young John Milton; he may even have met the ageing Shakespeare himself.

Even if Wotton had never mentioned Shakespeare to Leon, his chaplain William Bedell may have done. He and Leon enjoyed a close intellectual relationship; Leon taught Bedell Hebrew, Bedell introduced Leon to Christian interpretations of the Bible.[18] It would have been odd if one or more of Leon's learned English contacts hadn't mentioned Shakespeare to him at least in passing, probably pointing out that two of the bard's plays were set in Venice and a couple more in nearby Verona.[19] Particularly since Leon was something of a playwright himself, he is known to have written at least two plays, only one of which, *L'Ester*, has survived.

If Leon had heard of Shakespeare then we might wonder whether he had also heard of Shylock and indeed whether he had an opinion about Shakespeare's presentation of the character. It would be meaningless to ask if Leon thought that *The Merchant of Venice* was an antisemitic play; Christian hostility towards Jews was a given in his lifetime and the term antisemitism would not be coined for another 250 years or so (researchers predictably unable to agree on who used the term first). But it is not meaningless to wonder whether Leon would have found the play offensive towards Jews, or more pertinently, whether we should today.

Much has been written about whether Shakespeare's treatment of Shylock betrays his personal attitude towards Jews. It is an impossible question. As James Shapiro writes: '*The Merchant of Venice* is a play, a work of fiction, not a diary or a polygraph test; since no one knows what Shakespeare personally thought about Jews, readers will continue to make up their own minds about this question.'[20] We can listen to Antonio's characterization of Shylock as a devil, an evil soul, 'a villain with a smiling cheek', hear Solanio's 'dog jew' slur or the duke's 'inhuman wretch', and decide these are exactly the sort of insults one would expect from an antisemitic playwright. Alternatively we can hear Shylock's plaintive 'hath a Jew not eyes . . . if you prick us do we not bleed' and construe it as a demonstration of Shakespeare's sympathy for the ever-abused Jews. We can ask, as Stephen Greenblatt does, why, if Shakespeare was truly antisemitic, he doesn't exploit the ancient antisemitic libels – the poisoning of wells and the ritual murder of Christian children?[21] Or we can question why, if the play is not antisemitic, it turns on Shylock's heartless and vengeful demand for payment of a pound of Antonio's flesh, an allegation of Jewish usuriousness that has never been surpassed in English literature.

It is Frances Yates yet again who offers a perspicacious insight into what Shakespeare is doing in *The Merchant of Venice*.[22] In Act Three a succession of suitors turns up to seek the hand of the wealthy and desirable heiress Portia. Under the terms of her father's will each suitor is to be presented with three caskets, one of gold, another of silver and the third of lead. She must marry the man who successfully selects the chest in which her portrait is contained. The Prince of Morocco chooses the gold casket and fails. The Prince of Aragon opts wrongly for the silver container. It is the outlier of the group, the skint Bassanio on whose behalf Antonio has guaranteed a loan from Shylock, who wins Portia's suit by choosing the lead casket.

Yates points out that in occult thought lead is the governing metal of Saturn. The Venetian friar, Francesco Giorgi, who Yates argues was one of Shakespeare's influences when writing *The Merchant of Venice*, regarded Saturn as representing the religion of the Jews.[23] Saturn's name in Hebrew is Shabbetai, alluding to the *shabbat* or sabbath. It's about as Jewish an allusion as can be imagined.

She also notes that it has been suggested the three suitors who opened the three caskets represent three religions. The Prince of Morocco, who opened the golden casket, was no doubt a Muslim and the Prince of Aragon a Christian. By that reckoning Bassanio should be a Jew.

There is no suggestion of Bassanio's Jewishness in the play; it would spoil the entire plot if there were. Unless he was a former Jew, one whose family had converted to Christianity, a member of Venice's well-known Marrano community. Shakespeare knew one such converted Jew. His name, intriguingly, was Baptiste Bassano, one of Queen Elizabeth I's musicians. Does the similarity of names indicate that the fictional Bassanio is supposed to remind us of Bassano the converted Jew?

Or is the similarity of names because of Baptiste Bassano's daughter Aemilia?[24] The Oxford historian A. L. Rowse suggested that Aemilia Bassano had briefly been Shakespeare's lover, that she was the 'dark lady' of his sonnets.[25] And Shakespeare seems to have made a coded reference to Aemilia Bassano in two of his plays. She appears in *Othello* as Emilia and as Bassanio in *The Merchant of Venice*. These are the two plays that he set in Venice; they were first performed within a year of each other. This does not look like an accident. Perhaps Aemilia Bassano was on his mind at the time.

So if the suitor of the gold casket represents Islam and that of the silver Christianity, does his opening of the lead casket imply that Bassanio symbolizes the Jews; that the similarity of his name to Aemilia Bassano suggest that he was supposed to have come from a family converted to Christianity as her family had done? And if the fortunate Bassanio, one of the few characters to emerge from the drama innocent and unscathed, has Jewish ancestry, can *The Merchant of Venice* really be considered an antisemitic play?

The Lion's Rage

Leon Modena's life was full of disappointments. But there was one person he could take pride in. His student Joseph Hamiz, who had studied with him for years, who he loved like a son. Hamiz was not simply an erudite scholar of Talmud and rabbinic literature. He was also a distinguished medical student at the nearby University of Padua. Leon looked forward to a bright and distinguished future for him. Until the day he discovered that Joseph Hamiz had fallen under the spell of the Kabbalah.

Kabbalah was now so ubiquitous in the ghetto that it had entranced even the Christian residents of Venice. They would come in to buy amulets and talismans, to have spells written or hear protective blessings uttered, have their dreams interpreted or their horoscopes foretold. Leon Modena was as active as anyone else in the kabbalistic trade, he wrote amulets and had taught kabbalistic ideas. But he took great exception to the myths that he believed the kabbalists perpetuated, and to their rejection of the rationalism of Maimonides, the most outstanding of all medieval Jewish thinkers. Leon disputed the kabbalists' claims about the antiquity of their mystical system and regarded their challenge to Maimonides as a dumbing down of the Jewish intellectual tradition. He took exception to key kabbalistic ideas such as the migration of souls after death to another body and the assumption that the recital of particular prayers and formulae can cause God to act in certain ways. He rejected Kabbalah's fundamental concept of *sefirot*, the belief that God controls the world through the medium of ten divine attributes.

It is difficult for us to appreciate how Leon could challenge Kabbalah intellectually and still believe in the power of amulets and horoscope. But Leon lived at a time when magic and the occult were still taken seriously, even if they could not be accommodated into rational philosophy. He had faith in the power of his amulets, even if he thought that the theory lying behind them was nonsense.

Leon's great disappointment came when he realized that Joseph Hamiz was coming under the influence of those who taught and promoted Kabbalah in the ghetto. Leon was convinced they were in error, and he could not bear to see them leading his favourite pupil down the same mistaken path. He was an old man by now, 68 years of age, wracked by grief and misfortune, and feeling enraged by what he must have considered the intellectual gullibility of his pupil. He composed an anti-kabbalistic polemic as an outlet for his feelings. Entitled *Ari Nohem* ('A Lion Roars'), he addressed it to Joseph Hamiz, 'his beloved student, pleasant of speech, who looked at the works of those who call themselves kabbalists and open their mouths against the great eagle Maimonides'.[26]

Ari Nohem was a landmark work in the development of Jewish intellectual thought. In writing it, Leon used the same tools of historical criticism and religious scepticism that characterized the work of just a handful of early modern, European scholars. The Swiss-born Isaac Casaubon had made use of similar methods to show that the Hermetic literature and the Sybilline Oracles, mystical works long believed to have originated in darkest antiquity, were largely composed during the early centuries of the Common Era. Azariah dei Rossi, who we discussed earlier, challenged contradictions in the Talmud and rabbinic tradition over half a century before Leon wrote *Ari Nohem*. In Venice itself the friar Paolo Sarpi, who Leon knew, was refuting accepted assumptions about the historicity of the Catholic Church and the papacy. Yaacob Dweck, who wrote a comprehensive study of *Ari Nohem*, describes the book as an early Jewish exemplar of early modern scepticism.[27]

Ari Nohem was a closely argued scholarly work, an unremitting attack on the beliefs and presumed history of Kabbalah. But it failed in its avowed purpose. It did not convince Joseph Hamiz to abandon his interest in Kabbalah. It may even had strengthened his commitment, Hamiz may have read Leon's arguments and dismissed them as the disillusioned negativity of an embittered old man. Leon did not live long enough to follow Hamiz's career. In the years after Leon's death Hamiz edited a new edition of a major kabbalistic text, started to write a commentary on another, became an active follower of the kabbalist and false messiah Shabbetai Tzvi, and set off to travel to Jerusalem. He was never heard of again.[28]

Among the many books that Leon Modena wrote is a tirade against a man who was spouting heretical views. This time he knew the entire ghetto would agree with him. But reading his tirade leaves us wondering just how convinced he was himself by what he wrote.

More of a pamphlet really than a book, *Magen v'Tzina* (*Shield and Breastplate*) was composed as a reply to the rabbis of Hamburg. They had written to Leon asking how they should deal with one of their community who was challenging the fundamental beliefs and rituals of the Jewish religion. His name was Uriel da Costa, a *converso* who had been brought up in Portugal as a Catholic but had studied the Hebrew Bible and found that it reflected his outlook on life far more closely than the Gospels did. He converted to Judaism but almost immediately realized that the practice of the Jewish religion differed in many respects from the regulations set out in the Hebrew Bible. His response was to pose a series of questions to the Hamburg rabbis in which he challenged the fundamental beliefs of Judaism. He denied the immortality of the soul, argued against the authority of the rabbis, and urged that Jews return to following the literal words of the Bible rather than its interpretations.

Leon Modena wrote back to the rabbis of Hamburg with a detailed response to each of da Costa's points. He refused to mention da Costa by name, referring to him as the 'heretic from Hamburg' and as a 'foolish and stupid man, wise only in his own eyes'.[29] He told the Hamburg rabbis that unless he recanted Uriel da Costa should be excommunicated. His book *Magen v'Tzina* records his response to the Hamburg rabbis. He published it anonymously, even though everyone could tell who had written it. As well as advising that da Costa should be excommunicated in Hamburg, Leon carried out a separate, symbolic ceremony in the Ponentine synagogue in the ghetto, excommunicating Uriel da Costa in absentia.

The remarkable aspect of Leon Modena's response to the Hamburg rabbis is the strength of feeling that he showed in rebutting da Costa's claims, coupled with the wholly unnecessary, symbolic excommunication ceremony. It leaves us wondering whether Leon did not share some of the doubts articulated by da Costa and felt obliged to overreact in order to persuade himself of their falsity. Leon was a cultured man with friends and contacts in both Jewish and Christian society. He was widely read, he knew that da Costa's views were not particularly original, indeed that there were members of an entire branch of Judaism, the Karaites, who held similar views. It is not beyond the bounds of possibility that Leon Modena had a certain intellectual sympathy for da Costa's views, even if he could never accept them doctrinally. Perhaps he condemned da Costa with such force because the carefully articulated challenges to Judaism composed by the 'heretic from Hamburg' rang too true for him to contemplate.

Music and Culture in the Ghetto

SONGS OF SOLOMON

Musicians and dancers had a somewhat easier life than most in the ghetto. They did not always seem to be bound by the same restrictions or perhaps it is just that the Venetian authorities were more lax in dealing with them. We have heard already about Giuseppe from Mantua who was allowed to enter the houses of noblemen to teach their children to sing, dance and play musical instruments.[1] Madonna Bellina, whose existence we only know about from one letter, apparently played, sang and composed so wondrously as to become the delight of the city.[2] She and other artists like her were generally exempted from wearing the yellow head-coverings identifying them as Jews when entertaining the nobility.

Understandably some of the Jewish musicians of the ghetto didn't always treat the privileges they had been granted with the deference that the Venetian authorities expected. A singer by the name of Rachel was allowed to leave the ghetto at night to visit noble houses. A complaint was made that she, her father and brother would go to the houses of ordinary people where they would eat, drink and behave disreputably. As a result the *Cattaveri*, the three magistrates charged with overseeing the business activities of the Jews and keeping them socially apart from Christians, withdrew her privileges. Rachel paid no attention. A few years later she was in trouble once again, this time for going around the canals at night singing in a gondola.

Music played an important part in Leon Modena's life, but he neglected to say much about it in his autobiography. We know from synagogue records that he was appointed to the prestigious position of cantor of the Italian synagogue in the ghetto. To keep the job he had to be periodically re-elected by two-thirds of the synagogue board and confirmed by the entire membership. Yet the only mention he makes of it in his autobiography is in a list of twenty-six different professional activities that he appended toward the end of his book. The list is somewhat misleading, it is more of a list of skills than of individual jobs; he includes four different types of teaching and three separate genres of writing, each as a distinct profession.

Leon's position of cantor required him, in his unusually modest words, merely 'to sing prayers louder than all the others', but he was far more accomplished than that. He is said to have had a particularly pleasant tenor voice and he wanted to use it to do more than just chant the prayers as other cantors did. They, he said, made a laughing stock of themselves by braying like asses or shouting like dogs and crows. He maintained that every cantor was obliged to sing as pleasantly as possible, but that they no longer had the right skills because Jewish liturgical music had become a shadow of its former self since the destruction of the Jerusalem Temple a millennium and a half earlier.

Determined to raise the musical quality of synagogue services, Leon encouraged his congregation to join in with the singing and organized the more tuneful members into an ad hoc choir. On one occasion he controversially held a choral service in the Spanish Synagogue where musical instruments and an organ were played. It was the night of *Simhat Torah*, the festival that celebrates the end of the annual cycle of reading the Pentateuch. Well aware that the playing of musical instruments was prohibited on festivals and sabbaths, and that there was a particular sanction against the organ because of its association with church music, Leon relied on a legal opinion he had written some years earlier. Backed up by the full force of his rabbinic scholarship and religious authority, he had submitted on that occasion that *Simhat Torah* was as joyful an occasion as a wedding. If music was permitted at a wedding, he insisted, so too should it be permitted in a festival. To underline the joyous nature of the *Simhat Torah* celebration Leon made sure that the Christian population of Venice knew he was putting on a special event in the synagogue that evening. Dozens of them turned up, the visiting audience joining with the regular worshippers to hear and applaud the music until the synagogue service became a spectacle that carried on well into the night.

Among the hundreds of poems that Leon is known to have written, a good number were intended to be set to music. They include wedding odes, poems that include musical instructions within their stanzas, and one that states quite clearly in the introduction that the 'poet sings his own song'.[3] The poems may have been sung to well-known tunes or they may have had their own musical accompaniments composed separately. Unfortunately none have survived, other than one which fortuitously marks the highlight of Leon Modena's musical career. It is the fruit of the collaboration he forged with Salamone Rossi, the most distinguished Jewish composer of his age.

Rossi was lauded as the outstanding musical celebrity in Mantua, his home town. Patronized by the powerful Gonzaga family who ruled Mantua for nearly 400 years, he composed madrigals and instrumental works, played violin and conducted concerts at the ducal palace where his sister, 'Madama Europa', would also sing. He travelled to Venice at least three times between 1600 and 1628 to supervise the printing of his musical scores. While he was there he would take the time to meet up with Leon Modena, an old friend from years back.

It was probably Leon who put the thought into Rossi's mind of writing an opus of Hebrew songs, one that was written as if intended for the concert hall but in practice would be used in synagogue services. Such a work would enhance the congregation's enjoyment of the religious services, give them something to listen to other than the monophonic voice of the cantor, and provide them with an opportunity to join in the singing. All in all, a composition of that nature would further Leon's aim of raising the standard of music sung in the synagogue.

Few details have survived of the collaboration between the two men. It is probable that, like many Italian Jews, Rossi didn't know much Hebrew and that Leon advised him on which biblical and liturgical texts to select, showing him how to arrange them so that the congregation could respond at appropriate moments. He would have told him where he should accentuate individual words and how the liturgical score should be vocalized. It took the pair of them many years to bring the collaboration to a conclusion, largely due to Leon falling into a depression and losing interest in everything after the murder of his son Zebulun. Rossi is known to have said that he found the project particularly onerous.

Once the musical composition was finally completed Leon oversaw its printing and publication. He composed the preface and wrote a dedication on behalf of the composer, penned three dedicatory poems, introduced several others written by colleagues and associates for the occasion, inserted the legal opinion he had written justifying the use of music in the synagogue, and appended approbations by five rabbis.

His most difficult task was to prepare the work for printing, a process that was far from straightforward. The challenge was to align the musical notation which runs from left to right with the Hebrew words that are written in the opposite direction. Nobody had ever done such a thing before. Rossi opined that 'it was better for the readers to pronounce the letters backwards and read the words of the song, which are well known to all, in the opposite direction than to reverse the order of the musical symbols and have the singers move their eyes from right to left . . . lest they lose their minds'.[4]

When the work was finally completed it fell to Rossi to name it. He borrowed a tradition from rabbinic authors of punning on his own first name to create the title of the work. Salomone Rossi's opus became *Songs of Solomon*. It is now considered to be a formative work in the development of synagogue cantorial music. At the time it was sufficient that it fulfilled Leon's twin aims of enhancing the synagogue service and educating Jewish students in the science of music.

THE ACADEMY OF THE IMPEDED

If you had lived in Italy in the sixteenth or seventeenth century and had an interest in anything to do with culture or the intellect, you would almost certainly have been a member of an *accademia*. There were academies, or intellectual societies, in every major Italian city, some comprising hundreds of members, some just a handful of people. Academy members would meet to debate or study, perform or even publish their works. The Venice Ghetto had one such academy. It was called the *Accademia degli Impediti*, or Academy of the Impeded, so-called because its members were impeded by their life in the ghetto.

The *Accademia degli Impediti* was a musical society. It is believed to have been founded by refugee Jewish musicians who fled to Venice after the sacking of the ghetto in Mantua in 1628 during the War of Succession. The *maestro* of the academy, its musical director, was the ubiquitous Leon Modena. It was the singers and musicians who belonged to the academy who took part in the extravagant, choral *Simhat Torah* service in the ghetto's Spanish synagogue.

For its motto the *Impediti* took the phrase 'when we remembered Zion' from Psalm 137. The psalm tells of a group of Jewish captives sitting, weeping by the rivers of Babylon, their harps hanging on poplar trees.[5] The academy's emblem was three poplar trees with musical scores and instruments hanging on them. The intention, according to a letter composed by Leon Modena, was to convey the 'unhappy state of our captivity'.[6] Hence the name *Impediti*.

The members of the academy met twice a week to rehearse but their gatherings were short lived. Another devastating outbreak of bubonic plague in 1630, as bad as the one half a century earlier, took its toll on the *Impediti*. Several members died and the rehearsals became less and less frequent until Leon declared that the group no longer deserved to be called an academy. Eventually their activities petered out altogether and although Leon expressed the hope that they would one day resume, it appears that they never did.

The *Accademia degli Impediti* was adequate for a small group of musicians who wanted to rehearse and perform together, but it was not enough to assuage a growing hunger for secular culture among the intellectuals of the ghetto. Shortly after the *Impediti* began meeting, another circle with a far wider cultural remit was established. Based in the home of Sara Copia Sulam, a woman now widely regarded as Italy's leading poet of the age, the academy attracted both Jewish and Christian intellectuals, the latter regularly coming into the ghetto to meet with their hostess and her associates. Meanwhile outside the ghetto walls the celebrated *Incogniti* Academy, the largest and best known of all Italian intellectual circles, reached out to Jews who they hoped would offer them insights into their ancient wisdom and introduce them to their manuscripts and antiquities. Cross-cultural engagement between Jews and Christians in Venice, although still very much an elite encounter, had never been so commonplace.

It would be misleading to imagine that the lowering of cultural barriers between the faiths heralded an improvement in the lot of ordinary Jews living in the ghetto. Sadly, that was not the case. People like Leon Modena and Sara Copia Sulam had reputations and a standing that made their ideas and works interesting to intellectuals on the far side of the ghetto's walls. The same did not apply to the ordinary residents of the ghetto, whose lives were about to become even more abject and miserable than before.

The plague that broke out in 1630, the worst in living memory, killing 46,940 people in the entire city, merely added to the misery of life in the ghetto. Even before the plague started, living standards in the ghetto had been miserable, in large part due to the slum's dilapidated architecture. Overcrowding and the lack of space on the ground meant that the only way to increase accommodation was to build upwards. By the early part of the seventeenth century some of the tenements around the square were nine storeys high, subdivided horizontally and vertically into multiple dwellings, with ledges and balconies hanging out over the canals. Even so, the overcrowding was severe. Venetian archives describe narrow, confined apartments in which eight or ten people, sometimes more, were crammed together in buildings that were old, fragile and insanitary.[7] Standing on unstable, waterlogged ground their weight had to be kept as light as possible, requiring partitions between rooms and dwellings to be paper thin, ceilings low in height, and floors flimsy. The buildings were dark, many apartments had no fireplaces, and no proper means of sanitary disposal. Life in the ghetto was smelly and unhygienic. Even the bridges over the canals were unsafe.

Little wonder that disputes, arguments and fights broke out frequently. When in the spring of 1631 the plague seemed to have departed the ghetto while increasing in severity in the rest of the city, Leon Modena complained about the behaviour of his fellow residents. 'Only we Jews did not appreciate the miracle wrought for us and people in our communities continued to do evil in the sight of God by quarrelling, slandering, stealing, cursing, lying and swearing falsely. Thus God's anger was kindled against his people and they began to be affected by the plague [again].'

The more storeys that the Jews added to their tenements, the higher the ghetto towered over the rest of the city. And the higher the ghetto rose, the more the Venetian authorities worried about what the Jews could see. It wasn't that the Venetians were doing anything improper in their homes or trying to hide their secrets and possessions. It was that they felt uncomfortable about being overlooked by foreigners: by alien Jews. In 1560, when permitting some Jews from the grossly overcrowded *Ghetto Nuovo* to move into the *Ghetto Vecchio*, the authorities ordered the boarding up of all windows that overlooked the neighbouring Christian streets, making the dwellings even darker. They also required that all doors and balconies adjoining Christian houses be blocked up, and that a wall was built to further block the Jews' view.[8]

The authorities were not wholly insensitive to the overcrowding in the ghetto, or so it seemed. After the plague finally receded, they succumbed to pressure and extended the Jewish quarter into an area alongside the *Ghetto Nuovo*, allowing the construction of twenty new houses in what would be called the *Ghetto Nuovissimo*. It turned out however that, rather than trying to reduce overcrowding, the Venetian government's main motivation was to restore their tax revenues. The plague had depleted the Jewish population, so the only reliable way to restore the income the city collected from the ghetto was to let more Jews in.

The city's rapacity was confirmed by their decree that the new buildings were not for the use of people already living in the ghetto;

they were for newcomers only. The *Ghetto Nuovissimo* was to be inhabited exclusively by newly arrived Levantine Jewish merchants. Nobody from the other two ghettos could move there for at least three years. The ghetto Jews took little notice of the decree; even while construction was still going on there were reports that local Jews were renting and moving in to the new dwellings. The Jews of the ghetto were taxed to the hilt and lived in intolerable conditions but living among the commercially obsessed Venetians had taught them the necessity of looking out for themselves. Their victories over the system may have been small and few, but at least they were victories.

SARA COPIA SULAM'S CIRCLE

The poet Sara Copia Sulam spent her life confronting the twin disadvantages of being both a woman and a Jew in seventeenth-century Venice. The weapons that she mustered against those who sought to put her down were her wealth, her allure, her connections, and most of all her literary and musical talent. She was born as Sara Coppio sometime around 1592 into a prosperous family and spent her life in the more privileged echelons of ghetto society, marrying Jacob Sulam, a man from a similar background.[9] Her family, the Coppios, were relatives of Leon Modena's wife Rachel, her husband's brother was a patron of Salamone Rossi in Mantua. When Rossi was in Venice he would stay with Sara and Jacob.

Christian women had begun to emerge onto the cultural stage in Venice as writers, musicians and artists in the middle of the sixteenth century. By the time Sara was born, Venice had become a leading centre for women's writing. They did not have an easy time of it; the *accademias* were predominantly male and misogynistic, patronizing women writers and treating them as curiosities. Women often published their works under a male pseudonym to avoid abuse.

Sara's story is in part a cautionary tale about a prosperous but naïve young woman who lived a sheltered, parochial life in the ghetto, who yearned to be accepted in mainstream society. In her youth Sara had read an epic poem about the biblical Esther, written by a Genoese monk named Ansaldo Cebà. She was deeply moved by the poem and extravagantly wrote to its author, declaring her admiration and spiritual love for him. She told him that she carried his poem with her everywhere and slept with it under her pillow. She enclosed two sonnets with her letter and confided in Cebà that she had recently nearly died of a miscarriage. Cebà, deeply flattered by her attention, replied saying that he wished to maintain a correspondence with her and that he would like to convert her to Christianity. He told her that the feminine form of her family name Coppia indicated that they could be a couple. She responded by changing the spelling of her name to Copia and reminded him that he was a celibate monk and that she was married.

At this stage of their relationship their exchanges appear to be little more than banter, she doesn't seem to have been offended by his presumptuousness and it did not inhibit their correspondence. They exchanged fifty letters and sent each other gifts, portraits and sonnets by mail. The letters that Cebà wrote have survived, explaining how we know so much about their romantic pen-friendship. She, however, stipulated that her side of the correspondence be destroyed.

Despite never meeting her, Cebà praised her beauty and her golden tresses, he said her looks matched her grace. When he sent her a gift of fruit she detained the servant who delivered it, refusing to let him depart until he had heard her sing a musical rendition of Cebà's play *Esther*.

In 1618, around the same time as she initiated her correspondence with Cebà, Sara instituted her literary salon. From the very outset the salon attracted many more Christian participants than Jews; the names of ten Christian attendees and only two Jews are known.[10] Among the writers, artists and poets who attended the regular sessions were an archdeacon and a Venetian senator. The salon's agenda appears to have covered every aspect of art and culture; at their various meetings the members of the salon might decide to read poetry or literature, discuss politics, perform plays, discuss philosophy or play music. Because the ghetto gates were closed at night the salon was only able to meet at Sara's home during the day. It didn't seem to matter; Sara's wealth and standing were such that, despite the unsafe and unsavoury environment of the ghetto, she was able to welcome her guests into a salon suitably furnished and appointed for visitors who were used to their comforts.

Leon Modena was one of the few Jews who visited the salon regularly. Sara was a patron of his and when she showed him Cebà's poem about Esther it inspired him to write a new rendition of a play, composed some years earlier on the same subject, by the *converso* poet Solomon Usque. Leon entitled his play *L'Ester* and dedicated it to Sara.

It has been suggested that Leon adapted Usque's play to alert Sara to the dangers of corresponding with Cebà, warning her not to be swayed by his attempts to convert her to Christianity. Leon's version of the play casts the characters from the Bible story in a very different light to those in Cebà's epic. Cebà portrays Queen Esther as a faithful Christian, a role that he is trying to persuade Sara to adopt. Leon however stays closer to the biblical narrative, treating Esther as a model of resistance; a Jew who remains true to herself despite the pressures that are applied to her.[11]

Leon was right to urge Sara to be cautious about Cebà. As their correspondence progressed he grew increasingly unpleasant towards her. Jealous of her salon, which was too far from Genoa for him to attend, he took advantage of her naïvety and the far too effusive and obsequious letters she wrote to him. He began making sexual innuendos that soon turned into more overt advances, all the while denying that he meant anything by it because he was too old and ill. She expressed her displeasure at his language but kept the correspondence going, even when he suggested that she was sleeping with the men who attended her salon.

For all his unpleasantness Cebà did retract his accusations, or at least try to explain them away, whenever Sara rebuked him. She had far greater problems with some of the men who attended her salon. On the face of it, the fact that Christians were coming into the ghetto for intellectual discourse with Jews appears to be a welcome development in the cross-cultural fertilization of Venetian society. But when we consider how she was treated by some of the men who came (always men, we know of no women visitors to the salon), we may wonder whether any progress was being made at all.

The first sign of trouble in the salon was when Sara engaged one of her attendees, Numidio Paluzzi, to be her teacher. It was an act of generosity on her part. Paluzzi was a syphilitic Roman poet with no money of his own, who Sara supported in exchange for him teaching her two lessons each week. She paid him five scudi a week for the lessons and covered his rent, grocery and clothing bills.[12] Paluzzi showed his lack of gratitude by conspiring against her with his friend Alessandro Berardelli, an unscrupulous Roman writer and artist. They recruited her laundress and kitchen maid and between them systematically robbed Sara of her money, jewellery and other possessions. When she finally challenged them, they told her that a demonic spirit had visited the house and made off with her property.

She must have believed them because they came up with an even more outrageous scheme, forging letters to her from a fictitious French prince who asked her to send him her portrait. They persuaded her that the right thing to do would be to send him a gift with the portrait and suggested that a jewel-encrusted box would be fitting. They told her that they knew someone who would make it and that they would take care of the arrangements. Trustingly, she gave them as much money as they told her it would cost, they pocketed the cash and told her that the box had been made and sent to France.

They didn't get away with it. Their hubris got the better of them; they bragged too often and too loudly about their triumph. When word got back to Sara about what they had done she sacked Paluzzi and reported Berardelli, the prime mover in the fraud, to the authorities. He was sentenced to a term in the galleys.

Even after they had been caught neither man showed any contrition. Berardelli defamed her in a pamphlet called 'Sara's Feats' that he distributed across the city. Paluzzi slandered her in a poem. He died before it could be published, but Berardelli stepped in, edited and circulated it.

In 1621 Sara suffered a far more unsettling attack than the blatantly criminal activities of Paluzzi and Berardelli. It was launched by the archdeacon of Treviso, Baldassare Bonifaccio, one of Venice's most prominent intellectuals who she had always regarded as an enthusiastic member of her salon. The two of them used to vigorously debate theological matters, particularly the question of the immortality of the soul. It was a topic of profound interest to Christian thinkers at the time, one that was regularly discussed in academies. In 1621 Bonifaccio published a discourse on the subject, in which he falsely accused Sara of denying the soul's immortality. He wrote that she was worse than Eve who was responsible for the mortality of humans, because Sara gave ear to the 'pestiferous doctrine' of Aristotle.[13] After a long and convoluted argument in which he invoked the Bible, Plato, Greek mythology and medieval philosophers to justify his belief in the immortality of the soul, Bonifaccio told Sara that the only way he could save her was if she were to give up being a Jew and become a Christian.

Whether Bonifaccio's attack was drive by misogyny, antisemitism or sexual jealousy is impossible to know. Whatever it was, Sara wasn't cowed. A few days later she published a response. She called it a 'Manifesto' and dedicated it to her late father. She explained that she had written it hurriedly because she had only just recovered from a serious illness and did not know how much longer she had to live. Nor did she want to allow too much time to elapse between Bonifaccio's accusations and her rebuttal, lest there be too much gossip. Anyway, she said she was able to produce the 'Manifesto' quickly because she knew her own mind and did not need to do any research. Anyone reading Bonifaccio's discourse would instantly know how 'blunderingly its author defies others in a matter that nobody, whether a Jew or a Christian, is permitted to gainsay'. She wrote about her hurt and pain at what she considered to be Bonifaccio's betrayal, described his arguments as slander, reminded him that she had heard him describe himself as neither a philosopher nor a theologian, and accused him of audacity at wanting to 'put his hand in the pasta', at getting involved in matters beyond his expertise.[14] She appended four sonnets to her 'Manifesto', expressing her feelings through verse as well as prose.

Bonifaccio responded to Sara's 'Manifesto' in a condescending, long-winded display of mansplaining. He didn't address her arguments, told her he was her friend, called her Jezebel, and intimated that Leon Modena had corrected her work. From our perspective as outsiders, Bonifaccio fell far short of winning the argument.

Sara Copia Sulam closed her salon in 1624, probably because of the abuse she suffered from her male guests. It had been in operation for just six years. Nothing more was heard of her after this. It is known that she survived the great plague of 1630, because her gravestone states that she died on the Hebrew date of 5 Adar 5401, corresponding to February 1641 in the secular calendar. Leon Modena composed the rhyming Hebrew epitaph engraved on her tombstone; it can still be seen in the old Jewish cemetery on the Lido, remarkably well preserved.

PASSING THE TIME

The elite intellectual activities of the *Impediti* and Sara Copia Sulam's circle meant little to the mass of the ghetto's residents, who had neither the education nor the opportunity for such interests. Even the traditional Jewish cultural pursuit of religious study only occupied the attention of a small number of people, mainly rabbis and their students. The Hebrew printing workshops, with their scholarly staff of proof-readers and typesetters, bolstered by the prestigious rabbinic academy in nearby Padua, had helped turn Venice into one of Europe's most important European Talmudic and kabbalistic centres. The ghetto attracted rabbis and scholars from across the Jewish world but by and large they did not stay long, often using their time in Venice as a launch pad for the careers they would develop elsewhere. In any case their numbers were small. Most Venetian Jews looked for less demanding pastimes for their cultural and social entertainment.

We have seen how Leon Modena was obsessed by gambling; probably addicted. He was not the only one. Playing games of chance were a popular, though illegal, pastime in seventeenth-century Venice. The law threatened gamblers with banishment from the city and those working in casinos with having their nose and ears cut off, but the threat of physical violence doesn't seem to have dulled the Venetians' enthusiasm for playing the tables. We have no information to tell us how widespread gambling was within the ghetto, but we can surmise from Leon Modena's frequent references to what he calls games of chance, and the names of other gamblers that he mentions, that it was fairly common. We don't know where they played, whether Leon and his gambling associates got together for games in their own homes or whether they went into the city, to the up-market casinos and *ridotti*, where players donned masks so as not to be recognized. If they did go to the casinos, it could only have been during the day, when the ghetto gates were open.

Nor do we know much about public entertainments in the ghetto. Marin Sanudo had mentioned a comedy that was performed in the ghetto in March 1531.[15] If, as is generally assumed, this was a play put on for the annual carnival festival of Purim, then it is likely that similar performances would have taken place most years. The ancient tradition of the Purim *spiel*, or play, usually took the form of a farce or knockabout based on the biblical book of Esther. Solomon Usque's play about Esther, and Leon Modena's later adaptation of it, was probably intended as a traditional Purim *spiel* to be performed in the ghetto.

Public performances in the ghetto could only take place in the open air on the *campo* or in the synagogues. There was nowhere else large enough. We do hear of a theatre in the ghetto built by a wealthy Venetian resident, but only that Rabbi Sh'muel Aboab condemned it as a place of great sin, where children were taken and corrupted: 'If at least only adults went there. But what do they want of the little lambs? A great punishment awaits those who bring little children there.'[16] There is no other record of when it was built or how long it was in use for.

There were theatres in the city beyond the ghetto. The authorities had closed them towards the end of the sixteenth century, apparently because the Jesuits were selling tickets at extravagant prices, but when the ban was lifted in 1607 at least three auditoriums opened. Only the most privileged of Jews would have been able to attend evening performances, and to do so they would have had to bribe the guards or leave the ghetto with the assistance of powerful friends among the nobility. But Jews would almost certainly have been among the crowds which gathered during the day for the street theatres or at carnival time.

9

Politics and Diplomacy

GOVERNING THE GHETTO

One of the advantages of being compelled to live in the ghetto was that the Venetian Republic left the Jews alone to govern themselves, provided they stayed on the right side of the law. Jews living as outsiders in Christian or Muslim lands did not necessarily expect such a degree of autonomy: many centuries earlier the Talmud had decreed that Jews subject to foreign rule had to conform to the civil law of the lands in which they lived. But the Venetians had no interest in regulating the day-to-day lives of the Jews in the ghetto or to impose fiscal obligations upon them individually. As long as the residents of the ghetto fulfilled the terms of the charter permitting them to live in the city, in other words, as long as they paid their communal taxes, the Venetian authorities were quite content for them to regulate themselves.

The only complicating factor, as far as the Jews were concerned, was that the Venetian government regarded the Tedeschi, Levantine and the Ponentine, or Spanish and Portuguese, communities as separate entities, each with their own charters, privileges and obligations. The three communities differed too in their religious and cultural practices, with their own distinctive customs, synagogues, culinary habits and dress. When deciding on the best system of self-regulation the ghetto community had to take these differences into account.

The only visible feature uniting all three groups were the yellow head-coverings they were obliged to wear. And even these were no longer yellow. Imperceptibly the colours had shifted over the years. By the end of the seventeenth century many Levantine men were wearing red turbans, the Tedeschi wide-brimmed or flat red hats, and women just flashes of red in the shawls draped over their heads.

The principal governing body of the ghetto was the *Università Grande*, or Large Assembly. Membership was automatically granted to all men of sufficient financial standing; in 1607, for example, only those who paid tax of more than 12 ducats per year were admitted, just 129 of the total adult male population of 1,157. A body of that size was too unwieldy to manage the daily affairs of the ghetto, so the main function of the Large Assembly was to elect an executive, generally comprising no more than a dozen members, sometimes as few as six.

The three communities seem to have functioned almost as political parties, they each tended to vote as a bloc. The 12-ducat threshold for membership meant that the Tedeschi, who were the poorest community, were under-represented on the Large Assembly; it was the better-off Levantine and Ponentine merchants who dominated affairs. The balance of power between the three groups was restored somewhat when it came to electing the membership of the *Congrega Piccola*, the Small Assembly, where a form of proportional representation seems to have been applied.

The executive, or Small Assembly, was responsible for the upkeep of the ghetto infrastructure, security and sanitation. It maintained law and order, fining miscreants rather than cutting off noses or sending offenders to the galleys, as the Venetian government was wont to do. It passed sumptuary laws regulating the dress code in the ghetto and imposed restrictions on ostentatious feasts and parties. Occasionally it remonstrated with the Venetian government on behalf of residents who had been treated unfairly.

The main duty of the Small Assembly in practice was to find people who would fund and manage the pawnshops that the Tedeschi Jews were obliged to maintain under the terms of their charters. The poor of Venice relied on loans from the pawnshops for their daily expenses and the Venetian government required the Jews to run them as a condition of their residency in the ghetto. There were always voices outside the ghetto walls agitating for the Jews to be expelled and for the pawnshops to be replaced by the charitable Monti di Pietà loan banks that could be found in many Italian cities. The onus was on the Tedeschi to ensure that the pawnshops were run efficiently and fulfilled their purpose, so that they could continue to renew their charters and dwell in Venice.

The process for electing members of the Small Assembly was cumbersome and arcane – even for the seventeenth century. Various methods were used. In one, a quantity of balls equal to the number of voters were placed in a bag. All the balls, with the exception of a few, were of the same colour. Each voter drew a ball. When an irregularly coloured ball was drawn the voter who drew it had to nominate a candidate for election, whom the Assembly would then vote on. This process went on until all the positions had been filled. Another method was to draw names out of a hat and to vote on them in the order in which they had been drawn, presumably handing an advantage to those who were drawn first. Electors could vote for or against candidates, by placing a ball in the 'yes' or 'no' compartment of a voting box.

We don't need to look too closely at the government of the ghetto to realize that despite theoretically being representative it was in fact a plutocracy. One of the duties of the Large Assembly was to appoint an assessment committee who decided on the amount of tax that each family was liable to pay. Troublesome families could be excluded from the ghetto's governance by lowering their tax liability below the qualifying level. Conversely, power could be concentrated in the hands of the wealthiest simply by raising the tax threshold for membership. This explains why, despite the population of the ghetto rising from 1,157 in 1607 to around 3,000 just before the murderous plague of 1630, membership of the Large Assembly fell from 129 in 1607 to 125 in 1621.[1]

Serving on the tax-assessment committee was a position few wanted. Its members were obliged to interview each resident of the ghetto to assess their tax liability, a process that began with them walking around the ghetto and inspecting the houses to determine which of the residents were liable to pay tax. They put 'sneak boxes' on the walls for residents to denounce neighbours who were suspected of hiding from the committee in order to avoid assessment.

Once the assessment committee had made its list of potential taxpayers they conducted individual interviews with everyone on it, to ascertain their financial circumstances. Each assessment had to be agreed by at least six of the seven committee members. Then, when all the interviews were over and assessments finalized, the committee would add up the sums demanded to see if they had raised enough money to meet their commitments. If not, they would go back and raise the per capita assessment until they were confident they would have enough in the coffers to pay the ghetto's tax liability to the Republic. The process of assessment lasted for several weeks, during which time the members of the committee were locked away in a secure location and not allowed to leave the ghetto. It was not a job that many people wanted.

Apart from the laborious nature of assessing the financial position of thousands of people individually, there was the ever-present risk of personal conflict with those who felt they had been assessed unfairly. The committee did make sure that members were not obliged to assess their relatives, but they could do little more than that. The population of the ghetto was not large and the overcrowding was such that few of the residents were strangers to each other. Anyone with a grievance could easily seek out a member of the assessment committee to complain. The number of people willing to serve on the committee, or indeed to serve in any public office, was so small that the Assemblies instituted rules to stop people leaving town to avoid election or applying to a magistrate of the Republic for an exemption from office. One of the officers of the Small Assembly described his role as being that of a target in a shooting practice.[2]

Fortunately there were other, more rewarding ways for the public spirited to contribute to the well-being of the ghetto. There was always a need for philanthropy.

FELLOWSHIPS AND FRATERNITIES

Most people in the impoverished ghetto lived hand to mouth at very best, few had the money to cover the cost of emergencies, even fewer were able to plan ahead for unexpected events or family celebrations. They were not unusual in this; poverty was the norm for most people in early modern Europe, and every community had its informal support networks, its religious societies, fraternities or fellowships. In that sense community life was little different to today, except that the fraternities were more localized than the charities that we are used to and ritual played a far greater part in their activities.

The ghetto fraternities, or *hevrot*, covered nearly every imaginable need. There were societies which fed the poor, provided dowries for brides, buried the dead, clothed the impecunious, freed debtors, supported orphans and took care of the sick. Not all fraternities disbursed money, some performed religious acts, praying for the sick, reciting prayers for the dead, or just getting up earlier than most people in the morning to offer additional supplications on behalf of the community. The societies were formally organized, their members drawing lots to decide who would perform particular tasks, their officers usually chosen from those who could afford to carry the greatest burden.

Philanthropic and religious fraternities were a feature of Jewish life across Europe, but they were not confined to Jews. In Christian cities the *scuole* played the same role as the *hevrot* in the ghetto, but on a much grander and more visible scale. On Shrove Tuesday in 1581 the French essayist Michel de Montaigne watched in fascination as many of Rome's hundred or more fraternities marched in torchlit procession towards St Peter's, 'each man carrying a torch, and almost all of these of white wax. I think there passed before me twelve thousand torches at the least'.[3]

Renaissance Venice was a city of processions. The Venetians revelled in them. They were a spectacle. Consisting of hundreds or thousands of participants all bearing torches and dressed in the same colours, with the Doge and the senior officers of Church and State at the centre, they were far more than just a line of people shuffling along the road. The English traveller Fynes Moryson wrote that they were so frequent and performed with such great pomp that they surpassed every other city, not only in Italy, but in the whole world.[4]

There was, however, one annoyance that spoiled the Venetians' enjoyment of their ceremonies. The annoyance was the Jews who would watch and stare as the processions passed by. The Venetians were convinced that they were muttering curses and profanities under their breath as they gawped. On at least one occasion the ghetto Jews were formally accused of blaspheming as the sacraments were carried along the Cannaregio.

If the Jews of the ghetto did mutter under their breath, their outward behaviour showed no sign of it. Rather, they copied the parades of the *scuole*. *G'milut Hasadim*, dedicated to the relief of poverty and the largest of the Jewish fraternities, conducted their own torchlit processions to accompany funerals, insisting that all their members take part if the dead person had been one of the fraternity.

Some fraternities did not approve of such blatant copying of Christian Venetian practices. The society dedicated to providing dowries for poor brides tried banning torches from their processions. They prevailed for seventeen years, until the ban was dropped at the insistence of a new generation of members who were anxious to raise the visual image of their society.

Of all the fraternities of the ghetto, one stood out more than any of the others. It would have stood out anyway, just because of the amount of money which passed through its accounts; it handled far more than any other ghetto fraternity. But what made it noticeably different to any other philanthropic activity in the ghetto was the extent of its political involvement, its financial sophistication, and the dangerous nature of its work. Its name translates from the Hebrew as the Society for the Ransoming of Captives.

FREEING THE SLAVES

Moshe Zacuto arrived in Venice in 1645. Born in Amsterdam he travelled to Poland in his youth to study in a rabbinic seminar.

He then made his way to Italy, with the intention of crossing the Mediterranean and heading to the kabbalistic community of Safed, in Israel. He didn't make the journey. Instead, he was offered a position as a preacher in Verona. A few years later he set off again, making the short journey to Venice where he settled for the next quarter of a century in the ghetto. Zacuto has gone down in history as a preacher and one of the most important kabbalists of his generation, but he also wrote poetry and at least one play. Presumably none of these occupations generated enough revenue to support his family because he supplemented his income as a proof-reader and editor in the Hebrew printing workshops.

The play he wrote, based on the biblical patriarch Abraham, is the first known Hebrew biblical drama not to be written for the Purim festival or constructed around the life of Esther. It doesn't leave us any wiser as to whether plays, other than Purim *spiels*, were performed in the ghetto, because Zacuto probably wrote it before his arrival in Venice and it was not published during his lifetime.

As a poet Zacuto is best known for his narrative poem *Tofteh arukh*, or *Hell Made Ready*, an account of a journey through the underworld. The poem opens with the narrator believing that he is still alive, lying on his deathbed cursing the doctors and his servants for their incompetence. Then, in a Dantesque vision, he sees legions of damned souls in hell, all suffering their tortures and punishments. Finally he is conducted on a journey through the seven caverns of the underworld.

In the introduction to the poem Zacuto told his readers that what they are about to read is informed by a story in the Talmud. In fact, it draws more heavily on the mystical imagery and ideas of the Kabbalah, seasoned with more than a touch of Dante's *Inferno*, to which Zacuto owes a literary debt. *Tofteh arukh* is an outstanding example of the cross-fertilization of cultures in the ghetto: its imagery familiar to Christians with an interest in Kabbalah, its style recognizable by Jewish intellectuals conversant with Italian literature. Most importantly however, despite not being published until after his death, *Tofteh arukh* posthumously cemented Zacuto's reputation as one of the leading kabbalists of his age.[5]

It may have been the time that Moshe Zacuto spent in Poland which impelled him to take a special interest in the suffering of the Jews there. Or he may have decided that it was his life's mission to concentrate his energies on the religious imperative of rescuing captives. Either way, in the mid-seventeenth century when the Jews of Venice were conducting fundraising campaigns across Europe to ransom Jewish slaves and liberate captives, Moshe Zacuto was the man most often at the heart of the operation.

Piracy had been a problem in the Eastern Mediterranean for decades. Cargoes were seized, merchants, travellers and seafarers were taken into captivity, and the Venetian economy, which relied on maritime trade, was once again coming under severe strain. When, in 1586, the Turkish Sultan offered to ransom Venetian prisoners of war, the Republic ordered all the churches and charitable institutions in its territories to contribute to a central ransoming fund. The fund would supplement the ad hoc efforts that up to now had fallen to the Republic's charities and the captives' families. It did not, however, take responsibility for ransoming Jewish captives. The Republic left them for the Jews to take care of.

On 25 September 1609, four days before the Jewish New Year, the Small Assembly of the ghetto met to discuss the growing problem of Jews being captured and offered for ransom. They agreed that they would raise the sum of 500 ducats, which they would use to cover the ongoing costs of ransoming captives as they fell due.[6]

Jewish merchants were particularly at risk from piracy because they sailed both from Venice and the Ottoman Empire. The Venetian merchants were targeted by pirates setting off from the Barbary coast of North Africa. Those on Ottoman boats were targeted by the Knights of St John, who were engaged in a particularly profitable enterprise raiding Turkish shipping, seizing Jewish prisoners, and selling them as slaves on the island of Malta. The English traveller Philip Skippon reported seeing 'Jews, Moors and Turks' publicly sold in the market. 'A stout fellow may be bought (if he be an inferior person) for 120 or 160 scudi of Malta. The Jews are distinguished from the rest by a little piece of yellow cloth on their hats or caps. We saw a rich Jew who was taken about a year before, who was sold in the market that morning we visited the prison for 400 scudi and supposing himself free, by reason of a passport he had from Venice, he struck the merchant that bought him; whereupon he was presently sent hither, his beard and hair shaven off, a great chain clapped on his legs, and *bastinato'd* with 50 blows.'[7]

With the problem of Turkish piracy showing no signs of abating, the Society for the Ransoming of Captives adopted a more assertive policy than merely paying the kidnappers. They appointed local traders in Malta who would act as the society's agents on the ground. Their role was to identify those slaves who were Jewish and to negotiate the price of their ransom with the Knights.

The first negotiator to be appointed, Baccio Bandinelli, served for twenty years, from 1648 to 1668, without taking any payment for his services. When he retired a French judge named François Garsin took over, also working pro bono.[8] Those who took part in the complex business of transmitting the ransom money, through letters of credit from Venice to Malta, probably took a cut for their services, but neither Bandinelli, Garsin, nor his son who succeeded him did so. The Society for the Ransoming of Captives, acutely aware that none of the mediators were Jews, wrote to Bandinelli when he retired telling him that his merit would be all the greater before God for assisting captives who were not of his own people. When Garsin stepped down from his post, they wrote a testimonial saying that he worked tirelessly at all times for the benefit of the captives, without any thought of personal gain.

The Society for the Ransoming of Captives was the largest philanthropic fraternity in the ghetto. Like all fraternities it was funded through donations from its members, but it also levied a tax of between one-eighth and one-quarter per cent on Jewish merchants when they despatched or received goods from the Ottoman Empire. No matter how much money it raised, it was never enough.[9]

Three years after Moshe Zacuto arrived in Venice the Khmelnytsky uprising broke out in Ukraine. It led to the massacre of up to 20,000 of the 40,000 Jews in Ukraine and an untold number elsewhere in the Polish–Lithuanian Commonwealth. Thousands more were captured by Tatar raiding parties and sold in the slave markets of Istanbul.

The uprising led by the Cossack warlord Bogdan Khmelnytsky was a rebellion against the Polish nobility who ruled Ukraine. The Jews, who were always a target when trouble broke out, were the main casualty of the uprising. Largely because many of them were employed by Polish landowners to run the feudal estates where the Ukrainian peasants were exploited.[10]

The Small Assembly in the Venice Ghetto agreed with the Jewish community of Istanbul that they would divide the financial burden of liberating the slaves between them. Venice would raise funds to ransom the victims of the pirates in the Mediterranean and the Jewish slaves in Malta, while Istanbul would be responsible for those slaves captured by the Tatars and shipped across the Black Sea. It promised to be a neat division of resources, but the agreement rapidly proved unworkable. The number of Jewish slaves coming onto the market in Istanbul was far too great for the local community to cope with. They just didn't have enough money. So the leaders of the Istanbul Jewish community abandoned their agreement with Venice and sent their own representative to fundraise from the Jewish communities of Europe, effectively treading on Venice's toes. They even empowered their envoy to raise money in Venice itself.

The Istanbul Jews chose a man named David Carcassoni as their representative. He arrived in the ghetto in 1650 and met with Moshe Zacuto and his older colleague Sh'muel Aboab. Both men were rabbis in the ghetto and sat from time to time on the board of the Society for the Ransoming of Captives. Their importance to Daniel Carcassoni was that they were both connected to a fundraising network encompassing all the major Italian Jewish communities, and a global sweep of Sephardi congregations stretching from Bordeaux, Amsterdam, Antwerp and Hamburg in the north to Damascus in the East. Zacuto and Aboab gave Carcassoni the introductions that he needed, wrote letters endorsing his efforts, and sent him on his way.

Unfortunately, despite the connections that he was given, Carcassoni turned out not to be a particularly good fundraiser. The Istanbul Jewish community was deeply disappointed with his efforts. But his meeting with Zacuto and Aboab did have one benefit. The Jews of Venice realized that the crisis in Ukraine and Poland was so great that they could no longer rigidly adhere to their earlier commitment only to raise funds to free the victims of piracy in the Mediterranean. Refugees from Poland were streaming across Europe, many were turning up in Italy, and the Venetian philanthropists could no longer justify the claim that all the money they handled was earmarked for the captives of the Mediterranean and the slaves of Malta.

The additional burden of raising funds for the Polish Jews and those sold into slavery in Istanbul and Malta led to tensions between Italy's Jewish communities. In 1652 the Society for the Ransoming of Captives wrote an angry letter to their counterparts in Ancona. They accused them of not honouring their promise to send philanthropic funds to Venice, and of exacerbating their offence by telling Polish refugees in their town that they had no money because it had all been sent to the Venetian fund. The rabbi of the Ancona community fiercely denied the charge. He said that no Polish fundraiser or refugee had ever left Ancona empty handed. If the refugees were saying anything different it was because they were so desperate that they would make up any story if they thought it would give them a chance of getting more money.

The dispute between the Jews of Venice and Ancona illustrates the difficulty of turning well-meaning pledges and promises into hard cash. Moshe Zacuto had to send letters to all the Jewish communities of Italy, reminding them that two fundraisers from Lviv in Ukraine had been in Venice for a considerable time, waiting to receive money that had been promised to them. A while later Sh'muel Aboab wrote a similar letter to Ferrara, asking them to delay no longer in sending the money they had pledged.

In 1656 the Jews of the ghetto held a public day of fasting and mourning in support of the Jews of Poland, where a further round of massacres was underway.

THE JEW OF MALTA

When Elizabethan theatregoers watched *The Merchant of Venice* they might have wondered why the portrayal of Shylock was noticeably different from that of the other fictional Jew on the contemporary London stage. Barabas, the Jewish anti-hero of Christopher Marlowe's *The Jew of Malta*, is a character who seems intended to stir up and exaggerate all the anti-Jewish prejudices of Elizabethan English audiences. It is generally accepted by Shakespearean scholars that when he decided to write *The Merchant of Venice*, Shakespeare was influenced by Marlowe's play, written a few years earlier. Yet that influence does not seem to extend to the personalities of Shylock and Barabas. All that Shylock and Barabas really have in common is that they are both Jewish merchants who have an antagonistic relationship with the Christians amongst whom they live.

Christopher Marlowe was a colleague and mentor of the young Shakespeare, perhaps even a friend. They were rivals inasmuch as they competed to have their plays performed, but many scholars are of the opinion that they collaborated at times. A major academic publisher recently credited Marlowe as co-author on the title pages of all three parts of Shakespeare's *Henry VI*.[11]

The two men had very different personalities. The university-educated Marlowe lived a roistering, swashbuckling life. Before he wrote plays he spent a few years spying for the government and had been briefly imprisoned after being involved in a fatal fight. He was arrested in the Netherlands on suspicion of counterfeiting coins, was detained more than once for brawling, and was accused of sedition and blasphemous talk. In 1593 he was on the sixteenth-century equivalent of parole, when he was stabbed to death in a quarrel between friends, apparently over a bill for dinner. He was twenty-nine years old.[12]

There had been no university education for Shakespeare. He had moved directly from his home county of Warwickshire to London, a former grammar-school boy solely intent on furthering his writing career. An ambitious, hard-working young playwright, he seems to have kept himself to himself, not tempted by the vulgar delights and louche pleasures to be had in Bishopsgate in the heart of the city of London where he lived. Instead, he spent his time reading, observing and listening, mining London's culture and the lives of its residents for inspiration. As Robert McCrum puts it: 'Always competitive, with magpie instincts, he became, like the rogue Autolycus in *The Winter's Tale*, a snapper-up of unconsidered trifles.'[13]

Marlowe was a prime quarry for Shakespeare's magpie instincts. His influence on Shakespeare is well attested.[14] Apart from their differences, *The Merchant of Venice* and *The Jew of Malta* have much in common. Both are about Jewish merchants, aliens in their city, who are portrayed as avaricious. Both have daughters who are the sole children of their father, neither woman has a mother in the play. Both daughters fall in love with Christian men and convert to Christianity, both steal their father's money, one with her father's knowledge, one without.

But that is as far as it goes. Marlowe's treatment of Barabas is horribly antisemitic. The Jewish merchant's many crimes all reflect classic antisemitic tropes. Barabas is contemptuous of everyone, he murders at will, poisons nuns, spreads diseases, contaminates wells, he even kills his own daughter. There is none of this in Shylock, his one act of violence is to demand his pound of flesh. As we have seen this may be attributed to his sense of strict, unyielding justice. Even if we reject this idea and maintain that his demand for flesh was wholly for revenge, he nevertheless displays none of Barabas's gratuitous violence for the sake of self-enrichment.

In both dramas the plot turns on the daughter's handling of her father's money. In *The Jew of Malta* Barabas instructs his daughter Abigail to rescue his money. He had hidden it in his house, but the house had been confiscated and turned into a nunnery. Abigail pretends to convert to Christianity, becomes a nun, retrieves the money, and returns it to her father. She does so freely, 'to injure them that have so manifestly wronged us'. Later in the play, after she has become so repulsed by her father's behaviour she converts again, this time sincerely. 'My sinful soul, alas, hath paced too long the fatal labyrinth of misbelief, far from the son that gives eternal life.'[15]

Jessica's actions in *The Merchant of Venice* stand in direct contrast to Abigail's. Rather than rescuing her father's money she steals it so that she can elope with her lover Lorenzo. She converts to Christianity willingly, neither fraudulently nor through hatred of her father. She does it for love, that she might be with Lorenzo.

There are so many similarities between the representation of the Jewish characters in the two plays and so many glaring contrasts that it seems unlikely that Shakespeare was not reacting in his own way to Marlowe. Which leaves us wondering whether Shakespeare's more sympathetic treatment of his Jew was not a response to the virulence of Marlowe's antisemitism and, once again, whether the characterization of *The Merchant of Venice* as an antisemitic play can truly stand up to scrutiny.

Edging Towards Modernity

THE CONDITION OF THE JEWS

The Luzzatto family, who moved from Germany to Venice in the mid-fifteenth century, bore one of the most prominent names in the ghetto. Isaac Luzzatto, who was born around 1540, had been a mercantile trader with interests in maritime insurance and property rental. He sold *strazzaria*, the second-hand clothes and goods that were the mainstay of the domestic Venetian economy, and ran three of the pawnshops that the Tedeschi Jews were obliged to operate under their charter. A member of the Small Assembly, he had once served as its president and twice negotiated the Jewish moneylenders' charters with the Venetian government.[1]

His son Simone Luzzatto followed in his father's footsteps, taking part in his commercial activities even while it was apparent that his heart lay elsewhere. Like his father he helped to negotiate the renewal of the moneylenders' charters, in his case between 1639 and 1641. He succeeded Leon Modena as the ghetto's most illustrious rabbi but that is not what he is mainly remembered for today. Simone Luzzatto's legacy lies in the contribution he made to science, philosophy and religious tolerance.

Luzzatto did not write much and little is known about his personal life. He was born in 1582, probably, and spent his youth working alongside his father while studying the classic religious and rabbinic texts. As such his upbringing was fairly conventional. Less conventional, for a youth in the ghetto, was his study of science and mathematics. His contemporary, the scientist and doctor Joseph Delmedigo, wrote that Simone Luzzatto knew 'every aspect of the mathematical sciences and has entered all its chambers'. Delmedigo said that he did not know if Luzzatto had written on geometry or astronomy; it appears that he did not, or if he did his works are no longer extant. But we see glimpses of his attitude to science in his other works. He believed that one could not appreciate the wonders of God, nor even understand Jewish law, without mastering natural science, particularly astronomy. Kabbalah on the other hand was just another occult philosophy; it had no greater standing in his eyes than any other philosophical school.[2]

Simone Luzzatto was ordained as a rabbi at the relatively young age of 24 and for many years he served as the rabbi of the *Scuola Tedesca*, the German Synagogue in the ghetto. He succeeded Leon Modena as the head of the Venice Yeshiva, although we don't have much idea of what responsibilities the position entailed. The nature of the Venice Yeshiva remains one of the ghetto's mysteries, there is not enough information about it to form a picture of its activities or its role in communal life. The yeshiva in the ghetto could not have been large; after the plague of 1630 the entire population of the ghetto numbered little more than 2,500 souls.[3] It is unlikely that there were more than a handful of students in the yeshiva; there may even have been none at all, it may simply have been a forum for rabbis. As mentioned below,[4] being appointed head of the yeshiva appears to have been a mark of age and seniority rather than, for example, holding a chair in philosophy at nearby Padua University or being the principal of an academy for the training of rabbis.

Like many senior rabbis Simone Luzzatto wrote responses to legal questions raised by his congregants. The best known was his opinion that it was permitted for Jews in Venice to cross a canal by gondola on the sabbath. The document in which he wrote this opinion hasn't survived, we only know about it because it is quoted in an eighteenth-century rabbinic encyclopedia. He presented his ruling to the Small Assembly in the presence of the Venetian rabbis. They voted to overrule him and ordered that his ruling should not be shown to anyone, telling him that it was never wise to permit something that the masses thought was forbidden.[5] Of his legal opinions that have survived the most well-known is the rather turgid response to a dispute between rabbis over the technical fitness of a ritual bath in Rovigo, a town to the south-west of Venice.

Simone Luzzatto published his most important work in 1638. Entitled *Discourse on the State of the Jews and in particular those dwelling in the illustrious city of Venice*, it is generally known simply as the *Discorso*. The book owes its existence to the events surrounding the theft of gold cloth and silk from the Merceria in 1636, which had caused Leon Modena to flee to Padua and the ghetto community to be threatened with expulsion.

Simone Luzzatto had been caught up in those events. He was one of the rabbis who told the magistrates that it wasn't possible to excommunicate the three Jewish men connected with the robbery because they were either no longer in the city or in gaol. He began to write the *Discorso* following that meeting with the magistrates, while the threat of expulsion was still hanging over the ghetto. His immediate aim was to try to influence the Venetian government not to proceed with the threatened expulsion. However, he framed the book much more widely, as a far-reaching inquiry into the position of Jews in Christian society.

Written in Italian and intended to be read by the local Venetian nobility, Luzzatto's *Discorso* is a plea for religious and political toleration. He didn't concentrate on the ethics of tolerance, that to be tolerant is the right way to behave because it is just and fair. He was writing for Venetians, he knew they were more likely to be swayed by the argument that tolerance is both commercially and practically the most sensible approach.

Setting out his case under eighteen headings or 'Considerations', Luzzatto argued that the 'Jewish Nation' was a valuable asset for Venetian society. He accepted that there may be a few bad elements among the Jewish population (he had the recent robbery and bribery cases in mind), but insisted it was undoubtedly the case that the benefits the Jews brought to Venice vastly outweighed any possible disadvantages. 'Just as a well-cultivated terrain often produces useless and harmful herbs along with the harvest, a wise farmer does not abandon the intemperate and thriving soil for this single reason. He uproots the harmful plants and continues with the tiring work of tending to the good plants and keeping the useful ones alive . . . Thus, the crimes of a few people of this Nation are exaggerated by some people as intolerable misfortunes and unbearable calamities . . . whereas the continuous advantages and profits . . . are overlooked, ignored, and neglected.'[6]

The advantages which the Jews brought to Venice were more than just the taxes and duties that they paid. Presenting a case that might make later generations feel more than just a little uncomfortable, Luzzatto argued that the most important benefit the Jews brought to the city was the profit that they make from their mercantile trade. Trade, which he maintains is an almost unique feature of the Jewish nation, is beneficial not just because it opens up the flow of money and goods into the Republic, but because it helps to maintain peace between neighbouring states. Egypt and Syria, he says, never went to war with Italy because of their trading relationship. In contrast Barbary and Italy, who never had a commercial affinity, are constantly at each other's throats.

The weakness of this argument was that only a fraction of the residents of the ghetto were engaged in maritime trade. Luzzatto tried to deal with this by emphasizing the collective nature of Jewish society. Only some Jews were traders, but because commerce and moneylending were historically the only occupations permitted to Jews, all Jews had become well suited to trade. This can be proved, he said, by the fact they were commercially successful elsewhere and not just in Venice.

Turning to the question of Jewish exclusion from mainstream society, he claimed that the disadvantages under which Jews laboured were also to Venice's benefit. Being stateless, lacking political power, and forbidden from owning property made them 'submissive, humble and pliable'. As a result they fulfilled their contractual obligations to operate pawnshops in the city, even though the rates of interest they were permitted to charge did not even cover their overheads.

These particular qualities of the Jews should be harnessed, he insisted, to halt the commercial decline that was taking place in Venice. Just as a child continues to grow until it reaches its adult size, Venice had also reached a point at which it had ceased to expand. Having grown rich the citizens were no longer commercially motivated. Instead, foreigners came along to take advantage of the city's maritime location and mercantile resources. It made them prosperous but once they had grown rich they went back home, taking their money with them. The city did not benefit from their sojourn.

Unlike the foreigners, however, the Jews have nowhere else to go. And anyway they have no motivation to leave the city since Venice is one of the few places where they are treated well. 'One can boldly conclude,' he declared in an astonishing display of chutzpah, that 'it is more beneficial to the interests of the ruler and the citizens for commerce to fall into the hands of the Jewish Nation.' Barely one-third of the way through his *Discorso*, Luzzatto transformed his plea for tolerance, albeit only in passing, into a suggestion that the Republic give the Jews a monopoly on trade and leave them alone to get on with it.[7]

Throughout the *Discorso*, Luzzatto used nature as a metaphor for the arguments he was advancing. Earlier we saw him compare the criminal elements of Jewish society to a few harmful herbs in a well-tended field. Elsewhere he likened the distribution of taxes in society to the way in which nourishment flows into the body from the stomach. He pointed out that just as we only appreciate our good health when we are ill or notice the swift flow of water when it hits an obstacle, so the only time we recognize good things is when something goes wrong. David Ruderman notes that Luzzatto's frequent use of natural metaphors in this way suggests a familiarity with classical theories of nature and the Stoic philosophy of ancient Greece.[8] Luzzatto had mentioned the Stoics in the introduction to the *Discorso* where he compared the Jewish contribution to the

revenues of the state to an earthly vapour that feeds the sun, moon
and stars. He also mentioned the Greek philosopher Democritus in
the same passage, saying that 'The Jewish Nation should be allowed
to compare itself to Democritus's atoms in representing one particle
of a very numerous population.'[9]

This familiarity with classical philosophy and natural science
far exceeds anything taught in rabbinic training. It places Luzzatto
alongside those other scholars we have encountered who extended
the Jewish worldview beyond the bounds of the ghetto. Were it not
for the fact that the *Discorso* deals with Jewish life and the place of
the Jewish population in Venetian society, we might even conclude
that Luzzatto's secular and classical interests far outweighed
anything he gained from his religious education.

THE IMPACT OF THE *DISCORSO*

Luzzatto's *Discorso* was written as an address to the Venetian
government to counter a local threat of expulsion and to justify
the continued residence of the Jews in Venice. He indicated in
the title that the book was particularly about those Jews living in
Venice. He didn't confine himself to Venice though; the second
part of the book is much wider in scope, addressing the wider
topic of Jewish–Christian relations generally, and contributing to
the debate beginning to take place elsewhere in Europe about the
status and rights of Jews in Christian society.

In 1659, some years after Luzzatto wrote his *Discorso*, the Jews
of the ghetto were again under threat of expulsion. The details
of the charges against them are no longer known, but we know
something of why the threat was rescinded. A member of the
powerful Loredan family, believed to have been Gian Francesco
Loredan, mounted a powerful defence of the Jews in the Senate,
arguing against the expulsion. He used the *Discorso* to compose his
speech, citing its arguments about the economic utility of the Jews
and repeating some of the demographic information that Luzzatto
supplied in his treatise (though Loredan made some mistakes when
copying the figures).

Loredan reminded his colleagues that during the past quarter of a century Venice had been at war with the Ottoman Empire over the island of Crete. During that time the Jewish community had paid substantial taxes and duties into the Serenissima's coffers. Without the Jewish contribution it would have been impossible for the Republic to defend the island they had occupied for over 450 years against the Turks' predatory attacks. In the five years to 1649 alone the state had received 670,000 ducats from the Jews in rental payments, duties, support for the banks and voluntary donations. Loredan's assessment tallied with a similar claim made by the Jews that they had contributed 1.3 million ducats between 1644 and 1659.[10]

Some of the *Discorso*'s readers responded to the book very differently from Loredan. Only three years after the book appeared an anti-Jewish polemicist, Melchiore Palontrotti, wrote *A Brief Response to Simone Luzzatto*. It was indeed brief, just 13 pages in total. Most of it was just unoriginal anti-Jewish polemic, but Palontrotti did respond to a few of the points in the *Discorso*. He poured scorn on Luzzatto's claim that it was always better for the Venetian government to deal with the Jews because they were deferential and obedient, less likely than foreign merchants to become involved in disputes. Palontrotti retorted that of course the Jews were deferential, if they weren't they would be reviled all the more and driven out of town. He mocked Luzzatto's claim that the best way to ascertain the true nature of a kingdom was to see how it treated its Jews. Those rulers who treated Jews well, riposted Palontrotti, were merely doing their Christian duty, in the hope that the Jews might repent of their errors.[11]

A more erudite response to the *Discorso* came from Giulio Morosini. A converted Jew, he had been born as Samuel ben Nehemias, a member, so he said, of a very ancient and respected Jewish family. He wrote his book *Way of Faith* for both Christian and Jewish readers, composing a separate introduction for each group.

In the introduction he wrote for his Jewish readers he made up a rather unimaginative story about two Jewish brothers who had been brought up as Christians, presumably in Spain. One brother left his homeland and went to Venice where he lived as a Jew. The other brother visited him and tried to convince him to return to Christianity. Unable to resolve their differences they agreed that they would seek out the true interpretation of the messianic prophecy of the Book of Daniel. Whoever was wrong would adopt the faith of the other brother. Anxious to find out the meaning of the prophecy the Jewish brother visited a fictional rabbi who Morosini calls Simone Luzzatto. The rabbi confessed that the prophecy shows that the Messiah had already come and advised the brothers not to enquire further. The Jewish brother, now convinced that Daniel's prophecy cannot be reconciled to Judaism, converted back to Christianity. Morosini claimed to have attended that fictional event. He said it inspired him to convert to Christianity and to devote his life to persuading the Jews of Venice to do the same.

Most of *Way of Faith* is devoted to persuading Jews of the superiority of Christianity. Towards the end Morosini turns to Luzzatto's parable about the harmful plants in a well-tended field. He says that he is glad that Luzzatto acknowledges the sinful elements among the Jews. Luzzatto, he says, should also recognize that because of their rejection of Christianity, all Jews are mired in sin.[12]

Neither Morosini's criticism of the *Discorso* nor that of Palontrotti seems to have had much impact. They were not serious critiques. Yet it turned out that Luzzatto's work had far greater impact outside Italy, away from his critics. The *Discorso* was cited by, among others, the French jurist and author Montesquieu, the German philosopher Johann Gottfried Herder, and the English politician Joseph Addison.

It was in England where the *Discorso* had its most influential impact, part of the burgeoning debate as to whether the Jews should be readmitted to the country. Strictly speaking, the few Jews who lived in England during the sixteenth century and the first half of the seventeenth should not have been there. The law forbidding their presence had remained unchanged ever since their expulsion by Edward I in 1290. But in the seventeenth century pressure to allow them to return began to build. International commerce was expanding and English merchants were regularly trading with Jews in Amsterdam who lived freely and without restrictions. There were compelling commercial arguments in favour of allowing Jewish merchants and traders into England. Religiously too, it was being argued that England's political troubles at the time were the consequence of its laws against the Jews. God would only look kindly on the country if it allowed them to return.[13]

Menasseh ben Israel, Amsterdam's leading rabbi, held a similar view. He believed that the messianic age was imminent but would only be realized when the Jewish exile had spread to every corner of the world. It was essential therefore that the Jews be readmitted to England. He came to London in 1655 to deliver a written address to the Lord Protector, Oliver Cromwell. His pamphlet presented both the economic and theological cases for readmitting the Jews and drew on many of the arguments that Luzzatto had made in the *Discorso*. Menasseh did not mention the *Discorso* in his pamphlet but his use of it is apparent, he translated parts of it verbatim and replicated some of its key points.[14]

Sixty years later the Irish philosopher John Toland published a tract advocating the naturalization of the Jews in Great Britain and Ireland. He too made considerable use of the *Discorso* and declared that he intended to translate it. He never did translate it, however, but he was abundant in expressing his admiration for Luzzatto, describing him as 'a man of extraordinary learning and judgment, very acute, and not meanly eloquent'.[15]

THE CHARGE AGAINST SOCRATES

Luzzatto's only other major work reinforces the idea that secular philosophy was his overriding interest. He was the leading rabbi of his generation in Venice yet in his heart of hearts he considered himself to be a philosopher. Philosophy is a conventional interest for a rabbi, some of the leading rabbinic scholars in history wrote influential philosophic works, most notably Maimonides. Where

Simone Luzzatto diverges from the rationalist philosopher-rabbis who followed Maimonides is in his interest in Scepticism, the philosophical theory which questions the possibility of achieving knowledge through reason and the senses. If Luzzatto's book of philosophy actually reaches a conclusion, which for most readers is by no means certain, it is that ultimate truth can never be known, that there is a danger in relying too firmly on reason and the senses.

The title of Luzzatto's work is *Socrates, Or On Human Knowledge*. It is usually known by its shortened Italian title; *Socrate*. In its subtitle it claims to be *A Book That Shows How Deficient Human Understanding Can Be When It Is Not Led by Divine Revelation*. This suggests that, unlike the rational Maimonidean philosophers, reason plays very little part in Luzzatto's philosophy. But the subtitle is misleading; the book does not say much at all about Revelation.

The book is an enigma. Luzzatto was not the first learned Venetian Jew to write a book which had nothing to do with Judaism for an Italian readership; Leone Ebreo had done the same. But Ebreo was not the senior rabbi in Venice. And Ebreo's *Dialogues of Love* was a hugely popular and influential work, reprinted many times. Simone Luzzatto's *Socrate*, a reconstruction of the trial of Socrates, was barely known even in his own time. First printed in 1651 it was rarely mentioned in succeeding centuries and was next published in 2013. Historically and politically, Luzzatto was an important figure in the Venice Ghetto. His book *Socrate* almost certainly was not.

Dedicated to the Venetian Doge Francesco Molino and the 'wise men of the Council', the book is nevertheless a testimony to the range of Luzzatto's erudition and an outstanding example of how deeply the learning and culture of the outside world had penetrated the walls of the ghetto. His familiarity with the philosophers and thinkers of Rome and Greece is not wholly unexpected. Nor too is his knowledge of Stoicism and Scepticism. More surprisingly, he seems to be familiar with the works of the French sceptical essayist Montaigne (although he doesn't mention him by name) and had almost certainly read the works of Thomas More and Machiavelli. He summarizes Galileo's theories and the works of the physician Paracelsus, understands optics, Euclidean geometry and navigational techniques. None of this is unusual for an early seventeenth-century thinker in Christian society but far less probable in the Jewish world. It does contradict any suggestion that the ghetto was a backward place, cut off intellectually as well as physically from the rest of the world.

UNDERSTANDING THE TIMES

In 1648 a book of sermons was published in Venice. Entitled *Bina L'itim* ('Understanding the Times'), it was a collection of 76 homilies delivered in the ghetto by Rabbi Azariah Figo who had died the previous year. The book turned out to be so popular that it has been reprinted nearly fifty times since its first publication.

Born just three years before Simone Luzzatto, Azariah Figo, or Picho, was a man similarly interested in the natural world, who used examples of contemporary technology to illustrate the ideas he was trying to get across to his synagogue audiences. Unlike Luzzatto, however, he was conflicted by his interest in science. He complained that as a young man he had spent too long studying secular subjects, to the extent that he neglected his Talmudic and spiritual studies. He resolved to abandon his secular studies and devote himself exclusively to mastery of the religious sources. He wrote a commentary on the Talmud despite copies being in such short supply after the burning in 1553 that he had to borrow most of the volumes from neighbouring communities.

There is no doubt that to some degree Figo managed to recreate himself in the austere image associated with a rabbinic scholar wholly immersed in textual study. During his career he opposed the establishment of the theatre, which Rabbi Sh'muel Aboab also condemned,[16] and criticized his congregation for sexual laxity, dressing too opulently, religious leniency, and generally doing any of the things that make life too enjoyable. But he could not rid himself of the scientific and natural knowledge he had picked up in his youth, and when reading his sermons one gets the impression he didn't try too hard to put such things out of his mind.

He alluded in one sermon to the classical technique known as the Art of Memory. The technique, which involves associating mental images with the objects or ideas that one needs to remember, had a particular resonance for Venetians. They remembered the occult 'memory theatre' designed in the city by Giulio Camillo during the early part of the sixteenth century. It was intended to help those who entered it to retrieve any aspect of human knowledge, by referring to the relevant images and symbols in the theatre. Figo told his congregation that the Art of Memory was integral to the Jewish religious tradition, citing as an example the fringes on a prayer shawl which, when looked at, are intended to bring the commandments to mind.

Figo frequently reminded his audience of the benefits of contemporary medical treatments and of technologies like eyeglasses and telescopes that enhanced the benefits already provided by nature. But he made it clear that scientific knowledge alone was not enough. He pointed out that doctors are liable to make mistakes, that imperfect knowledge can be dangerous. Science, he believed, was only valuable when accompanied by observation. It was Revelation that provided this observation, truth can only be known through revealed experience of the divine.[17]

Unlike Simone Luzzatto, Azariah Figo turned partly away from the scientific revolution taking place in the secular world. He saw science as useful but only as a technological aid, not as an intellectual pursuit. The intellect could only be satisfied by the study of the religious literature.

Figo broke no new ground and was not a cultural or intellectual trendsetter. If anything this enhances rather than diminishes his significance. His importance can be discerned by the popularity of his sermons. They suggest that he understood the intellectual needs of his congregation, that he knew how to reach ordinary people, those who were not scholars or philosophers, at their own level. If so, he was more a man of the ghetto than those at the forefront of its cultural renaissance.

OCCULT MISDEEDS

Leon Modena's grandson Isacco Levi was in trouble. He was now the preacher at the Italian Synagogue and a man whose wide interests spanned magic, alchemy and the occult. A report had reached the Inquisition in Venice that he had been involved in an occult ritual to catch a thief who had stolen a girdle from a certain Francesco Basilio of the San Samuele district. The ritual, known as *esperimento dell' inghistera,* was typically performed using a bowl of water, candles and an innocent person: either a child, a virgin or a pregnant woman (she wasn't considered innocent but her foetus was). When it was performed properly the ritual would conjure up a white angel who would truthfully answer questions about the whereabouts of demons and malefactors such as the person who had stolen Francesco Basilio's girdle. The *esperimento dell' inghistera* had been performed in Venice for many years. The Inquisition frowned upon it because it involved the reprehensible act of divination, but generally they took no action. In Isacco Levi's case, however, they took action. He was divining on behalf of a Christian, an act strictly prohibited to Jews, and they suspected that he was also involved in the far more serious offence of demon worship.

The Inquisition accused Isacco Levi of performing the *esperimento* by placing a bowl of water on a tripod together with a piece of paper on which was written a Hebrew formula. He put a candle at each of the three feet of the tripod and asked two boys to tell him what they saw in the water. They told him that they could see a king, dressed in black, sitting on a throne and holding a book. Isacco told them to address the king, telling them exactly what to say. When they had finished their address the king showed them an image of the thief, told them that he was a tailor, and gave them the initials of his name. We don't know if the thief was identified and caught, but that is how the events are set down in the Inquisition's records.[18]

The accusation of witchcraft was only the start of Isacco Levi's misfortunes. Three years later the Inquisition raided his home. They found a quantity of occult books and kabbalistic Hebrew texts as well as a work by the condemned Florentine friar Giralomo Savanarola. The Inquisition summoned Giulio Morosini, the convert who would write a criticism of Simone Luzzatto's *Discorso*, to tell them what was in the Hebrew books.[19]

That seems to be as far as matters went. For reasons we cannot know, the investigation into Isacco Levi was never concluded. Maybe a bribe was paid, perhaps the Inquisition's attention was diverted towards other matters. For whatever reason the file remains open in the Inquisition's records.

MADNESS

At the end of 1665 reports arrived in the ghetto from Jerusalem. They declared that the Messiah had finally come. Jews had been expecting him for centuries, belief in the Messiah's impending arrival had furnished them with hope during the long years of exile and persecution. The arrival of the Messiah would usher in a new utopian era. He would set the world aright, restore the Jewish nation to their ancient homeland and wipe away their tears.

Similar reports had circulated before, but this time it seemed far more credible. This was not just a vague rumour about something somebody had heard or seen; the Messiah was an identifiable person, a man named Shabbetai Tzvi, who had been anointed by a prophet in Jerusalem while enwrapped in a fiery cloud. An angel's voice had been heard coming out of the cloud as he was being anointed. The prophet who had anointed the Messiah, a previously unknown man named Nathan of Gaza, was circulating devotional manuals to be read in the synagogues. The masses could not contain their enthusiasm. Already people from as far afield as Egypt, Smyrna and the Balkans were packing up their lives and heading to Jerusalem. It was even whispered that the armies of the Ten Lost Tribes were winning great victories against their enemies in Persia, Arabia and North Africa. Rabbis were calling for repentance in advance of the cosmic transformation about to take place.

The announcement that the Messiah had arrived in the person of Shabbetai Tzvi led to the greatest outbreak of mass delusion in

Jewish history. The first stirrings of the movement had begun in the summer of 1665, when Nathan of Gaza announced that he had had a mystical vision in which he saw the face of Shabbetai Tzvi engraved upon the heavenly throne. It was revealed to him there and then that Shabbetai Tzvi was the Messiah and that Nathan's mission was to declare his arrival to the world. Within weeks a mass frenzy had broken out on a scale and of an intensity greater than anything ever experienced before, anywhere.

Not everyone succumbed to the madness. A deep rift opened up in the Jewish world, violent in its expression and devastating in its impact. Riven between those who believed that Shabbetai Tzvi was the Messiah, come at last to redeem Israel, and those who were certain he was a false messiah, a charlatan, a madman. Families were torn apart, preachers denounced each other, rabbis condemned their communities, congregations ostracized their rabbis, polemicists printed rebuttals and counter-rebuttals. Meanwhile those who believed the Messiah had arrived sold their possessions and waited anxiously for him to summon them. Those who could not wait set off for the Holy Land and crowded into the narrow streets of Jerusalem.

The following September, little more than a year after the turmoil broke out, Shabbetai Tzvi converted to Islam. Ten years later he was dead. The frenzy died with him, though the repercussions carried on for decades. They can still be discerned in some quarters.

One of the first reports to reach Venice about the arrival of the Messiah came in a letter sent to Rabbi Solomon Hay Saraval. Like many of the early communications about the Messiah, the writer was reticent about disclosing too much. He wrote simply that he had seen many good signs but what he had seen may not be committed to paper. Everything, he said, now depended upon repentance.

The letter was less than informative but it was enough to arouse great excitement. Venice, always a hub of communication between Jewish communities, soon took a lead in spreading the word. Travellers excitedly departed from the ghetto bearing great news, others arrived daily bringing reports of new wonders. There were even stories of Christians elsewhere in Italy who had converted to Judaism. It wasn't long before word reached the Venetian authorities that something of great significance was happening in the Jewish world and that the Jews in the ghetto seemed to be at the heart of it. They had heard reports from Ferrara that four Christians had been arrested for declaring the only true religion to be that of Moses, that in the Vatican it was rumoured that the Antichrist had come, that in Venice itself illiterate Christians were now studying with rabbis. Fearing for the stability of their own community the Venetian authorities demanded that the leaders of the ghetto communities tell them what was going on. The ghetto leaders, themselves uncertain as to whether or not the rumours were true, said they knew nothing.[20]

Shortly afterwards an emissary from the messianic movement in Jerusalem arrived in the ghetto. He had come to deliver a bundle of letters containing instructions from the Messiah. The new rules imposed a ban on attending theatres and masques and disclosed new penances that were to be recited daily. They delivered a severe warning that all were to behave chastely. Chastity, wrote the author of a letter recording the messenger's arrival, was a great thing to demand.

The news of the alleged messiah's arrival divided the rabbis of Venice just as it did the Jewish world at large. Rabbi Sh'muel Aboab was now the head of the yeshiva, a body which seems to have grown larger in size and authority than in earlier days. Aboab was a man of even temperament and diplomatic caution. He is unlikely to have believed Tzvi's claim to messiahship nor to have approved of the ecstatic and enthusiastic behaviour of some of the movement's members. But he did not condemn the messianic movement and he did approve of its call to repentance, an activity which, from a rabbinic point of view, is never a bad thing.

Aboab's attitude, as far as we can make out, was to try to maintain harmony within the ghetto and wait to see how things worked out. He was concerned though about the impact on the Venetian citizenry of the stories that were circulating in the ghetto. He was fearful that triumphalist displays by Shabbetai Tzvi's more exuberant followers might provoke anti-Jewish disturbances in the city. When asked by the rabbi of nearby Verona for advice on how to react to the new events he recommended caution and restraint, not discussing the events in public and wherever possible calming the more excitable elements in his town.

Aboab's rabbinic colleague Moshe Zacuto, was equally inscrutable in his attitude to the false messiah. Shabbetai Tzvi made extensive use of Kabbalah in his rituals and in the so-called miracles that he worked, introducing heretical and even pornographic elements into his kabbalistic activities. Zacuto, who was one of Italy's leading kabbalists, recognized the extent to which the false messiah had corrupted Kabbalah. He didn't condemn Tzvi's use of Kabbalah though, because he was won over by the idea that the present moment was one of grace, in which conflict and division should be kept to a minimum. Instead, he treated Tzvi's excesses leniently, as if they were nothing more than errors.

Modern scholars are divided over Zacuto's attitude to Shabbetai Tzvi. Some hold that Zacuto was an enthusiastic follower of the false messiah, others believe that he was an unyielding opponent. Gershom Scholem, whose masterly biography of Shabbetai Tzvi remains unrivalled after more than half a century, regards Zacuto's faith in Tzvi as 'essentially that of a doubter and it is not surprising that he forsook it immediately after Shabbetai's apostasy'.[21]

Overall, the rabbis of Venice were confused as to how to respond to the reports and stories they were hearing. They wrote letters to their counterparts in Jerusalem and Constantinople asking for information about what was going on. The letter to Constantinople described the agitated conversations and arguments in the streets of the ghetto and asked the Turkish rabbis to confirm whether this time was indeed one of glad tidings or whether the rumours that were circulating were nothing more than fantasy. Moshe Zacuto was one of the six rabbis of the yeshiva who signed the letter. Sh'muel Aboab did not sign. The way the letter was drafted, and its despatch following a day of fasting and repentance in the ghetto, suggests that they were expecting an optimistic answer.

The rabbis of Venice waited anxiously for replies to their letters. They heard nothing from Jerusalem, but they did finally receive a response from Constantinople. Written in a cryptic style, presumably in case it fell into the wrong hands, it said that the merchandise about which the Venetian rabbis had inquired had been investigated and found to be perfect. It would yield great profit and the rabbis of Venice were urged to quieten the quarrelling parties and eliminate all doubt concerning the matter. In other words the Constantinople rabbinate stood firmly and squarely behind Shabbetai Tzvi.[22]

Among the residents of the ghetto the atmosphere was fevered. The believers, those who had no doubt that the Messiah had arrived, vastly outnumbered the faithless, who they called infidels. Fights broke out in the synagogues over the introduction of new prayers that the believers were expected to recite.

When the letter from Constantinople finally arrived the members of the ghetto's Small Assembly summoned the rabbis to discuss it. One of Leon Modena's grandsons, a rabbi by the name of Isaac Levita, described the meeting in his autobiography. Levita wrote that a violent quarrel broke out between the lay elders of the ghetto who wanted to keep the letter a secret and some rabbis who demanded it was published. The meeting descended into chaos, with the Small Assembly insisting that the rabbis only had control over religious matters and the rabbis demanding the right to voice an opinion on any subject they desired.

Finally, the rabbis stormed out and went off to issue a proclamation to the ghetto. Levita did not disclose what had been written in the rabbis' proclamation, but the Small Assembly declared its content invalid. They issued an edict that from now on no rabbi was to be addressed by the traditional honorific of 'our master'. Anyone disobeying the edict risked excommunication and a fine of 200 ducats.[23]

Meanwhile Shabbetai Tzvi had made his fateful final journey to Constantinople, where he had been arrested and would ultimately convert to Islam. One of his followers, a man named Moses Nahmias, journeyed from Venice to the fortress in Gallipoli where the Sultan had ordered the Messiah to be detained. He told Tzvi that many people were speaking ill of the Messiah and asked whether it was permissible to shed the blood of those who slandered him. Tzvi told him that it was.

THE PROPHET ARRIVES

Shabbetai Tzvi's conversion to Islam severely wounded the messianic movement but it did not finish it off. His most ardent followers explained it as part of a grand plan, a necessary prelude to the ultimate redemption that the Messiah would bring about at its due time. His prophet, Nathan of Gaza, kept the faith, justifying the apostasy and travelling to Jewish communities to fortify the believers.

He arrived in Venice in 1668. According to the Sabbatean faithful in the ghetto, the rabbis had asked the Venetian government to deny him entry to the city, but their request had been denied. The rabbis then threatened excommunication on anyone who even spoke to Nathan, let alone allowed him into their home.

Rabbi Sh'muel Aboab went to meet Nathan on his arrival and told him he would not be allowed into the ghetto because his presence might stir up unrest or even violence. According to the Sabbatean believers, Rabbi Moshe Zacuto also went to see him and after a lengthy conversation confessed that, although he had studied Kabbalah for 38 years, Nathan was better versed in the subject than he. Whether it was at Zacuto's urging or through some other means, Nathan secured an invitation to the palace of two Venetian nobles. He stayed there for two days while the nobles procured an order from the government to the Small Assembly demanding that he be admitted to the ghetto.

Nathan stayed in the ghetto for a fortnight while the rabbis cross-examined him. They recorded their conclusions in a lengthy document in which they declared that Nathan had been unable to give satisfactory answers to their questions. Indeed, they said, he was so ashamed in their presence that he could hardly speak. They said that he had admitted to being possessed by an evil spirit and since he had not wilfully acted wickedly, they had resolved not to punish him severely. They would not excommunicate him, but they would publish their account of the proceedings and circulate it to all Jewish congregations in order to discredit him.

They made Nathan sign a retraction, saying he was mistaken in believing that Shabbetai Tzvi was the Messiah. After he left Venice, Nathan protested that he had been forced to sign under duress, and that the believers should take no notice of his retraction or of any of the statements issued by the Venetian rabbis.

The publication of the rabbis' conclusions led to another round of argument in the ghetto. The believers condemned the rabbis; even Moshe Zacuto was execrated. The tolerance that he had shown towards the messianic movement at the beginning had turned to outright condemnation after he heard of Tzvi's apostasy, and the Messiah's supporters treated him with no greater respect than they did any other rabbi.

The believers printed their condemnation of the rabbis and circulated it widely. Zacuto responded to them angrily. Calling them deceitful fools, he accused the believers of damaging the reputation and commercial interests of the ghetto traders through their madness, of increasing the risk of apostasy among those former followers of Shabbetai Tzvi who now felt betrayed and disappointed, and of endangering the physical security and safety of the ghetto by stirring up the incredulity and hostility of their Christian neighbours.

As for Nathan, he went on his way. The believers in the ghetto gradually returned to their former lives, but bad feeling between members of the two groups persisted for the rest of their lives. The damage could not be undone.

Decline

MONEY PROBLEMS

By the closing decades of the seventeenth century the power, prestige and wealth of the Venetian Republic were all in decline. The lengthy struggle beginning in 1645 to defend the island of Crete against Turkish invaders culminated in 1669 with the withdrawal of the Venetian flag. It was followed in 1684 by yet another war against the Turks, this time lasting for fifteen years. Many died and the city's treasury was depleted. The Republic was weakened politically too; the kingdoms of northern Europe no longer considered Venice a formidable continental power as they once had done. Commercially, French, German and English merchants had muscled in on the Mediterranean trade that the Republic once regarded as its own, causing further financial distress. Recovery was impeded by the soaring costs of exporting goods from the city, costs that were themselves a consequence of the toll the wars had taken upon the Venetian merchant fleet. Venice was deeply in debt, paying interest of up to 14 per cent on its loans.[1]

Whenever the Venetian government needed money, their first port of call was always the Jews of the ghetto. Between 1669 and 1700 the ghetto community paid taxes, charges and loans into the city treasury, amounting to the enormous sum of 800,000 ducats, the equivalent today of tens of millions of pounds. In the first week of 1700 the Senate demanded a further loan from the Jews of 150,000 ducats. And so it went on. For the ghetto, with a total population of no more than 5,000, such sums were unachievable.[2] Forbidden to pawn property or to own real estate the Jews had no assets they could sell to meet the Senate's demands. They had to borrow whatever they could, much of it from the nobles and wealthy citizenry of Venice. Their debts piled up, with interest accruing. The only bright light in this bleeding dry of the ghetto's population was that the Jews were now free of the threat of expulsion. The Serenissima had no intention of throwing the Jews out while they still owed money to the city and its nobles.

Like the city itself the ghetto was bankrupt. Yet they were still obliged to maintain the pawnshops. They had been running at a loss for years because the rate of interest the shop owners were allowed to charge was never sufficient to cover the operating costs of the business. And so, in 1706 the Tedeschi community petitioned the government to allow foreign Jews to live in the ghetto for limited periods of time. They would be charged an annual tax. The authorities agreed.

Always anxious to find additional ways of extracting money from the ghetto, the Venetian authorities came up with a new solution. It had been known for a long time that although the Jewish communities always had trouble paying their dues and taxes to the city, there was private money in the ghetto in the hands of a few wealthy families. For nearly a hundred years the Senate had tried to prevent wealthy families from leaving Venice, taking their assets with them. Now they tightened the screw. They appointed a magistrate to investigate any family which wished to leave, with the intention of obstructing their departure as much as possible. No longer continually threatened with expulsion, the Jews were now almost forcibly detained in the ghetto.[3]

As the ghetto's financial situation continued to worsen, the Senate cast around for new ways to bring the situation under control. They appointed Inquisitors to oversee all the various statutory bodies that had control over the ghetto. The idea was that one overarching authority would have a broader perspective on the financial crisis and be able to implement more effective solutions. The Inquisitors delved into every aspect of the ghetto's finances, even seizing 2,500 ducats from the Society for the Ransoming of Captives. It prevented the charity from continuing its work and caused an outcry in the ghetto.

Unfortunately, although the archives have preserved extensive records of the deliberations and resolutions of the Venetian authorities, there is very little record of events on the ground. While we generally know what the Republic decided to do, we often do not know what actually happened. Other than seizing the assets of the Society for the Ransoming of Captives, it is hard to tell from the little evidence available what difference the appointment of the Inquisitors made to the financial situation in the ghetto.

Meanwhile, the permission that had earlier been granted to allow foreign Jews into the ghetto was beginning to backfire. Seeing that foreign Jews were liable only to pay a personal tax and were not obliged to contribute to the communal tax that the Senate demanded, ghetto families began to change their status, declaring themselves to be foreigners. This created further tensions with the government and conflict among the Jews themselves. It was bound to happen. The greater the number of ghetto Jews who declared themselves to be foreigners, the fewer the number of natives who remained to share the communal tax burden.

In 1732 the *Cattaveri*, the magistrates who oversaw the ghetto's activities, submitted a report to the Doge. They told him that the Jews of the ghetto had abandoned their former submissive obedience and were now seeking as much advantage as they could. They reported that the barriers between Jew and Christian seemed to be breaking down, that Jews now seemed to be owning property and some even had Christian servants. A number of years earlier, noting that members of both faiths were socializing inappropriately, eating and drinking together and submitting to the many temptations of the city, the *Cattaveri* had banned the sale of Jewish wine to Christians. They had hoped that this would put an end to the shenanigans. In fact, it had made little difference and now the *Cattaveri* were obliged to tell the Doge that their efforts had failed. There was now even a Hebrew printing shop in the ghetto, in direct contravention of the ongoing prohibition against Jewish printers. The Jews had even chosen their own censor to inspect the books being published, despite this being an office that was supposed to be appointed and overseen by the authorities. The censor they had appointed was a convert from Judaism and the *Cattaveri* did not trust his decisions. They suspected that he was open to bribery. Bewailing the fact that the censor, the typesetter and the editor were all Jews or former Jews, they had no idea what scandals may have arisen or were yet to arise.

Towards the end of the 1730s the financial crisis in the ghetto was brought under a degree of control. The *Università Grande*, the Jews' governing assembly, submitted a debt-reduction proposal to the Senate that would result in the ghetto's creditors receiving a proportion of the money they owed. Once two-thirds of the creditors had been reimbursed with two-thirds of the money they were owed, it would become far easier to deal with the remaining debt. The Senate approved the proposal and instructed the Inquisitors to oversee the plan.

The plan was a good one, but the *Università Grande* hadn't yet raised the money to implement it. They despatched the leading rabbi in the ghetto, Jacob Raphael Saraval, and the merchant Jacobo Belilios, sending them on a fundraising mission to London, Amsterdam and the Hague. The two men did well. They raised several thousand pounds, to be repaid over ten years, with the interest payments to be overseen by the Inquisitors.[4]

Over the next few years a further series of measures were implemented to try to restore financial stability to the ghetto. The loophole that allowed ghetto residents to declare themselves foreigners was removed and the distinction between the Levantine, Tedeschi and Ponentine communities was formally abandoned. From now on the Jews in the ghetto would be treated as a single community, all under one charter, with the same responsibilities and privileges.

THE LAST SCHOLARS

The financial crisis was not the only symptom of the ghetto's decline. Venice's diminishing status as a global and maritime power lessened the magnetic appeal of both the city and the ghetto. Intellectually too the ghetto's reputation was receding. Scholars of repute visited less frequently; original thinkers were scarcely to be found. The ghetto no longer seemed able to produce sages and scholars of the calibre of their predecessors. Even the oddballs, prophets and false messiahs stopped coming.

Well, not quite all. Moses Hayyim Luzzatto is regarded today as one of the most important early modern Jewish ethical thinkers. But in his youth in the ghetto he was regarded as something of an oddity. He was deeply involved in Kabbalah and claimed that he had a mystical *maggid*, a disembodied voice that spoke to him. He gathered a circle of disciples around him and told them about the heavenly voice that he heard. He warned them not to breathe a word of it to anyone, but one of his disciples let the secret out. It caused an uproar among the rabbis. The memory of the Shabbetai Tzvi affair was still fresh in their minds, and the last thing that the rabbis of Venice wanted was the emergence of another would-be charismatic to seduce the masses into believing he was the Messiah.

Word of Luzzatto's activities reached Moses Hagiz, the son of one of Shabbetai Tzvi's most determined and forceful opponents. He wrote to the rabbis of Venice warning them to rein Luzzatto in. When he was challenged, Luzzatto denied having any messianic pretensions and carried on much as before, meeting his disciples and absorbing the kabbalistic ideas the *maggid* was planting in his head. He was only 23 years old and probably had little idea of the consternation he was causing.

The Venetian rabbis resorted to the only sanction available to them. They excommunicated him. Luzzatto, believing that rabbis and teachers were to be obeyed whether they were right or wrong, accepted the decree, signed the document of excommunication and left town. He travelled first to Frankfurt, then Amsterdam and finally Israel.

With hindsight, leaving Venice was the best thing that could have happened to Moses Hayyim Luzzatto. Once he was away from the ghetto he began writing prolifically, changing his field of interest from mysticism to ethics. His book *Path of the Upright*, which he wrote in Amsterdam, is a classic of Jewish ethical literature. He was probably the most talented and charismatic person to emerge from the Venice Ghetto in the eighteenth century. But the ghetto he'd grown up in was no longer the sort of place where those possessed of unconventional or charismatic talent could easily survive. The malaise of decline was everywhere.

This didn't mean that the ghetto was full of ignorant or poorly educated people. Families continued to send their brightest sons to study medicine in Padua as they had done for generations. Rabbis and theologians still came to the ghetto to have their scholarly works printed on the city's Hebrew presses, even if their numbers were fewer than in times gone by. And the ghetto still produced talented people. It's just that in many cases the talent at which they excelled was more mercantile than bookish.

One of the few who bucked the trend was Jacob Raphael Saraval, the rabbi who had earlier been sent on a fundraising trip to Holland. Known as a preacher, musician, liturgical poet and translator of Hebrew works into Italian, Saraval spent the early part of his life in the ghetto in Venice until being appointed as the rabbi of nearby Mantua in 1752. Saraval began his writing career by collaborating with a colleague, the rabbi and playwright Simone Calimani, on an Italian translation of and commentary on the ancient Hebrew ethical tract *Chapters of the Fathers*. His most powerful work was his forceful, anonymous *lettera apologetica*, his response to an antisemitic polemic written by the lawyer Giovanni Battista Benedetti of Ferrara.[5]

Cast in the same mould as Leon Modena but enjoying a less troubled and painful life, Saraval was an erudite man with a network of contacts reminiscent of those of his seventeenth-century predecessor. Benjamin Kennicott, the English Bible philologist and scholar, published one of Saraval's letters to him in his landmark book on the authoritative text of the Hebrew Bible.

Around 1772 Saraval was contacted by members of the Amsterdam Jewish community. They told him that they were commissioning the Austrian composer Christian Giuseppe Lidarti to write an oratorio based on the biblical book of Esther. They asked Saraval to write a Hebrew libretto for the work based on Handel's English version. They knew of Saraval's literary skills from the letters that he had recently published describing his earlier fundraising trip and travels in Holland. Still in circulation today, the seven letters are more than just an early Hebrew travel diary. They describe the advantages and pleasures of life in a country which, unlike Italy, was a bastion of religious tolerance and plurality. Saraval describes Holland with an almost messianic fervour. A new edition of his letters was printed in 2005.[6]

Saraval accepted the commission for the libretto. It involved translating part of Handel's English into Hebrew, a task that doesn't seem to have bothered him at all. He wrote the Hebrew libretto in rhymed verse, using the iambic tetrameter with which Jewish audiences were familiar from some of the more popular songs they sang in synagogue. Much of the libretto consists of quotes taken directly from the Hebrew Bible, but masterly reworked by Saraval to fit the rhyme and metre. Premiered in 1774 it became the first oratorio to be sung wholly in Hebrew.

The great tragedy in Saraval's life came on 31 May 1776 when his daughter attended a wedding in Mantua. There had been three weddings in the Mantuan Jewish community that day and the guests from all the celebrations crowded together for a party in a third-floor apartment in the ghetto. The flimsy building was unable to bear the weight of such a crowd. It collapsed killing 66 people, including Saraval's daughter.

Saraval wrote an elegy in Hebrew lamenting the event. He described the details of the tragedy in the preface but kept a promise he had made not to name the building or its owner. Grieving over the sudden transformation of a day of celebration into one of mourning he declared that the event would be commemorated as a day of fasting for the entire community and of thanksgiving for the 52 people who had survived.[7]

THE LAST MERCHANTS

One man who possessed more than his fair share of mercantile wizardry was Isaac Treves. He came to Venice from Constantinople in 1724 and settled with his family in the *Ghetto Vecchio*, the section of the ghetto that had been set aside for the Levantine merchants in 1541. He came from a prosperous trading and banking family. His father owned a large and successful business in Constantinople and Isaac Treves spotted an opportunity to open a branch in Venice, to act as a bridge for trade between Turkey and London. He set himself up in Venice then sent two of his four sons, Joseph and Pellegrin, to open an office for the family business in London. Shortly afterwards he set up a further trading arm in the Baltic countries. Isaac Treves remained in the ghetto, with the aim of transforming his family's ambitions from wealth creation to elevating their social standing and status.

We can get a sense of Isaac Treves's status from a picture painted in the 1730s by Bartolomeo Nazari. The painting, entitled *Isaac Treves and his Captains*, shows a bewigged Treves seated in his study wearing an ermine-lined gown. His left elbow is resting on the table that forms the centrepiece of the picture. The table is covered in a plush, red Turkish carpet, symbolizing the firm's origins in Constantinople. To Treves's right is a boy, presumably the eldest of his four sons. He has his right arm around the boy, resting his hand on his shoulder as if to allude to the line of succession. A footman is adjusting the boy's coat, suggesting the scrupulous care that is being lavished upon him. Behind them is the boy's mother. Since the title suggests that this is a business rather than a family portrait, the presence of Madame Treves probably indicates that she played a role in the business.

On the left-hand side of the picture stand four gentlemen who must be the captains alluded to in the painting's title. A merchant with four captains in his permanent employ is clearly a man of significant wealth. But his business interests extend beyond ships. For seated at the edge of the table is a young man in a pose typically used to portray a banker at his counting table. But this banker has no money before him. Instead he is writing letters, copying from a couple of bound ledgers that sit on the table. The implication is that the Treves's enterprise is so solid and respected that it conducts its international trade through letters of credit. The global nature of the business is confirmed by the slightly askew picture of a ship on the wall at the back.[8]

In 1773 Salomon Treves, one of the two sons who had remained in Venice, rented a *palazzo* outside the ghetto. He paid the princely price of 500 ducats a year. It was a sign that the status of the Jews in Venice was gradually, if unofficially, changing. Salomon Treves was one of a small cohort who, by virtue of their status and wealth, were becoming known as 'separate Jews', managing to live beyond the ghetto walls and exempt from wearing the distinctive yellow or red cap. There was still a long way to go but the word emancipation hung tentatively in the air.

In 1780 Salomon's son Giuseppe Treves married Benedetta Bonfil. The Bonfils were just as prosperous as the Treveses and equally keen on social advancement. The two families merged their banking businesses and the young couple moved into a *palazzo* just outside the ghetto. Technically the *palazzo* was incorporated into the *Ghetto Nuovissimo*, but it is unlikely that the Treves–Bonfil family ever considered themselves ghetto dwellers; they now owned the largest company in Venice. One of their vessels was the first to sail under a Venetian flag to America, carrying flour to the New World and returning with a cargo of sugar and coffee.[9]

In 1811 Napoleon ennobled Giuseppe Treves, making him the first Italian Jew to receive the title of Baron. The Treves dei Bonfili family have remained prominent in Italian life ever since. The *palazzo* bearing their name is no longer on the fringes of the *Ghetto Nuovissimo*. In 1827 the family bought the Palazzo Barozzi, the home since the twelfth century of an aristocratic Venetian family. They renovated the building and renamed it the Palazzo Treves de Bonfili. The pink palace looks onto the Grand Canal, just a short distance from Piazza San Marco.

THE LAST CONFLICT

As the eighteenth century wore on the Venetian Republic's economy continued to worsen. The city was deeply in debt, the highest offices of state were in the hands of a few immensely rich families, a sense of decadence, corruption and dissolution was palpable. The Senate was in crisis. Technically the Doge was the highest authority in the Republic, but everyone knew that the real power in the Serenissima lay in the unelected hands of Andrea Tron, the loud, reactionary son of a wealthy industrialist. Tron, a bully who made no secret of his xenophobic leanings, dominated the Republic's politics. They called him *el paron*, the patron.[10]

It was Tron who led the calls for economic reform. The Jews, he and his allies argued, controlled too much of the Republic's trade. They dominated the market in grains and oils, shutting out the Venetian merchants who were now at a gross disadvantage. The only solution was for the Jews to be banned from the trade in olive oil. Tron's leverage over the Senate was such that they did not need much persuasion. They introduced a new protectionist policy excluding Jews from buying oil.

The consequences were swift and devastating. Prices soared, a thriving black market sprung up, the farmers on the Venetian island of Corfu, who no longer received their subsidies from the Jewish traders, were up in arms. The Senate set up two inquiries into the matter. When they reported, one called for the status quo to be restored, the other expressed confidence in the new policy saying that the chaos was all the fault of the Jews.

After much argument and soul searching the Senate opted to put things back the way they had been before. The free market was restored, Jews could once again deal in oil.

It was a setback for Tron and his protectionism but it wasn't a defeat. The discord within the Senate did not quieten down. The *Cattaveri*, anxious not to give ground to the Jews, reinforced the prohibitions against Christians and Jews mixing socially; prohibitions that some people had been regularly flouting for years and that had become largely unenforceable.[11]

In 1777 the Jews' charter to trade and reside in the city came up for renewal. Two years earlier the new Pope, Pius VI, had issued an edict tightening the restrictions imposed on Jews living in the Papal States. As an independent state Venice was not bound to enforce the regulations in the edict, and in any event their overriding concerns as always were commercial not religious. Nevertheless, the new edict helped darken the anti-Jewish mood, impeding the charter negotiations. It was grist to Andrea Tron's mill.

The new charter contained 96 clauses. Many of them concerned matters such as taxation and the management of the pawnshops, which were little different to the provisions of earlier charters. Far more onerous, however, were the new restrictions on trade and commerce which Tron had managed to drive through. In order to stop Jewish manufacturers from selling directly to the public and thereby undercutting Christian retailers, Jews were henceforth banned from manufacturing. All unlicensed Jewish manufacturing facilities were to be torn down immediately, those workshops that had licences were to be closed within two years, or as soon as their licences expired. The only exception was for those factories that made goods not manufactured by Christians.

The charter also definitively clarified the legal standing of the Jews in Venice. It established the principle that Jews could never enjoy the right of being a Venetian subject. Nor could they enjoy any privileges reserved for Venetians, though they were given the protection of the Venetian authorities both at home and overseas when trading.[12] The consequence was, as the *Cinque Savi alla Mercanzia*, the Five Sages of Commerce, pointed out, that the Jews were merely merchants in the Venetian marketplace, albeit under public protection. The overall effect of the charter prompted one modern historian to declare that it reduced 'a once prosperous and useful community to the status of rag-and-bone merchants'.[13]

SHYLOCK RETURNS

The Merchant of Venice was not performed for most of the seventeenth century. The title page of the first edition of the play, printed in 1600, stated that it had already been performed 'divers times' and it is known that King James I watched it in 1605. But from the time of Shakespeare's death in 1616 and for the rest of the century Shylock was absent from the English stage. Oliver

Cromwell's parliament had ordered the closure of all theatres in 1642 but they were reopened eighteen years later, upon the Restoration and the accession of Charles II. Shylock's absence from the stage was far longer than that. By the time Shylock returned the Jews of the Venice Ghetto would have not recognized him at all. The ghetto was vastly different from the days of Anselmo del Banco, and Shylock was now being played in a way far removed from that which Shakespeare intended.

Shylock returned to the theatre in 1701. His was the title role in *The Jew of Venice*, a stripped-down, comical adaptation of Shakespeare's play written by George Granville, a poet and politician who eventually became Britain's Secretary for War. Granville's Shylock displays the worst aspects of Shakespeare's character, but to comic effect. He has none of the complexity of Shakespeare's Shylock and elicits neither sympathy nor fury from the audience. He is a buffoon who appears on stage sporting a large nose and red hair, whose most memorable scene is to propose a toast to money.

Unlike Shakespeare, Granville wrote at a time when Jews were legally allowed to live in England. Oliver Cromwell had admitted them to the country in 1656 and attitudes towards them were beginning to soften somewhat. The millenarian belief that Christ would not return until all the Jews were converted was gaining ground, suggesting that a more welcoming manner towards them was appropriate. There was also a growing interest in the Mosaic legislation of the Pentateuch; Sabbatarians for example were keeping their day of rest on a Saturday rather than on a Sunday. Jews were becoming both theologically necessary and a little more interesting to the English.[14]

But such views were not widespread. To most people Jews were still as demonic as they always had been. Unable to relate to them on a personal level and certainly unwilling to socialize with them, the native English are likely to have regarded the Jews as oddities. They would have spoken about them with a mixture of antipathy and amusement, public attitudes that Granville exploited in his portrayal of Shylock.[15]

It wasn't until 1741 when Charles Macklin played the part that Shylock was restored to a serious, three-dimensional character. The long-dormant *Merchant of Venice* was about to be revived and Macklin researched his part thoroughly. He studied the mannerisms and behaviours of the Jews in London, visited their places of business, researched the costumes they wore in sixteenth-century Venice, and devoured Josephus's *History of the Jews* (the fact that it had been written some 1,500 years before Shakespeare mattered little to him). The Shylock that Macklin played was fearsome and intense, passionate and unyielding. It was not a sympathetic portrayal, but it was a performance that struck terror into the hearts of the audience. One critic wrote that 'there was such an iron-visaged look, such a relentless, savage cast of manners, that the audience seemed to shrink from the character'.[16] King George II, who could not sleep after watching Macklin's performance, suggested to Prime Minister Robert Walpole that he should use Macklin whenever he wanted to frighten the House of Commons. The character of Shylock came to define Macklin. He continued to play the part in the same style for fifty years and only retired at the age of 89 when he could no longer remember his lines.

If George Granville's Shylock reflected the popular view of Jews in his time as strange and alien, Macklin's portrayal forty years later tells us that their image was now far more sinister.

Macklin's portrayal of Shylock came towards the end of a lengthy national controversy over the naturalization of foreigners. A bill allowing foreigners to become British subjects had been passed by Parliament in 1709, but the outcry was so fierce that it was repealed three years later. Various attempts were made to revive the bill during the following decades and in 1753 a Jewish banker named Joseph Salvador petitioned Parliament to allow Jews to be naturalized without taking the Christian Holy Sacrament. The government agreed and in April of that year Parliament passed the Jewish Naturalization Act with little fuss. In the streets, however, feelings were very different. Opposition to what they called the 'Jew Bill' was fierce and clamorous. The newspapers railed against it, angry sermons were preached in the churches, public meetings disintegrated into anarchy. By November the government realized that the mood in the country was firmly against them. They repealed the bill.

Every good protest movement needs a villain to focus attention upon and the recent revival of *The Merchant of Venice* offered up an unrivalled knave in Shylock. One polemicist, railing against the 'exorbitant avarice' of the Jews, said that it put him in mind of *The Merchant of Venice*. Another foresaw an England ruled by Jews 100 years hence, where performances of *The Merchant of Venice* would be banned. Various satirical works appeared in which Shylock was plotting mastery over the English or planning revenge over Christians. He turned up in political cartoons, was spoofed in the theatre, and apparently even haunted the fears and imaginations of hard-working Englishmen. James Shapiro quotes an article in the *London Evening Post* in which a farmer complained of having had no sleep for three nights because he believed that the farm he rented was about to be sold to a Jew and he had heard that Jews circumcise all their tenants. Apparently the previous week two strange-looking men had come to inspect his farm. One of them was called Shylock.[17]

By the mid-eighteenth century Shylock was considered in the same light as Marlowe's Jew of Malta, as an avaricious, heartless villain. It was a far more superficial appreciation of the Venetian moneylender than Shakespeare's nuanced, allegorical anti-hero.

THE GATES COME DOWN

On 12 May 1797 the Venetian Senate bowed to pressure from Napoleon. Its members approved the French occupation of the city and surrendered their powers to a French-controlled, provisional government. It was the end. The Venetian Republic was no more, never to rise again.

A few weeks later, on 9 July, the Jews of the ghetto, who Napoleon had now elevated to the status of citizens, were summoned to a meeting in the Spanish synagogue. They were addressed by the president of the provisional government. He announced that forthwith there was to be 'no visual appearance of a separation' between the Jews and the other citizens of Venice.[18] The gates of the ghetto were to be dismantled forthwith; the district itself was to be renamed as *Contrada dell'Unione*, the Quarter of the Union. He called for a collection of 200 hundred ducats to formalize the opening up of the ghetto, saying that the money would be distributed among the Christian poor of the adjoining neighbourhoods. The crowd erupted with cheers and cries of 'Long live brotherhood, Democracy and the Italian nation.' A collection was immediately taken up. It realized 314 ducats, enough to keep 300 families in food for a week, and was distributed to the poor as the president had indicated.

The following afternoon a large crowd of ghetto residents, French soldiers and onlookers gathered in the ghetto square. An order was given to a group of workmen who proceeded to pull down the four ghetto gates, one by one. The sound of the falling gates was drowned out by the cheers of the crowd. The leader of one of the French military battalions looking on reported that 'as soon as the gates were brought to earth, people of both sexes without distinction wove joyful democratic dances in the midst of the square . . . the rabbis danced too, dressed in Mosaic garb, which roused the Jewish citizens to still greater fervour'.[19]

As soon as the workmen had finished demolishing the gates, gangs of young men rushed forward, picked up the broken timbers and conveyed them to the centre of the square. They built a pyre and threw the remains of the gates upon it. The local news-sheet declared that it was a fine sight 'to watch the hatchet bravely swing to splinter a base barbaric prejudice. Citizen Vivante jumped up on the wall and harangued the crowd. The music, the sound of the hatchet blows, the confusion and excitement of the crowd made it impossible to hear his heartfelt words.'[20]

The ghetto was no more, but for the time being the Jewish citizens of Venice remained in their old derelict and dilapidated homes. The Jewish governing council, the *Università Grande*, had been dissolved when the Jews were accepted as full citizens of Venice, but that summer its former secretary, Saul Levi Mortara, carried out a census of those still in the ghetto. He found that there were 421 Jewish family groups made up of 820 men and 806 women. Just over 30 families were the descendants of the Levantine merchants who still traded across the Mediterranean in wheat, oil and sugar. Another 85 families worked as second-hand fabric merchants, buying and selling at the Rialto, the commercial heart of the city. Some 47 individuals worked as teachers or religious functionaries. Everyone else was either engaged in menial work, in domestic service, or was not employed at all. The ghetto had gone, but the poverty remained.

The liberation of the ghetto did not last long. In October of the same year Napoleon ceded Venice to Austria. Two months later the ghetto lost its designation as *Contrada dell'Unione* and took back its old name. The Jews lost the civil liberties they had briefly enjoyed. But the gates were never replaced. That much at least had improved.

Epilogue

On the north-west wall of the *campo*, the main square of the *Ghetto Nuovo*, are seven bronze bas-relief panels. Created by the artist Arbit Blatas they depict the deportation, enslavement and murder of the Jews of Venice during the Shoah.

There were around 1,300 Jews in Venice before the outbreak of World War II. They were fully integrated into Venetian life with the same rights and privileges as all other Italian citizens. They could live where they wanted and work in whichever professions or occupations they chose. The ghetto was still the centre of community life; it was where the synagogues still stood and there was now a Jewish school and an old-age home. The Jews of the city went to the ghetto regularly to buy kosher meat and food, in that respect the area was little different to a Jewish district anywhere else in the world. The ghetto as a place of confinement was simply an historical memory.

The Jews of Italy were stunned in 1938 when Mussolini's fascist government announced the introduction of racial laws. Suddenly they could no longer attend schools, own businesses, work in the civil service, be employed in the professions, or marry non-Jews. They were even banned from the beaches of the Lido. The Venetian Jews were not forced back into the ghetto, but in all other respects they found themselves outsiders once again.

When Mussolini's government fell and the Nazis entered Venice in 1943, they ordered Giuseppe Jona, the president of the Venetian

Jewish community, to hand over the names of all the Jews in the city. Jona was 77 years old. He had practised as a doctor until he was barred under the racial laws. He had spent his career preserving life, he was not the sort of man to collaborate in the destruction of it.

The Nazis gave Giuseppe Jona two days to hand over the list of names. He spent the time destroying every single document he could find relating to the Jewish community. He warned the Jews to escape if they could, if not he told them they should hide. When he had done as much as he believed he could do, he wrote his will and committed suicide. The Germans never got their list of names.

Two days later, when the Nazis raided the ghetto they found just over 100 people. In total, during the two years that the Nazis occupied Venice, they deported 243 Jews. Giuseppe Jona had taken his own life to save more than 1,000 others.

Walk around the ghetto today and you will see plaques on walls and inscriptions on paving stones in memory of deportees. Giuseppe Jona is commemorated on one inscription in the *campo* as a 'master of rightness and goodness' who 'led the community of Venice with a high sense of dignity and lavished on it the treasures of his great soul'. Adolfo Ottolenghi, the infirm and nearly blind rabbi of Venice, who was murdered in Auschwitz, is revered on another inscription. Other plaques commemorate people whose names are only remembered because their families refused to allow them to be erased from history.

The ghetto today is not a place of sadness. It is a vibrant destination, a must-see for tourists, perhaps the only group of streets anywhere in the world outside Israel which still retains half a millennium of unbroken Jewish history. It has two kosher restaurants, a Jewish museum and five synagogues, three of which at the time of writing are undergoing a major restoration. Architecturally, the ghetto looks little different from the way it did in the sixteenth century, though the buildings are, one hopes, less fragile and the long alleyways more sanitary.

As for the few hundred Jews who still live in Venice, they are no longer pawnbrokers or ship-owning merchants. They are just like everybody else. They do the same jobs, raise their children in the same way, have the same joys and fears, share the same successes, and experience the same insecurities.

The history of the ghetto is now inseparable from the wider history of Venice, the small city that was once one of the wealthiest and most powerful states in Europe. Its inhabitants still call it the Serenissima despite it being less serene these days; the 14 million tourists who visit each year make sure of that. But Venice remains one of the most astonishing cities on earth.

As for Shylock, he still turns up from time to time. In 2016, on the 500th anniversary of the founding of the ghetto, *The Merchant of Venice* was staged in the *campo*. Shylock was played by five different actors, four men and one woman. Which just goes to show that, 500 years after he didn't exist, Shylock's true identity remains as enigmatic as ever.[1]

Acknowledgements

This book is indebted to a multitude of people, most of whom I have never met. First and foremost there are the many academics and scholars whose invaluable research I drew on for elements of the story; their names are listed in the Bibliography and Endnotes.

Then there are all the people who I did meet, whose names I don't know, who didn't even necessarily know that they were helping me write a book, but without whose help it would have been far harder to write it. They include the dedicated staff of the British Library, the patient waiters of the Ba'Ghetto Restaurant in the Venice Ghetto, the unbelievably helpful experts in the Ghetto museum and bookshop, and the anonymous passers-by from whom I sought information while I was exploring the Ghetto.

I am especially grateful to those I do know, who helped with information, documents, translations and just conversations. Thank you so much to Assam Dadon, Melody Dadon, Shula Dadon, Bernard Eder, Jason Rosenblatt, Shaina Trapedo, Robert Winston and Lucy Wiseman, with humble apologies to anyone I have overlooked.

And thank you once again to my wise and outstanding publisher Robin Baird-Smith and to your consummately professional team at Bloomsbury. To Sarah Jones for your continual support, prompt responses and good humour even when I ask stupid questions, to Richard Mason for your accurate, thorough and eagle-eyed copy-editing, to Guy Holland for your careful proofreading, to Kate

Inskip for a thorough and comprehensive index. Also thanks to Mila Melia Kapoor for the energetic and dynamic way you are publicising the book, to Sarah Head for your marketing talent, your graphics and your seemingly effortless ability to cruise through the baffling world of social media. I must also thank Rachel Nicholson and Lizzy Ewer in Publicity and Marketing respectively, and Allison Davis, Hubert Adjei-Kontoh and Rachel Ewen in Bloomsbury's New York offices. And a special thanks to Yehudit Singer Freud and Shari Wright Pilo for your promotional expertise and help. As always, it has been a delight to work with you all.

Finally, I have been remiss in the past in not thanking Claudia Rubenstein and her dedicated team at the tremendous Jewish Book Week, without doubt London's most important and well-attended literary festival. You have invited me back time and again and I have not acknowledged you in any of my books. So to Claudia, Sarah Fairbairn, Sarah Gluckstein, Suzannah Okret and all your volunteers, thank you so much. You are all tireless, enthusiastic and supportive, and the work you do is incredible.

Writing a book, for me anyway, requires copious amounts of solitude and thinking time. It's easy to fall into the trap of thinking it is easiest to write when alone. But that is to overlook the support and encouragement of those who matter the most; the interest they show, the questions both casual and probing, the challenges and assertions, the disagreements and those rare, uplifting occasions when they say 'yes you are right'. So to Josh, Mollie, Melody, Louis, Samantha, Daniel, Claire, Eli, Bonnie, Leo and Dylan, once again, thank you for everything.

And finally and most importantly of course to Karen, without whom I couldn't have written this, or any, of my books. I do value your support and faith in me, even though I don't tell you often enough.

Sunny (!) London, June 2023

Notes

CHAPTER I – CROSSING THE LAGOON

1 Cedric Cohen-Skalli, *Don Isaac Abravanel: An Intellectual Biography*, trans. Avi Kallenbach. Waltham, MA: Brandeis University Press, 2021.

2 Exodus 15: 1–19.

3 Don Isaac Abarbanel, *Introduction to the Book of Kings*.

4 Cohen-Skalli, *Don Isaac Abravanel*, p. 266.

5 John Julius Norwich, *A History of Venice*. London: Allen Lane, 1977.

6 The question of whether Jewish women as well as men had to wear a distinguishing mark needs further investigation. See Benjamin Ravid, 'From Yellow to Red: On the Distinguishing Head-Covering of the Jews of Venice', *Jewish History*, vol. 6, nos. 1/2, *The Frank Talmage Memorial Volume* (1992), pp. 179–210, n. 34.

7 Richard Kearney, *Strangers, Gods and Monsters: Interpreting Otherness*. London: Routledge, 2002.

8 Josephus, *Against Apion* 1, § 227–50.

9 James Shapiro, *Shakespeare and the Jews*. New York: Columbia University Press, 1996.

10 Robert Bonfil, *Jewish Life in Renaissance Italy*. Berkeley, CA: University of California Press, 1994.

11 Ibid.

12 Eliyahu Capsali, *Seder Eliyahu Zuta*, vol. 2, ed. Aryeh Shmuelevitz et al. Jerusalem: The Ben Tzvi Institute of Yad Ben Tzvi and the Hebrew University, 1977, p. 277.

13 Ibid.

14 Ibid., p. 284.

15 David Malkiel, 'The Ghetto Republic', in *The Jews of Early Modern Venice*, ed. Robert C. Davis and Benjamin Ravid. Baltimore, MD: Johns Hopkins University Press, 2001.

16 Diary of Marin Sanudo quoted in Brian Pullan, *Rich and Poor in Renaissance Venice: The Social Institutions of a Catholic State to 1620*. Cambridge, MA: Harvard University Press, 1971, p. 484.

17 Rossella Pescatori, 'The Myth of the Androgyne in Leone Ebreo's *Dialoghi d'amore*', *Comitatus*, vol. 38 (2007), pp. 1–14.

18 Translated by Raymond Scheindlin, 'Judah Abrabanel to His Son', *Judaism*, vol. 41 (1992), pp. 190–9. A full translation of the whole poem, by Dan Almagor, Barbara Garvin and Dan Jacobson, was published in *The Jewish Quarterly*, no. 48 (Winter 1992–3), pp. 55–60.

19 Among his patients were the Viceroy of Naples and the scholarly papal legate, Cardinal San Giorgio.

20 A 1986 article argued that *Dialoghi d'amore* had first been written in Hebrew around 1502. More recent scholarship tends not to agree. Arthur M. Lesley, 'The Place of the *Dialoghi d'amore* in Contemporaneous Jewish Thought', in *Ficino and Renaissance Neoplatonism*, ed. Konrad Eisenbichler and Olga Zorzi Pugliese. Toronto: Dovehouse Editions, 1986.

21 Leone Ebreo, *Dialogues of Love*, trans. Damian Bacich and Rossella Pescatori. Toronto: University of Toronto Press, 2009, p. 325.

22 G. Veltri, *Renaissance Philosophy in Jewish Garb*. Leiden: Brill, 2009, 2018.

23 Brian Ogren, 'Sefirotic Depiction, Divine Noesis, and Aristotelian Kabbalah: Abraham ben Meir de Balmes and Italian Renaissance Thought', *Jewish Quarterly Review*, vol. 104, no. 4 (2014), pp. 573–99.

CHAPTER 2 – CONFRONTATION AND SEGREGATION

1 Brian Pullan, *Rich and Poor in Renaissance Venice*.

2 Patricia H. Labalme and Laura Sanguineti White, eds, *Venice, città excelentissima: Selections from the Renaissance Diaries of Marin Sanudo*, trans. Linda L. Carroll. Baltimore, MD: Johns Hopkins University Press, 2008, p. 338.

3 Among the other theories are that the word derives from the Hebrew meaning for divorce or separation, from *getto* meaning

a jetty or, in order to explain how the soft 'g' of *geto* ('foundry') became hard, from *ghetta*, a substance used in refining metal, something also done in a foundry. Sandra Debenedetti-Stow, 'The Etymology of "Ghetto": New Evidence from Rome', *Jewish History*, vol. 6, nos. 1/2 (1992), pp. 79–85; Cecil Roth, 'The Origin of Ghetto: A Final Word', *Romania*, vol. 60, no. 237 (1934), pp. 67–144; Benjamin Ravid, 'From Geographical Realia to Historiographical Symbol: The Odyssey of the Word Ghetto', in David B. Ruderman, ed., *Essential Papers on Jewish Culture in Renaissance and Baroque Italy*. New York: New York University Press, 1992, pp. 373–85.

4   Labalme and White, eds, *Venice, cità excelentissima.*

5   *Venice: A Documentary History, 1450–1630*, eds David Chambers, Brian Pullan and Jennifer Fletcher. Toronto: University of Toronto Press, 2001, p. 338.

6   Jeremiah 31: 31–3.

7   A. Jessop and M. R. James, *The Life and Miracles of St William of Norwich*, Cambridge, 1896, quoted in Gavin I. Langmuir, 'Thomas of Monmouth: Detector of Ritual Murder', *Speculum*, vol. 59, no. 4 (1984), pp. 820–46. https://doi.org/10.2307/2846698.

8   Shapiro, *Shakespeare and the Jews.*

9   Ibid., p. 73.

10   Donatella Calabi, *Venice and Its Jews*. Milan: Officina Libraria, 2017, p. 7.

11   Ibid.

12   Pullan, *Rich and Poor in Renaissance Venice.*

CHAPTER 3 – CROSSING BOUNDARIES

1   Haim Gottschalk, *The Formation of the House of Bomberg*, https://www.academia.edu/31885035, 2017.

2   Joseph R. Hacker and Adam Shear, eds, *The Hebrew Book in Early Modern Italy*. Philadelphia, PA: University of Pennsylvania Press, 2011. The Hebrew bibles read *k'ari*; the Complutensian and other Christian bibles read *k'aru*.

3   Hacker and Shear, *The Hebrew Book in Early Modern Italy.*

4   Claudia Rosenzweig, *Bovo D'Antona by Elye Bokher. A Yiddish Romance: A Critical Edition with Commentary*. Leiden: Brill, 2015.

5 Ibid., p. 21.

6 Francis X. Martin, 'The Writings of Giles of Viterbo', *Augustiniana*, vol. 29, nos. 1/2 (1979), pp. 141–93; John W. O'Malley, *Giles of Viterbo on Church and Reform: A Study in Renaissance Thought*. Leiden: Brill, 1968.

7 Hebrew is written with vowels for educational purposes and to assist people who are not too familiar with the language. But classical Hebrew texts, and most publications in modern Hebrew, do not contain vowels.

8 The same string of consonants, with different vowels or a change of accent, can for example mean 'they built', 'his son', or 'among us'.

9 Christian D. Ginsburg, *Sefer Masoret Hamasoret*. London: Longmans, Green & Dyer, 1867, pp. 97–8.

10 Ibid., p. 96.

11 Psalm 119: 66; Proverbs 16: 24 (Levita has inverted the word order in the quote from Psalms).

12 Ginsburg, *Sefer Masoret Hamasoret*.

13 Deena Aranoff, 'Elijah Levita: A Jewish Hebraist', *Jewish History*, vol. 23 (2009), pp. 17–40.

14 The major works that Elia Levita wrote in the Cardinal's employ were *Sefer Habahur*, *Perek Eliyahu*, *Sefer Ha-Harkava*, and *Luah B'Dikduk HaPoalim V'haBinyan*.

15 Pullan, *Rich and Poor in Renaissance Venice*.

16 Ginsburg, *Sefer Masoret Hamasoret*.

17 Ibid., p. 23.

18 Ishmaelites is a cognomen for Muslims, who trace their origins to the biblical Ishmael, son of Abraham.

19 Moti Benmelech, 'History, Politics, and Messianism: David Ha-Reuveni's Origin and Mission', *AJS Review*, vol. 35, no. 1 (2011), pp. 35–60.

20 Katrin Kogman-Appel, 'Illuminated Bibles and Re-Written Bibles: The Place of Moses dal Castellazzo in Early Modern Book History', *Ars Judaica*, no. 2 (2006), pp. 1–18.

21 Ibid.

22 Elkan Nathan Adler, *Jewish Travellers*. London: Routledge, 1930, p. 269.

23 I Chronicles 5: 26 where the name is given as Till'gat Pilneser.

24 *Monumenta Saeculi XVI.: Historiam Illustrantia*, vol. 1, quoted in Benmelech, 'History, Politics and Messianism', p. 40.

25 Ibid.

26 Molcho's principal works are *Sefer HaMifa'or* (Salonika, 1529) and *Hayat Kane* (Amsterdam, 1660)

27 Edward Hutton, *Pietro Aretino, the Scourge of Princes: With a Portrait after Titian.* London: Constable, 1922.

28 Edward Gelles, *The Jewish Journey: A Passage Through European History.* London: I. B. Tauris, 2015.

CHAPTER 4 – CONCORD AND DISPUTE

1 Labalme and White, eds, *Venice, città excelentissima*, p. 342.

2 Pier Cesare Ioly-Zorattini, 'Jews, Crypto Jews and the Inquisition', in Davis and Ravid eds, *The Jews of Early Modern Venice.*

3 Benjamin Ravid, 'Christian Travelers in the Ghetto of Venice: Some Preliminary Observations', in Stanley Nash, ed., *Between History and Literature: Studies in Honor of Isaac Barzilay.* B'nei B'rak: Hakibbutz Hameuhad, 1997, pp. 111–50, esp. p. 119.

4 Leviticus 18: 16.

5 Deuteronomy 25: 5–10.

6 The words Kabbalah and Kabbalist can be spelt with a 'K' or a 'C'. Conventionally, the 'C' spelling is applied to Christian Cabbala, the 'K' to the Hebrew original from which it is derived.

7 Hacker and Shear, *The Hebrew Book in Early Modern Italy.*

8 Frances A. Yates, *Giordano Bruno and the Hermetic Tradition.* Chicago, IL: University of Chicago Press, 1964.

9 'Venice: June 1530', in *Calendar of State Papers Relating to English Affairs in the Archives of Venice, Volume 4, 1527–1533*, ed. Rawdon Brown. London: Her Majesty's Stationery Office, 1871, pp. 244–6. http://www.british-history.ac.uk/cal-state-papers/venice/vol4/pp244–246.

10 Ibid., pp. 246–50.

11 For the history of Henry VIII's Talmud and the question over which of the three surviving English copies it was, see my book *The Talmud: A Biography.* London: Bloomsbury Continuum, 2014.

12 *The Merchant of Venice*, Act 4, scene i.

13 The kabbalistic Sefirot in this triad are *Gevurah*, representing Justice, *Hesed*, representing Love, and *Tiferet*, Mercy. Kabbala is not a science; every Sefirah has several names and various qualities.

14 Emily Cannon, *Comparative Synagogue Architecture in the Venetian Ghetto, 1500–1800*. Medford and Somerville, MA: Tufts University, 2014.

15 Benjamin Arbel, 'Jews in International Trade: The Emergence of the Levantines and Ponentines', in Davis and Ravid, eds, *The Jews of Early Modern Venice*, pp. 73–96.

16 Letter from Hieronymo Feruffino, ambassador of the Duke of Ferrara, dated 23 July 1550, quoted in Chambers et al., eds, *Venice: A Documentary History, 1450–1630*, p. 345.

17 Pullan, *Rich and Poor in Renaissance Venice*.

18 Arbel, 'Jews in International Trade'.

CHAPTER 5 – MORE TROUBLE

1 Pullan, *Rich and Poor in Renaissance Venice*.

2 Marvin J. Heller, *Further Studies in the Making of the Early Hebrew Book*. Leiden: Brill, 2013.

3 Pullan, *Rich and Poor in Renaissance Venice*, quoting on p. 517 from Paschini Pio, *Venezia e l'Inquisizione Romana da Giulio III a Pio IV*. Padua: Antenore, 1959, pp. 65–6.

4 Paul F. Grendler, 'The Destruction of Hebrew Books in Venice, 1568', *Proceedings of the American Academy for Jewish Research*, vol. 45 (1978), pp. 103–30.

5 For a fuller treatment of medieval and early modern Christian attitudes to the Talmud, see my book *The Talmud: A Biography*. London: Bloomsbury Continuum, 2014.

6 Thomas Coryate, *Coryat's Crudities: Hastily Gobbled Up in Five Months Travels in France, Savoy, Italy . . . Switzerland &c.* (London: 1611).

7 Deuteronomy 33: 2.

8 31 October–1 November 1553.

9 Printed in Abraham Menahem Rapaport, *Minhah Belulah*, Verona, 1594, p. 203b. (It is missing from the 1820 Hamburg edition.) See also Marvin J. Heller, *Abraham Menahem ben Jacob ha-Kohen Rapa mi-Porto (Rapaport) Ashkenazi: A Renaissance Rabbi of Interest*, 2021. https://seforimblog com/2021/03/abraham-menahem-ben-jacob-ha-kohen-rapa-mi-porto-rapaport-ashkenazi-a-renaissance-rabbi-of-interest.

10 This is also missing from the 1820 Hamburg edition.

11 Benjamin Ravid, '*Cum Nimis Absurdum* and the Ancona Auto-da-Fé Revisited: Their Impact on Venice and Some Wider Reflections', *Jewish History*, vol. 26 (2021), pp. 85–100.

12 Bonfil, *Jewish Life in Renaissance Italy*, p. 110.

13 Grendler, 'The Destruction of Hebrew Books in Venice'.

14 Ibid.

15 Guido Bartolucci, '"Hebraeus semper fidus": David de' Pomis e l'apologia dell'ebraismo tra volgare e latino', in *Umanesimo e cultura ebraica nel Rinascimento italiano*, eds. Stefano U. Baldassarre and Fabrizio Lelli. Florence: Angelo Pontecorboli, 2016.

16 See above, pp. 86–7.

17 Norwich, *History of Venice*, p. 481.

18 Pullan, *Rich and Poor in Renaissance Venice*, p. 537, quoting the Venetian State Archives of 18 December 1571.

19 1 Samuel 8: 11–18.

20 Exodus 18: 21.

21 Bartolucci, '"Hebraeus semper fidus"'.

22 David de Pomis, *De Medico Hebraeo* (Venice, 1587), in H. Friedenwald, *The Jews and Medicine* (Baltimore, MD: Johns Hopkins University Press, 1944), pp. 40–4, quoted in M. Lindsay Kaplan, *The Merchant of Venice, Texts and Contexts*. New York: Palgrave, 2002, p. 220.

23 Journal of the House of Commons: April 1571, https://www.british-history.ac.uk/no-series/jrnl-parliament-eliz1/ pp. 155–80.

24 Pomis, *De Medico Hebraeo*, quoted in Kaplan, *The Merchant of Venice*, p. 219.

25 *The Merchant of Venice*, Act I, scene iii, l. 131.

26 Ibid., I, iii, 170.

CHAPTER 6 – STABILITY AND FRICTION

1 Arbel, 'Jews in International Trade'.

2 D. Bilić, 'Daniel Rodriga's Lazaretto in Split and Ottoman Caravanserais in Bosnia', in A. A. Payne, ed., *The Land between Two Seas*. Leiden: Brill, 2022.

3 Bernard Dov Cooperman, 'Portuguese *conversos* in Ancona: Jewish Political Activity in Early Modern Italy', in *Iberia and Beyond: Hispanic Jews Between Cultures*. Newark, DE: University of Delaware, 1997.

4 Benjamin Ravid, 'The First Charter of the Jewish Merchants of
  Venice, 1589', *AJS Review*, vol. 1 (1976), pp. 187–222.
5 Chambers et al., eds, *Venice: A Documentary History, 1450–1630*.
6 Ravid. 'The First Charter of the Jewish Merchants of Venice',
  p. 201.
7 Simone Luzzatto, *Discorso circa il stato de gl'hebrei et in particolar
  dimoranti nell'inclita Citti'a di Venetia* (Venice, 1638), quoted in
  Arbel, 'Jews in International Trade', p. 90.
8 Brian Pullan, '"A Ship with Two Rudders": "Righetto Marrano"
  and the Inquisition in Venice', *The Historical Journal*, vol. 20, no. 1
  (1977), pp. 25–58.
9 Ioly-Zorattini, 'Jews, Crypto Jews and the Inquisition', pp. 97–116.
10 Pullan, '"A Ship with Two Rudders"'.
11 Ioly-Zorattini, 'Jews, Crypto Jews and the Inquisition'.
12 Pullan, *The Jews of Europe and the Inquisition of Venice*.
13 Howard Adelman, 'Jewish Women and Family Life, Inside and
   Outside the Ghetto', in Davis and Ravid, eds, *The Jews of Early
   Modern Venice*, pp. 143–65.
14 Brian Pullan, 'The Conversion of the Jews: The Style of Italy',
   Bulletin of the John Rylands Library, vol. 70, no. 1 (1988),
   pp. 53–70.
15 Chambers et al., eds, *Venice: A Documentary History, 1450–1630*,
   pp. 339–40.
16 Elliott Horowitz, 'Speaking of the Dead: The Emergence of the
   Eulogy among Italian Jewry of the Sixteenth Century', in David
   B. Ruderman, ed., *Preachers of the Italian Ghetto*. Berkeley, CA:
   University of California Press, 1992, pp. 129–62.
17 Robert Bonfil, 'Some Reflections on the Place of Azariah de
   Rossi's *Meor Enayim* in the Cultural Milieu of Italian Renaissance
   Jewry', in Bernard Dov Cooperman, ed., *Jewish Thought in the
   Sixteenth Century*. Cambridge, MA: Harvard University Press,
   1983, pp. 23–48.

CHAPTER 7 – THE LION WHO ROARED

1 Grendler, 'The Destruction of Hebrew Books in Venice'.
2 Yaacob Dweck, *The Scandal of Kabbalah: Leon of Modena,
  Jewish Mysticism, Early Modern Venice*. Princeton, NJ: Princeton
  University Press, 2011.

3 Mark R. Cohen. *The Autobiography of a Seventeenth-Century Venetian Rabbi: Leon Modena's Life of Judah*. Princeton, NJ: Princeton University Press, 1988, p. 91.

4 Ibid., p. 108. The 'silver' that Leon saw was in fact copper arsenide.

5 Leon's grandson refers to him as head of the yeshiva, but it is not certain what this means. The yeshiva in Venice was probably an assembly of rabbis rather than a teaching establishment as it is today. If so, Leon's status would have been that of the most senior or highly respected member of the yeshiva. See Howard Ernest Adelman, *Success and Failure in the Seventeenth-Century Ghetto of Venice: The Life and Thought of Leon Modena, 1571–1643*. PhD Thesis, Brandeis University, 1985, p. 705.

6 Cohen, *The Autobiography of a Seventeenth-Century Venetian Rabbi*, p. 141.

7 Ibid., pp. 143–5.

8 Ibid., p. 152.

9 Ibid., p. 131.

10 Cecil Roth, 'Leone da Modena and England', *Transactions (Jewish Historical Society of England)*, vol. 11 (1924–7), pp. 206–27.

11 Mark R. Cohen, 'Leone da Modena's *Riti*: A Seventeenth-Century Plea for Social Toleration of Jews', *Jewish Social Studies*, vol. 34, no. 4 (October 1972), pp. 287–321; Cristiana Facchini, 'The City, the Ghetto and Two Books: Venice and Jewish Early Modernity', in *Quest: Issues in Contemporary Jewish History, Journal of Fondazione CDEC*, October 2011.

12 Cohen, 'Leone da Modena's *Riti*'.

13 Jason P. Rosenblatt, *Renaissance England's Chief Rabbi*. Oxford: Oxford University Press, 2006.

14 Cohen, *The Autobiography of a Seventeenth-Century Venetian Rabbi*, p. 170.

15 See Cecil Roth, 'Leone da Modena and his English Correspondents', *Transactions (Jewish Historical Society of England)*, vol. 17 (1951–2), pp. 39–43.

16 Coryate, *Coryat's Crudities*, quoted in Kaplan, *The Merchant of Venice, Texts and Contexts*, p. 144.

17 https://shakespearedocumented.folger.edu/resource/document/sir-henry-wotton-writes-sir-edmund-bacon-discusses-burning-globe.

All is True was one of Shakespeare's last plays. It was known in the printed editions as *The Famous History of the Life of King Henry the Eighth.*

18 Adelman, *Success and Failure in the Seventeenth-Century Ghetto of Venice.*

19 *Othello* and of course *The Merchant of Venice* are both set in Venice. Verona is the setting for *Romeo and Juliet* and *The Two Gentlemen of Verona.*

20 Shapiro, *Shakespeare and the Jews*, p. 121.

21 Stephen Greenblatt, *Shakespeare's Freedom*. Chicago, IL: University of Chicago Press, 2010.

22 Frances A. Yates, *The Occult Philosophy in the Elizabethan Age.* London: Routledge & Kegan Paul, 1979.

23 See above, pp. 78–80.

24 She later found fame as the poet Emilia Lanier.

25 *The Times*, 2 July 1973.

26 Leon of Modena, *Ari Nohem*, ed. Nehemiah Libovitz. Jerusalem, 1939.

27 Dweck, *The Scandal of Kabbalah.*

28 Ibid.

29 *Magen v'Tzina*, ed. A. Geiger. Bratislava, 1856, p. 1a.

CHAPTER 8 – MUSIC AND CULTURE IN THE GHETTO

1 See above, p. 111.

2 Don Harrán, 'Jewish Musical Culture: Leon Modena', in Davis and Ravid, eds, *The Jews of Early Modern Venice*, p. 214.

3 Don Harrán, '"Dum Recordaremur Sion": Music in the Life and Thought of the Venetian Rabbi Leon Modena (1571–1648)', *AJS Review*, vol. 23, no. 1 (1998), pp. 17–61.

4 Ibid.

5 The trees in Psalm 137: 2 are often translated in English as willows, but the Hebrew word can also be translated as poplars.

6 Evelien Chayes, 'Crossing Cultures in the Venetian Ghetto: Leone Modena, the Accademia degli Incogniti and Imprese Literature', *Bollettino di italianistica, Rivista di critica, storia letteraria, filologia e linguistica*, vol. 2 (2017), pp. 62–88.

7 Quoted in Calabi, *Venice and Its Jews*, p. 34.

8 Diana E. Katz, *The Jewish Ghetto and the Visual Imagination of Early Modern Venice*. Cambridge: Cambridge University Press, 2017.

9 Don Harrán in *Sarra Copia Sulam: Jewish Poet and Intellectual in Seventeenth-Century Venice*, Chicago, IL: University of Chicago Press, 2009, estimates her birth year as 1600. Lynn Lara Westwater in *Sarra Copia Sulam: A Jewish Salonnière and the Press in Counter-Reformation Venice*, Toronto: University of Toronto Press, 2020, and Howard Tzvi Adelman in 'Sarra Copia Sullam', *Shalvi/Hyman Encyclopedia of Jewish Women*, Jewish Women's Archive, 2001, https://jwa.org/encyclopedia/article/sullam-sara-coppia, opt for 1592.

10 Westwater, *Sarra Copia Sulam*.

11 Scordari, Chiara Carmen, 'Behind Multiple Masks: Leon Modena's Diasporic Tragedy *L'Ester* in Seventeenth-Century Venice', *Skenè. Journal of Theatre and Drama Studies*, vol. 6, no. 2 (2020), pp. 53–70.

12 Adelman, *Success and Failure in the Seventeenth-Century Ghetto of Venice*.

13 Harrán, *Sarra Copia Sulam*.

14 Ibid., p. 321.

15 See above, p. 71.

16 Israel Zinberg, *A History of Jewish Literature: Italian Jewry in the Renaissance Era*, trans. B. Martin. Philadelphia, PA: Jewish Publication Society of America, 1974, p. 178.

CHAPTER 9 – POLITICS AND DIPLOMACY

1 Calabi, *Venice and Its Jews*; Malkiel, 'The Ghetto Republic', in Davis and Ravid, eds, *The Jews of Early Modern Venice*.

2 Pullan, *Rich and Poor in Renaissance Venice*.

3 Michel de Montaigne, 'Travel Journal', quoted in Elliot Horowitz, 'Processions, Piety and Jewish Confraternities', in Davis and Ravid, eds, *The Jews of Early Modern Venice*, pp. 231–47.

4 Ibid.

5 Michela Andreatta, 'Out of Your Senses: The Baroque World of Moses Zacuto's Tofteh "Arukh"', in Yeshaya Joachim et al., 2019, *The Poet and the World: Festschrift for Wout Van Bekkum on the Occasion of His Sixty-Fifth Birthday*. Berlin: De Gruyter, 2019.

6 Adam Teller, *Rescue the Surviving Souls: The Great Jewish Refugee Crisis of the Seventeenth Century*. Princeton, NJ: Princeton University Press, 2020.

7 Minna Rozen, *The Mediterranean in the Seventeenth Century: Captives, Pirates and Ransomers*. Palermo: Associazione 'Mediterranea', 2016, p. 32.

8 Ibid.

9 Cecil Roth, *Venice*. Philadelphia, PA: Jewish Publication Society of America, 1930.

10 Teller, *Rescue the Surviving Souls*.

11 BBC News, Entertainment and Arts, 26 October 2016, https://www.bbc.co.uk/news/entertainment-arts-37750558.

12 Charles Nicholl, 'Marlowe [Marley], Christopher (bap. 1564, d. 1593), playwright and poet', *Oxford Dictionary of National Biography*. Oxford: Oxford University Press, 2004.

13 Robert McCrum, *Shakespearean: On Life & Language in Times of Disruption*. London: Picador, 2020, p. 99.

14 Robert A. Logan, *Shakespeare's Marlowe: The Influence of Christopher Marlowe on Shakespeare's Artistry*. Aldershot: Ashgate, 2007.

15 Christopher Marlowe, *The Jew of Malta*, Act 3, scene iii, ll. 58–68.

CHAPTER 10 – EDGING TOWARDS MODERNITY

1 Benjamin Ravid, 'The Venetian Context of the Discourse', in Giuseppe Veltri and Anna Lissa, eds, *Simone Luzzatto, Discourse on the State of the Jews*. Berlin: De Gruyter, 2019.

2 Ibid.

3 Calabi, *Venice and Its Jews*.

4 See p. 224, note 5.

5 Isaac Lampronti, *Pahad Yitzhak*, quoted in Ravid, 'The Venetian Context of the Discourse', p. 245.

6 Veltri and Lissa, eds, *Simone Luzzatto, Discourse on the State of the Jews*, p. 11.

7 Ibid., p. 41.

8 David B. Ruderman, *Jewish Thought and Scientific Discovery in Early Modern Europe*. New Haven, CT, and London: Yale University Press, 1995.

9 Veltri and Lissa, eds, *Simone Luzzatto, Discourse on the State of the Jews*, p. 13.

10 Pullan, *The Jews of Europe and the Inquisition of Venice*.

11 Benjamin Ravid, '*Contra Judaeos* in Seventeenth-Century Italy: Two Responses to the *Discorso* of Simone Luzzatto by Melchiore Palontrotti and Giulio Morosini', *AJS Review*, vol. 7 (1982–3), pp. 301–51.

12 Ibid.

13 Edgar Samuel, 'The Readmission of the Jews to England in 1656, in the Context of English Economic Policy', *Jewish Historical Studies*, vol. 31 (1988), pp. 153–69.

14 Benjamin Ravid, '"How Profitable the Nation of the Jewes Are": The Humble Addresses of Menasseh ben Israel and the *Discorso* of Simone Luzzatto', in Jehuda Reinharz and Daniel Swetschinski, eds, *Mystics, Philosophers and Politicians*. Durham, NC: Duke University Press, 1982, pp. 159–80.

15 John Toland, *Reasons for Naturalizing the Jews in Great Britain and Ireland on the same foot with all other nations. Containing also a defense of the Jews against all vulgar prejudices in all countries*. London, J. Roberts, 1714, quoted in Luzzatto, *Discourse*, p. 249.

16 See above, p. 160.

17 David Ruderman, *Jewish Preaching and the Language of Science: The Sermons of Azariah Figo*, in Ruderman, ed., *Preachers of the Italian Ghetto*.

18 Pullan, *The Jews of Europe and the Inquisition of Venice*.

19 Dweck, *The Scandal of Kabbalah*.

20 Gershom Scholem, *Shabbetai Tzvi, The Mystical Messiah 1626–1676*. Princeton, NJ: Princeton University Press, 1973.

21 Ibid., p. 503.

22 D. J. Halperin, *Sabbatai Zevi: Testimonies to a Fallen Messiah*. Oxford: Littman Library of Jewish Civilisation, 2007.

23 Scholem, *Shabbetai Tzvi*.

CHAPTER 11 – DECLINE

1 Norwich, *History of Venice*.

2 Pullan, *The Jews of Europe and the Inquisition of Venice*.

3 Riccardo Calimani, *The Ghetto in Venice*, trans. Katherine Silberblatt Wolfthal. New York: M. Evans and Company, 1987.

4 Roth, *Venice*.

5 Jacob Raphael ben Simḥah Judah Saraval, *Lettera Apologetica a Sua Eccellenza Il Signor Marchese N. N. Amico Del Signor Avvocato Giovambattista Benedetti Di Ferrara Scritta Dal Signor.* Mantua, 1775.

6 Jacob Raphael ben Simḥah Judah Saraval, *Viaggi in Olanda: 1737–1771.* Milan: Edizioni Il polifilo, 2005.

7 Jacob Raphael ben Simḥah Judah Saraval, *Kinat Sofdim.* Mantua, 1777.

8 Martina Massaro, 'I Treves dei Bonfili tra collezionismo, imprenditoria e cosmopolitismo', in Donatella Calabi and Martina Massaro, eds, *Gli Ebrei, Venezia e L'Europa tra Otto e Novecento.* Venice: Istituto Veneto di Scienze, Lettere ed Arti, 2018.

9 Roth, *Venice.*

10 Norwich, *History of Venice.*

11 Calimani, *The Ghetto in Venice.*

12 Ravid, Benjamin, 'The Sephardic Jewish Merchants of Venice, Port Jews, and the Road to Modernity', in *From Catalonia to the Caribbean: The Sephardic Orbit from Medieval to Modern Times.* Leiden: Brill 2018.

13 Norwich, *History of Venice,* p. 602.

14 David S. Katz, *Philo-Semitism and the Readmission of the Jews to England, 1603–1655.* Oxford: Clarendon Press, 1982.

15 Catherine A. Craft, 'Granville's Jew of Venice and the Eighteenth-Century Stage', *Restoration and Eighteenth-Century Theatre Research,* vol. 2, no. 2 (1987), p. 44.

16 William Cook, *Memoir of Charles Macklin,* cited in John Gross, *Shylock: A Legend and Its Legacy.* New York: Simon & Schuster, 1992.

17 Shapiro, *Shakespeare and the Jews.*

18 Calimani, *The Ghetto in Venice,* p. 249.

19 Ibid., p. 251.

20 Ibid., p. 252.

EPILOGUE

1 Bassi, Shaul, and Carol Chillington Rutter, eds, 'The Merchant in Venice: Shakespeare in the Ghetto'. Studi e ricerche (2021).

Bibliography

Adelman, Howard Ernest. *Success and Failure in the Seventeenth-Century Ghetto of Venice: The Life and Thought of Leon Modena, 1571–1643*. PhD Thesis, Brandeis University, 1985.

Adelman, Howard Tzvi. 'Sarra Copia Sullam', *Shalvi/Hyman Encyclopedia of Jewish Women*, Jewish Women's Archive, 2021, https://jwa.org/encyclopedia.

Adler, Elkan Nathan. *Jewish Travellers*. London: Routledge, 1930.

Andreatta, Michela. 'Out of Your Senses: The Baroque World of Moses Zacuto's Tofteh "Arukh"', in Yeshaya Joachim et al., *The Poet and the World: Festschrift for Wout Van Bekkum on the Occasion of His Sixty-Fifth Birthday*. Berlin: De Gruyter, 2019.

Appleton, William Worthen. *Charles Macklin: An Actor's Life*. Cambridge, MA: Harvard University Press, 1960.

Aranoff, Deena. 'Elijah Levita: A Jewish Hebraist', *Jewish History*, vol. 23 (2009), pp. 17–40.

Baricci, Erica, 'La scena "all'ebraica" nel teatro del Rinascimento', *ACME Annali della Facoltà di Lettere e Filosofia dell'Università degli Studi di Milano*, vol. 33, issue 1 (January–April 2010).

Bartolucci, Guido. '"Hebraeus semper fidus": David de' Pomis e l'apologia dell'ebraismo tra volgare e latino', in *Umanesimo e cultura ebraica nel Rinascimento italiano*, eds Stefano U. Baldassarre and Fabrizio Lelli. Florence: Angelo Pontecorboli, 2016.

Benmelech, Moti. 'History, Politics and Messianism: David Ha-Reuveni's Origin and Mission', *AJS Review*, vol. 35, no. 1 (2011), pp. 35–60.

Berger, David. '*Cum Nimis Absurdum* and the Conversion of the Jews', *The Jewish Quarterly Review*, vol. 70, no. 1 (1979), pp. 41–9.

Bettan, Israel. 'The Sermons of Azariah Figo', *Hebrew Union College Annual*, vol. 7 (1930, pp. 457–95.

Bilić, D. 'Daniel Rodriga's Lazaretto in Split and Ottoman Caravanserais in Bosnia', in *The Land between Two Seas*. Leiden: Brill, 2022.

Bonfil, Robert. 'Some Reflections on the Place of Azariah de Rossi's *Meor Enayim* in the Cultural Milieu of Italian Renaissance Jewry', in Bernard Dov Cooperman, ed., *Jewish Thought in the Sixteenth Century*. Cambridge, MA: Harvard University Press, 1983, pp. 23–48.

Bonfil, Robert. *Jewish Life in Renaissance Italy*. Berkeley, CA: University of California Press, 1994.

Calabi, Donatella. *Venice and Its Jews*. Milan: Officina Libraria, 2017.

Calimani, Riccardo. *The Ghetto in Venice*, trans. Katherine Silberblatt Wolfthal. New York: M. Evans and Company, 1987.

Cannon, Emily. *Comparative Synagogue Architecture in the Venetian Ghetto, 1500–1800*. Medford and Somerville, MA: Tufts University, 2014.

Chambers, David, Pullan, Brian, and Fletcher, Jennifer, eds. *Venice: A Documentary History, 1450–1630*. Toronto: University of Toronto Press, 2001.

Chayes, Evelien. 'Crossing Cultures in the Venetian Ghetto: Leone Modena, the Accademia degli Incogniti and Imprese Literature', *Bollettino di italianistica, Rivista di critica, storia letteraria, filologia e linguistica*, vol. 2 (2017), pp. 62–88.

Cohen, Mark R. *The Autobiography of a Seventeenth-Century Venetian Rabbi: Leon Modena's Life of Judah*. Princeton, NJ: Princeton University Press, 1988.

Cohen, Mark R. 'Leone da Modena's *Riti*: A Seventeenth-Century Plea for Social Toleration of Jews', *Jewish Social Studies*, vol. 34, no. 4 (October 1972), pp. 287–321.

Cohen-Skalli, Cedric. *Don Isaac Abravanel: An Intellectual Biography*, trans. Avi Kallenach. Waltham, MA: Brandeis University Press, 2021.

Cooperman, Bernard Dov. 'Portuguese *conversos* in Ancona: Jewish Political Activity in Early Modern Italy', in *Iberia and Beyond: Hispanic Jews Between Cultures*. Newark, DE: University of Delaware, 1997.

Davis, Robert C. and Ravid, Benjamin, eds. *The Jews of Early Modern Venice*. Baltimore, MD: Johns Hopkins University Press, 2001.

Dweck, Yaacob. *The Scandal of Kabbalah: Leon of Modena, Jewish Mysticism, Early Modern Venice*. Princeton, NJ: Princeton University Press, 2011.

Ebreo, Leone. *Dialogues of Love*, trans. Damian Bacich and Rossella Pescatori. Toronto: University of Toronto Press, 2009.

Facchini, Cristiana. *The City, the Ghetto and Two Books: Venice and Jewish Early Modernity*. Milan: Fondazione Centro di Documentazione Ebraica Contemporanea, 2011.

Finlay, Robert. 'The Foundation of the Ghetto: Venice, the Jews and the War of the League of Cambrai', *Proceedings of the American Philosophical Society,* vol. 126, no. 2 (1982), pp. 140–54.

Gelles, Edward. *The Jewish Journey: A Passage Through European History.* London: I. B. Tauris, 2015.

Ginio, Alisa Meyuhas. *Jews, Christians and Muslims in the Mediterranean World after 1492.* London: Frank Cass, 2002.

Gluck, A. *Judah Abrabanel's Philosophy of Love and Kabbalah.* Lewiston: The Edwin Mellen Press, 2012.

Goodman, Martin. *A History of Judaism.* London: Allen Lane, 2017.

Grendler, Paul F. 'The Destruction of Hebrew Books in Venice, 1568', *Proceedings of the American Academy for Jewish Research*, vol. 45 (1978), pp. 103–30.

Gross, John. *Shylock: A Legend and Its Legacy.* New York: Simon & Schuster, 1992.

Hacker, J. and Shear, A, eds. *The Hebrew Book in Early Modern Italy.* Philadelphia, PA: University of Pennsylvania Press, 2011.

Halperin, D. J. *Sabbatai Zevi: Testimonies to a Fallen Messiah.* Oxford: Littman Library of Jewish Civilisation, 2007.

Harrán, Don. '"Dum Recordaremur Sion": Music in the Life and Thought of the Venetian Rabbi Leon Modena, (1571–1648)', *AJS Review*, vol. 23, no. 1 (1998), pp. 17–61.

Harrán, Don. 'A Tale as Yet Untold: Salamone Rossi in Venice, 1622', *Sixteenth Century Journal*, vol. XL, no. 4 (2009), pp. 1,091–107.

Harrán, Don. 'Tradition and Innovation in Jewish Music', in *Essential Papers on Jewish Culture in Renaissance and Baroque Italy*, ed. David Ruderman. New York: New York University Press, 1992, pp. 474–501.

Harrán Don. 'Madonna Bellina "Astounding" Jewish Musician in Mid-Sixteenth-Century Venice', *Renaissance Studies*, vol. 22, no. 1 (2008), pp. 16–40.

Harrán, Don. *Sarra Copia Sulam: Jewish Poet and Intellectual in Seventeenth-Century Venice.* Chicago, IL: University of Chicago Press, 2009.

Heller, Marvin J. *Further Studies in the Making of the Early Hebrew Book.* Leiden: Brill, 2013.

Heller, Marvin J. *Abraham Menahem ben Jacob ha-Kohen Rapa mi-Porto (Rapaport) Ashkenazi: A Renaissance Rabbi of Interest,* 2021. https://seforimblog com/2021/03/abraham-menahem-ben-jacob-ha-kohen-rapa-mi-porto-rapaport-ashkenazi-a-renaissance-rabbi-of-interest

Horowitz, Elliott. 'Speaking of the Dead: The Emergence of the Eulogy among Italian Jewry of the Sixteenth Century', in David B. Ruderman, ed., *Preachers of the Italian Ghetto*. Berkeley, CA: University of California Press, 1992, pp. 129–62.

Hutton, Edward. *Pietro Aretino, the Scourge of Princes: With a Portrait after Titian*. London: Constable, 1922.

Kamen, Henry. *The Spanish Inquisition: A Historical Revision*. London: Weidenfeld & Nicolson, 1997, pp. 18–28.

Kaplan, Lindsay M. *The Merchant of Venice: Texts and Contexts*. New York: Palgrave, 2002.

Kaplan, Yosef, ed. *Religious Changes and Cultural Transformations in the Early Modern Western Sephardic Communities*. Leiden: Brill, 2019.

Katz, David S. *The Jews in the History of England, 1485–1850*. Oxford: Clarendon Press, 1994.

Katz, David S. *Philo-Semitism and the Readmission of the Jews to England, 1603–1655*. Oxford: Clarendon Press, 1982.

Katz, Diana E. *The Jewish Ghetto and the Visual Imagination of Early Modern Venice*. Cambridge: Cambridge University Press, 2017.

Kaufmann, D. 'Elia Menachem Chalfan on Jews Teaching Hebrew to Non-Jews', *The Jewish Quarterly Review*, vol. 9, no. 3 (April 1897), pp. 500–8.

Kearney, Richard. *Strangers, Gods and Monsters: Interpreting Otherness*. London: Routledge, 2002.

Labalme, Patricia H. and White, Laura Sanguineti, eds. *Venice città excelentissima: Selections from the Renaissance Diaries of Marin Sanudo*, trans. Linda L. Carroll. Baltimore, MD: Johns Hopkins University Press, 2008.

Liptzin, Solomon. *A History of Yiddish Literature*. New York: Jonathan David, 1985.

Luzzatto, Simone. *Discourse on the State of the Jews*, eds Giuseppe Veltri and Anna Lissa. Berlin: De Gruyter, 2019.

Malkiel, David Joshua. *A Separate Republic: The Mechanics and Dynamics of Venetian Jewish Self-Government, 1607–1624*. Jerusalem: Magnes Press, 1991.

Martin, Francis, X. 'The Problem of Giles of Viterbo: A Historiographical Survey (Continuation)', *Augustinian*, vol. 10, nos. 1/2 (1960), pp. 43–60; of Viterbo, 'Augustiniana', vol. 29 nos. 1/2 (1979), pp. 141–93.

Massaro Martina. 'I Treves dei Bonfili tra collezionismo imprenditoria e cosmopolitismo', in *Gli Ebrei Venezia e L'Europa tra Otto e Novecento*, eds Donatella Calabi and Martina Massaro. Venice: Istituto Veneto di Scienze Lettere, 2018.

Melamed, Abraham. 'The Myth of Venice in Italian Renaissance Jewish Thought', *Italia Judaica Proceedings of the I International Congress*, pp. 401–13; Ministero per i beni culturali e ambientali, Rome, *Bari 1981*, 1983.

Melamed, Abraham, 'Jethro's Advice in Medieval and Early Modern Jewish and Christian Political Thought', *Jewish Political Studies Review*, vol. 2, nos. 1–2 (Spring 1990).

Netanyahu Benzion, *Don Isaac Abravanel, Statesman and Philosopher*. Ithaca, NY: Cornell University Press, 1998.

Norwich, John Julius. *A History of Venice*. London: Penguin, 2012.

Ogren, Brian. 'Leone Ebreo on *prisca sapientia*: Jewish Wisdom and the Textual Transmission of Knowledge', in *Umanesimo e cultura ebraica nel Rinascimento italiano*, eds Stefano U. Baldassarre and Fabrizio Lelli. Florence: Angelo Pontecorboli, 2016.

Pescatori, Rosella. 'The Myth of the Androgyne in Leone Ebreo's *Dialoghi d'amore*', *Comitatus*, vol. 38 (2007), pp. 1–14.

Pullan, Brian. 'Charity and Usury: Jewish and Christian Lending in Renaissance and Early Modern Italy', *Proceedings of the British Academy*, vol. 125 (2004), pp. 19–40.

Pullan, Brian. *The Jews of Europe and the Inquisition of Venice, 1550–1670*. Oxford: Blackwell, 1983.

Pullan, Brian. 'The Conversion of the Jews: The Style of Italy', *Bulletin of the John Rylands Library*, vol. 70, no. 1 (1988), pp. 53–70.

Pullan, Brian. '"A Ship with Two Rudders": "Righetto Marrano" and the Inquisition in Venice', *The Historical Journal*, vol. 20, no. 1 (1977), pp. 25–58.

Pullan, Brian. *Rich and Poor in Renaissance Venice: The Social Institutions of a Catholic State to 1620*. Cambridge, MA: Harvard University Press, 1971.

Pullan, Brian, 'Sefirotic Depiction, Divine Noesis and Aristotelian Kabbalah: Abraham ben Meir de Balmes and Italian Renaissance Thought', *Jewish Quarterly Review*, vol. 104, no. 4 (2014), pp. 573–99.

Ravid, Benjamin. '*Contra Judaeos* in Seventeenth-Century Italy: Two Responses to the *Discorso* of Simone Luzzatto by Melchiore Palontrotti and Giulio Morosini', *AJS Review*, vol. 7 (1982–3), pp. 301–51.

Ravid, Benjamin. '"How Profitable the Nation of the Jewes Are": The Humble Addresses of Menasseh ben Israel and the *Discorso* of Simone Luzzatto', in Jehuda Reinharz and Daniel Swetschinski, eds, *Mystics, Philosophers and Politicians*. Durham, NC: Duke University Press, 1982, pp. 159–80.

Ravid, Benjamin. 'Christian Travelers in the Ghetto of Venice: Some Preliminary Observations', in Stanley Nash, ed., *Between History and Literature: Studies in Honor of Isaac Barzilay*. B'nei B'rak: Hakibbutz Hameuhad, 1997, pp. 111–50.

Ravid, Benjamin. '*Cum Nimis Absurdum* and the Ancona Auto-da-Fé Revisited: Their Impact on Venice and Some Wider Reflections', *Jewish History*, vol. 26 (2021), pp. 85–100.

Ravid, Benjamin. 'Popular Religion in the Early-Modern Ghetto of Venice', in Jeffrey Stackert, Barbara N. Porter and David P. Wright, *Gazing on the Deep: Ancient Near Eastern and Other Studies in Honor of Tsvi Abusch*. Bethesda, MD: CDL Press, 2010.

Ravid, Benjamin. 'From Yellow to Red: On the Distinguishing Head-Covering of the Jews of Venice', *Jewish History*, vol. 6, nos. 1/2, *The Frank Talmage Memorial Volume* (1992), pp. 179–210.

Ravid, Benjamin. 'How "Other" Really Was the Jewish Other? The Evidence from Venice 2008', in William Andrews and David N. Myers, eds, *Acculturation and Its Discontents: The Italian Jewish Experience between Exclusion and Inclusion*. Toronto: University of Toronto Press, pp. 19–55.

Ravid, Benjamin. 'The Establishment of the Ghetto Vecchio of Venice 1541', *Proceedings of the World Congress of Jewish Studies* (1973), pp. 153–67.

Ravid, Benjamin. 'The Sephardic Jewish Merchants of Venice, Port Jews, and the Road to Modernity', in *From Catalonia to the Caribbean: The Sephardic Orbit from Medieval to Modern Times*. Leiden: Brill, 2018.

Ravid, Benjamin. 'Venice and its Minorities', in *A Companion to Venetian History*, ed. E. Dursteler. Leiden and Boston: Brill, 2013.

Ravid, Benjamin. 'The First Charter of the Jewish Merchants of Venice 1589', *AJS Review*, vol. 1 (1976), pp. 187–222.

Ravid, Benjamin. 'Venice' in Fred Skolnik and Michael Berenbaum, eds, *Encyclopaedia Judaica*, 2nd edn, vol. 20, pp. 499–504; Detroit: Macmillan, 2007.

Raz Krakotzkin, Amnon. 'Persecution and the Art of Printing Hebrew Books in Italy in the 1550s', in R. Cohen, N. Dohrmann, A. Shear and E. Reiner (eds), *Jewish Culture in Early Modern Europe: Essays in Honor of David B. Ruderman*. Pittsburgh, NJ: Hebrew Union College Press, 2014, pp. 97–108.

Rosenblatt, Jason P. *Renaissance England's Chief Rabbi*. Oxford: Oxford University Press, 2006.

Rosenzweig, Claudia. *Bovo D'Antona by Elye Bokher, A Yiddish Romance: A Critical Edition with Commentary*. Leiden: Brill, 2015.

Roth, Cecil. *History of the Jews in Italy*. Philadelphia, PA: The Jewish Publication Society of America, 1946.

Roth, Cecil. 'Leone da Modena and England', *Transactions (Jewish Historical Society of England)*, vol. 11 (1924–7), pp. 206–27.

Roth, Cecil. 'Leone da Modena and his English Correspondents', *Transactions (Jewish Historical Society of England)*, vol. 17 (1951–2), pp. 39–43.

Roth, Cecil. *Opportunities that Pass*. London: Vallentine Mitchell, 2005.

Roth, Cecil. *Venice*. Philadelphia, PA: Jewish Publication Society of America, 1930.

Roth, Cecil. 'The Origin of Ghetto: A Final Word', *Romania*, vol. 60, no. 237 (1934), pp. 67–144.

Rozen, Minna. *The Mediterranean in the Seventeenth Century: Captives, Pirates and Ransomers*. Palermo: Associazione 'Mediterranea', 2016.

Ruderman, David B. *Early Modern Jewry: A New Cultural History*. Princeton, NJ: Princeton University Press, 2010.

Ruderman, David B. 'The Italian Renaissance and Jewish Thought', in A. Rabil, ed., *Renaissance Humanism: Foundations, Forms and Legacy. Volume 1: Humanism in Italy*. Philadelphia, PA: University of Pennsylvania Press, 1988, pp. 382–433.

Ruderman, David B. 'The Impact of Science on Jewish Culture and Society in Venice (with Special Reference to Graduates of Padua's Medical School)', in Gaetano Cozzi, ed., *Gli Ebrei e Venezia secoli XIV–XVIII*. Milan: Edizioni Comunità, 1987, pp. 417–48.

Ruderman, David B. *Jewish Thought and Scientific Discovery in Early Modern Europe*. New Haven, CT, and London: Yale University Press, 1995.

Ruderman, David B., ed. *Essential Papers on Jewish Culture in Renaissance and Baroque Italy*. New York: New York University Press, 1992.

Ruderman, David B., ed. *Preachers of the Italian Ghetto*. Berkeley, CA: University of California Press, 1992.

Samuel, Edgar. 'The Readmission of the Jews to England in 1656, in the Context of English Economic Policy', *Jewish Historical Studies*, vol. 31 (1988), pp. 153–69.

Scholem, Gershom. *Shabbetai Tzvi The Mystical Messiah 1626–1676.* Princeton, NJ: Princeton University Press, 1973.

Scordari, Chiara Carmen. 'Behind Multiple Masks: Leon Modena's Diasporic Tragedy *L'Ester* in Seventeenth-Century Venice', *Skenè. Journal of Theatre and Drama Studies*, vol. 6, no. 2 (2020), pp. 53–70.

Seidel, Esther. 'The Concept of Philosophy in the Sixteenth Century: Leone Ebreo and the Italian Renaissance', *European Judaism: A Journal for the New Europe*, vol. 35, no. 2 (2002), pp. 97–105.

Shapiro, James. *Shakespeare and the Jews.* New York: Columbia University Press, 1996.

Shmuelevitz, Aryeh, Simonsohn, Shlomo and Benayahu, Meir, eds. *Eliyah Capsali Seder Eliyahu Zuta* (Hebrew). Tel Aviv: Tel Aviv University, 1983.

Shulvass, Moses Avigdor. *The Jews in the World of the Renaissance.* Leiden: Brill, 1973.

Stow, Kenneth R. 'The Papacy and the Jews: Catholic Reformation and Beyond', *Jewish History*, vol. 6, nos. 1/2 (1992), pp. 257–79.

Stow, Kenneth R. *Catholic Thought and Papal Jewry Policy, 1555–1593.* New York: Jewish Theological Seminary of America, 1977.

Tartaglia, Rachele, ed. *Venice, the Jews and Europe, 1516–2016.* Venice: Marsilio, 2016.

Teller, Adam. *Rescue the Surviving Souls: The Great Jewish Refugee Crisis of the Seventeenth Century.* Princeton, NJ: Princeton University Press, 2020.

Torbidoni, Michela. 'Pomis David ben Isaac de', *Encyclopedia of Renaissance Philosophy online.* ed. Springer, 2018/Giuseppe Veltri, *Renaissance Philosophy in Jewish Garb.* Leiden: Brill, 2009, 2018.

Weil, Gerard E. *Elia Levita: Humaniste et Massorete (1469–1549).* Leiden: Brill, 1963.

Westwater, Lynn Lara. *Sarra Copia Sulam: A Jewish Salonnière and the Press in Counter-Reformation Venice.* Toronto: University of Toronto Press, 2020.

Yates, Frances A. *Giordano Bruno and the Hermetic Tradition.* Chicago, IL: University of Chicago Press, 1964.

Yates, Frances A. *The Occult Philosophy in the Elizabethan Age.* London: Routledge & Kegan Paul, 1979.

Zinberg, Israel. *A History of Jewish Literature: Italian Jewry in the Renaissance Era*, trans. B. Martin. Philadelphia, PA: Jewish Publication Society of America, 1974.

Index

*A Right Excellent and Famous Comedy
    Called the Three Ladies of London*
    (R. Wilson)   103–4
*A Short Discourse Showing the Divine
    Origins of the Venetian Republic*
    (D. de Pomis)   100–1
Abarbanel, Benvenida   65
Abarbanel, Don Isaac   7–11, 14, 23,
    24, 54, 101
Abarbanel, Joseph   23
Abarbanel, Judah   26
Abarbanel, Judah Leon, see Ebreo, Leone
Abarbanel, Samuel   65
Aboab, Rabbi Sh'muel   160, 170–1,
    185, 190–1, 193
accademia and salons, 16th and 17th
    century Italian   151–2, 154–9
Accademia degli Impediti   151
Addison, Joseph   182
Adelkind, Cornelius   51, 91
Al-Farabi   27
alchemy   128
Alexandria   15
Alfonso V of Portugal, King   8
Amsterdam, Jewish community   5, 183,
    201
Anafesto, Paoluccio   20
Ancona   67, 68, 108, 171
Anne Boleyn   77
Antiochus IV Epiphanes   16–17
antisemitism and persecution   1, 3, 5,
    13–15, 17–18
  in 18th century England   207–8
  accusations of monstrousness and
    child murder   16–17, 38–9

burning of the Talmud   91–3, 95–6,
    120, 123, 185
Christian/Catholic Church   2–3, 17,
    22–3, 38–40, 91–7, 100 (*see also*
    Inquisitions)
Cum nimis absurdum Papal Bull   93–5,
    97–8, 117
expulsion and threatened
    expulsion   7, 8–9, 14–15, 16,
    17, 40, 44–6, 59, 66, 80, 84,
    85–6, 87, 100, 107, 125, 133,
    177, 180–1, 182–3
fear of 'otherness'   15–17, 38–9
The Merchant of Venice (W. Shakespeare)
    79, 141, 142–3, 174
pre-Christian   15–17
rise of Nazism   211–12
see also Inquisitions; Venetian
    Republic
Antwerp, Belgium   86, 108
Arabic philosophy   27
Aramaic language   55
Aretino, Pietro   68
Ari Nohem/ 'A Lion Roars' (L. Modena)
    144–5
Aristotle   25, 27
Art of Memory technique   186
Arthur, Prince of Wales   74
Arukh   60
Arzila, Morocco   8
Ashkenazi Jewish tradition   53, 120
Auschwitz   212
Austria   210
Averroes   27
Avicenna   27

Bacon, Francis 40
Bacon, Sir Edmund 140
Bandinelli, Baccio 169
banking *see* moneylending/banking,
    Jewish
Barabas (fictional character) 172, 173–4
Basilio, Francesco 187
Bassano, Aemilia 142–3
Bassano, Baptiste 142
Battle of Agnadello (1509) 20
Battle of Lepanto (1571) 99–100, 107
Bedell, William 140
Belilios, Jacobo 198
Bellina, Madonna 147
ben David, Rabbi Hiyya Meir 51
ben Hayyim ibn Adonijah, Jacob 60
ben Israel, Menasseh 183
Benedetti, Giovanni Battista 200
Berardelli, Alessandro 157
the Bible
    Bomberg and da Prato 49–50
    Book of Esther 17, 154–5, 156, 160,
        201
    Book of Kings 9, 62
    Deuteronomy 92, 102
    English Usury Bill (1571) 102
    Five Books of Moses, dal Castellazzo
        woodcuts 63
    Hebrew 49–50, 56, 60–1, 63, 75,
        100–1, 200, 201
    Hebrew grammar 55–6, 61
    Italian translation of Ecclesiastes 98–9
    Latin/Vulgate 56
    marriage and divorce 74, 76
    Meor Einayim/ 'Light of the Eyes'
        (A. dei Rossi) 104–5
    model for the Venetian Republic
        100–1
    Pentateuch 63, 148, 206
    Psalm 22 50
    Psalm 137 151
    Rabbinic editions 49–50, 60
    Song at the Red Sea 9
    Uriel da Costa's arguments 145–6
    see also Talmud
Bina L'itim/ 'Understanding the Times'
    (A. Figo) 185–6

Blatas, Arbit 211
blood libel, English 38–9
Bodleian Library, Oxford 64
Boldu, Antonio 118
Bomberg, Daniel 49–52, 60, 77, 86, 90
Bonaparte, Napoleon 203, 208–9, 210
Bonfil family 203
Bonifaccio, Baldassare 157–8
Boswell, William 138
Bovo d'Antona (E. Levita) 53–4
Bragadin, Alvise 90
Bragadin, Marcantonio 99
Bragança, Duke of 8
Bruno, Giordano 26
Buovo of Antona (aka Bevis of
    Hampton) 53
Buxtorf, Johannes 135

Calimani, Simone 200
Camillo, Giulio 186
Canterbury, Thomas Cranmer,
    Archbishop of 74
Capsali, Eliyahu 19–21, 35
Carcassoni, David 170–1
Casaubon, Isaac 144
Catherine of Aragon 74, 76, 138
Cattalan, Sabbadin 132
Cattaveri magistrates, Venetian 147,
    197–8, 204
Cebà, Ansaldo 154–5, 156
censorship of Hebrew texts 96–7, 198
Cervantes 26
Charles I of England, Scotland and
    Ireland, King 138
Charles II of England, Scotland and
    Ireland, King 206
child murderers, Jews portrayed as
    16–17, 38
Chiusi, Bishop of 98
Christian Church/Catholicism 7, 14,
    15, 25, 32, 37, 50, 52, 54, 144
    antisemitism 2–3, 17, 22–3, 38–40,
        91–7, 100 (*see also* Inquisitions)
    belief in Jewish monstrousness 16–17,
        38–9
    Catholic Church and Kabbalah 55,
        75, 167

Council of Trent 96
Counter-Reformation 89–90, 117, 136
Cum nimis absurdum Papal Bull 93–5, 97–8, 117
Elie Levita on 57–8
Jewish conversions to 36–8, 40–1, 66–7, 72, 77, 84–7, 107–10, 117–19, 145–6, 181–2
King Henry VIII of England 74–5, 76–7
Leon Modena's *Riti* 135–7
Protestantism 37, 38, 75, 89–90, 93–4
punishment of interfaith intimacy with Jews 72–3
scuole – ghetto fraternities 165–6
see also Bible; Inquisitions; Popes
Christian Hebraists 55–7, 59, 75, 135, 138
Christian Talmudists 6
Cinque Savi alla Mercanzia/'Board of Trade,' Venetian 82–3, 108–11, 205
Collegio, the Venetian 11, 31, 91
Congrega Piccola/Small Assembly, Venetian ghetto 162, 168, 170, 175, 177, 192
Constantinople 10, 45, 96, 99, 191–2
Contrada dell'Unione/'Quarter of the Union' 209–10
conversos, Christian 66–7, 72, 85–7, 107–10, 145–6
see also Marranos/New Christians
Cooperman, Bernard Dov 109
Coryate, Thomas 92, 139–40
Council of Ten, Venetian Republic 11, 12, 63, 71, 72, 92, 101, 108, 114, 116, 132–3
Council of Trent 96
Counter-Reformation 89–90, 117, 136
Cretan War (1645–1669) 181, 195
Croke, Richard 74–5, 76, 77
Cromwell, Oliver 183, 205–6
Cum nimis absurdum, Papal Bull 93–5, 97–8, 117
Cyprus 96, 99, 108

d'Orléans, Duc 134
da Costa, Uriel 145–6
da Fano, Rabbi Menahem Azariah 119, 121, 125–6
da Gama, Vasco 10, 45
da Prato, Friar Felice 49–51
da Viterbo, Cardinal Egidio 52, 54–5, 55–9, 64–5
dal Castellazzo, Moses 5, 62–3
De Arcanis Catholicae Veritatis (Galatino) 118
de Balmes, Abraham 26–8, 50, 60, 61
De Harmonia Mundi 26, 75, 77–80
De Medico Hebraeo (D. De Pomis) 101–3, 104, 105
De Pomis, Rabbi, David 97–9, 100–4, 105–6
de Selve of Lavour, Bishop George 60–1
dei Rossi, Rabbi Azariah 104–5, 119, 120–2, 144
del Banco, Anselmo 6, 29–30, 31, 32, 33–5, 41, 44, 54–5, 63
see also Meshullam, Asher
del Banco, Vita 29–30
della Mirandola, Pico 26
Delmedigo, Joseph 176
Democritus 180
di Arezzo, Fra Giovan Maria 31
di Friceli, Abram 44
Dialoghi d'amore/'Dialogues of Love' (L. Ebreo) 25–6, 184
Discorso/'Discourse on the State of the Jews' (S. Luzzatto) 177–83
divorce and Jewish law 74, 76, 116–17, 138
doctors/physicians, Jewish 17, 23, 26, 34–5, 68, 94, 97–8, 101–2, 105–6, 212
Doge, Venetian 12, 20, 37, 76, 101, 165–6, 184, 197–8, 204
Dolfin, Zacaria 31–2, 34
Donne, John 26, 140

Easter 30–1, 39
Ebreo, Leone/Abarbanel, Judah Leon 6, 23–6, 27–8, 54, 61, 98, 184
Edward I of England, King 40, 182
Edward VI of England, King 37

Egypt 16
Eliano, Giovanni Battista 117
Elizabeth I of England, Queen 37,
40, 77
England 14, 37, 38, 39–41, 74–8, 103,
138, 182–3, 205–8
Esecutori contro la bestemmia,
Venetian 96–7
esperimento dell' inghistera 187–8
Esther, Book of 17, 154–5, 156, 160,
201
exorcism 115

Ferdinand I of Naples, King 9
Ferdinand and Isabella of Spain, King
and Queen 7, 8, 14, 24
Ferrara 87, 107–8
Ferrara, Duke of 85
Figo, Rabbi Azariah 185–6
Foxe, John 40
France 15, 19, 67, 208–10
fraternities/*hevrot*, ghetto 165, 166,
169, 170–1

Gaffarel, Jacques 136–7
Galatino (aka Pietro Colonna) 118
gambling 126, 129–30, 131, 133, 135,
159–60
Garsin, François 169
George II of England, Scotland and
Ireland, King 207
ghetto, defined 1, 31–2
Ghetto Nuovo 31–3
Giorgi/Zorzi, Francesco 75, 76, 77–80,
142
Giuseppe from Mantua 111–12, 147
Giustiniani, Marco Antonio 90–3,
119–20, 123
G'milut Hasadim 166
gods/divinities and 'otherness' 17
Gradenigo, Paolo 119
Grand Council, Venetian 11, 101
Granville, George 206
Greece, Ancient 15, 16
Gregory XIII, Pope 101
Grillo, Joseph 128
Grimaldi, Cardinal 26–7, 28
Grotius, Hugo 138

Hagiz, Moses 199
Halfon, Rabbi Elijah Menahem 6,
67–8, 76
Haman 17
Hamburg, rabbis of 145–6
Hamiz, Joseph 143, 144, 145
Handel, George Frideric 201
Harvey, Gabriel 40
Hasmonean kingdom 17
Hebrew grammar 54, 55–6, 58–9, 60
Hebrew language 27, 55–6
Henry III of England, King 41
Henry VI (W. Shakespeare) 172
Henry VIII of England, King 6, 37,
74–7, 138
Herder, Johann Gottfried 182
hevrot ghetto fraternities 165, 166,
169, 170–1
Historia de gli Riti Hebraici (*Riti*),
(L. Modena) 135–9
History of the Jews (Josephus) 207
Hiyya Meir ben David, Rabbi 51
Holy Roman Emperors/Empire 19,
21, 59, 67
House of Catechumens, Venetian 117
House of Converts, Chancery
Lane 40–1

ibn Tibbon, Moses 27
ibn Tibbon, Samuel 27
Incogniti Academy 152
Inferno (Dante) 167
Inquisitions 52, 108
Congregation of the Inquisition 91
Portuguese 69, 82, 84, 86, 114
Spanish 69
Venetian 72, 90, 116
Abraham Righetto 113–14
black slave boy, Samuel
Maestro 114–15
conversions to Christianity 117–19
exorcism 115
Gaspare Ribiera 112–13
ghetto finances 196–7
Giuseppe from Mantua 111–12
interfaith intimacy 72–3
Isacco Levi 187–8
the Riti (L. Modena) 136–7

Isaac Treves and his Captains
  (B. Nazari) 202–3
Isserles, Rabbi Moshe 91, 120
Istanbul, Jewish community in 170–1
Italian Renaissance 4
Italian Synagogue, Venice 148, 187

James VI of Scotland and I of England,
  King 135, 205
Jerusalem 188, 189, 190
  168BCE, invasion of 16–17
Jesus Christ, death of 38–9
The Jew of Malta (C. Marlowe) 172,
  173–4
Jew of Venice (G. Granville) 206
Jewish community, 20th century
  Venetian 211–12
Jewish community, modern
  Venetian 212–13
Jewish ghetto community, Venetian
  1–2
  18th trade/manufacturing
    embargoes 204, 205
  accademia and salons 151–2, 154–9
  accusations of Turkish conspiracy 96
  bubonic plague (1630) 151, 152–3,
    176
  cultural renaissance/
    enlightenment 4–5, 23, 47, 61
  enforcement of hats and badges 4,
    14, 52, 68, 162, 203
  expansion of the ghetto 82–4
  false Messiah, Shabbetai Tzvi 188–94,
    199
  financial crisis 195–8
  Fondaco dei Turchi 2
  French occupation of Venice 208–10
  ghetto gates dismantled 209
  Ghetto Nuovo and Nuovissimo 31–2,
    41–2, 83–4, 109, 153–4, 203,
    211
  Ghetto vecchio 83–4, 153, 202
  hevrot ghetto fraternities 165, 166,
    169, 170–1
  influx of Paduan Jews 21, 22–3
  invasion of the League of
    Cambrai 19–21

Jewish scholarship 74–7, 159, 176,
  190
  law and courts 116–17
Levantine merchants 81, 82–5, 109,
  121, 154, 161–2, 198, 202–3,
  210
living conditions 152–4
money lending/pawnbroking and
  banking services 2–3, 18–19,
  21–2, 30, 45, 83, 89, 109, 110,
  119, 162–3, 175, 178, 196, 202–3
music and entertainment 71–2,
  147–51, 156, 159–60, 167
occupation (*see also above* money
  lending/pawnbroking and
  banking services)
occupations in the ghetto 42–3, 44,
  46, 80, 83, 94, 97, 178, 205
Ponentine settlers 109, 111, 146,
  161–2, 198
printing and Hebrew
  publications 49–54, 60–1, 63,
  75, 77, 90–3, 96–7, 119–20,
  123–5, 131–2, 159, 167, 198
punishment of sexual intimacy with
  Christians 72–3
rabbis 51, 67–8, 74, 76, 90–1, 92,
  97–9, 100–4, 105–6, 116–17,
  119–22, 126–37, 139–40,
  143–6, 148–50, 159, 176–7,
  187–8, 189, 190–2, 193–4,
  198, 199, 209 (*see also* Aboab,
  Rabbi Sh'muel; Figo, Rabbi
  Azariah; Luzzatto, Rabbi Simone;
  Modena, Rabbi, Leon; Saraval,
  Rabbi Jacob Raphael; Zacuto,
  Rabbi Moshe)
restrictions and segregation 2–4,
  13–14, 28, 31–5, 41–4, 46–7,
  52, 59, 71, 80, 83, 90, 94–7,
  110, 196, 203, 208–9
self-government - *Università Grande*
  and *Congrega Piccola* 161–4,
  168, 170, 175, 177, 192, 194,
  198, 209–10
study of Kabbalah 124–6, 143–5,
  167, 199

synagogues   32, 33, 43, 80–1, 120,
    121, 128, 134–5, 146, 148–50,
    151, 160, 176, 187, 192, 208–9,
    211, 212
  taxes and levies against   20, 22, 29–
    30, 33, 35, 46, 80, 84, 89, 110,
    153, 162, 163–4, 181, 195–7
  the Tedeschi/German settlers   2,
    13–14, 53, 83–4, 109, 110,
    161–3, 175, 176, 196, 198
  threats of expulsion   44–6, 59, 80,
    85–6, 87, 100, 107, 133, 177,
    180–1
  Venetian charters on occupation and
    trade   22, 30, 46, 80, 84, 89,
    94–5, 111, 161, 162–3, 175,
    198, 204–5
  yeshiva   176, 190
  see also Abarbanel, Don Isaac; Aboab,
    Rabbi Sh'muel; Figo, Rabbi
    Azariah; Luzzatto, Rabbi Simone;
    Modena, Rabbi Leon; Rodriga,
    Daniel; Saraval, Rabbi Jacob
    Raphael; Sulam, Sara Copia;
    Zacuto, Rabbi Moshe
Jewish Naturalization Act/'Jew Bill'
    (1753), English   207–8
Jewish population, Padua   4, 20–1, 46
Jewish Travellers (E. Adler)   64
João II of Portugal, King   8
João III of Portugal, King   65, 66
Jona, Giuseppe   211–12
Josephus, Flavius   16, 207
Judah Leon see Ebreo, Leone
judaizing, crime of   113
Julius II, Pope   55

Kabbalah   26, 55, 56, 75, 78–80, 93,
    124–6, 143–5, 167, 176, 191,
    199
Karaites Judaism   146
Katzenellenbogen, Rabbi Meir   90–1,
    119–20
Katzenellenbogen, Rabbi Samuel
    Judah   119–22
Kearney, Richard   15–16
Kennicott, Benjamin   200–1

Khmelnytsky, Bogdan   170
Khmelnytsky uprising, Ukraine
    169–70
Kimhi, David   50
Klemperer, Israel   95
Knights of St John   168–9

law and courts, Jewish   115–16
League of Cambrai   19–21, 54
Leicester, Robert Dudley, Earl of   40
Leicester's Commonwealth   40
L'Ester (L. Modena)   156, 160
letter apologetica (J.R. Saraval)   200
Levantine Jewish merchants   81, 82–5,
    111, 154, 198, 202, 210
Levi, Isacco   131–2, 187
Levita (aka Elye Bokher), Elia   6, 52–5,
    56–61
Levita, Isaac   192
Lidarti, Christian Giuseppe   201
London Evening Post   208
London, John Stokesley, Bishop
    of   74–5, 76–7
Lopez, Roderigo   40
Lord Chamberlain's Men   103
Loredan, Gian Francesco   180–1
Loredan, Pietro di Lorenzo   118
Louis XII of France, King   20, 44
Lovato, Ruffino   22–3
Luria, Isaac   124, 125
Luzzatto, Isaac   175
Luzzatto, Moses Hayyim   199–200
Luzzatto, Rabbi Simone   6, 111,
    132–3, 175–80, 181–5

Maccabees   17
Machiavelli   185
Macklin, Charles   207
Maestro, Samuel   115
Magen v'Tzinal 'Shield and Breastplate'
    (L. Modena)   145–6
maggid   199
Maimonides   90, 137, 143, 144,
    183–4
Maltese slave trade   168–9, 170, 171
Mantino, Jacob   68, 75, 76
Manuel of Portugal, King   14

Marlowe, Christopher   172–4
Marranos/New Christians   85–7,
       107–8, 110
Mary of England, Queen   37
Masoret Hamasoret (E. Levita)   57, 61
Maximilian I, Holy Roman
       Emperor   21
Medices, Friar Sixtus   102
'memory theatre', Venice   186
Menda, Yehuda   40
Mendes (aka Doña Gracia Nasi),
       Beatrice Nasi   86–7, 99
Mendes (aka Reyna Nasi), Brianda   87
Mendes (aka Joseph Nasi), João   86, 87
   see also Nasi, Joseph
Mendes, Diego   86
Meor Einayim (A. dei Rossi)   104–5,
       119, 120–2, 125–6
Merchant of Venice (W.
       Shakespeare)   35–6, 37–8, 41,
       78–80, 103, 141–3, 172, 173,
       174, 205–8, 213
Meshullam (del Banco), Hayyim   21, 29
Meshullam, Asher
   see Anselmo, del Banco
Meshullam, Diamante   65–6
Meshullam, Jacob   35–7, 41
Meshullam, Salamon   36
Meshullam, Simon   63
Messiahs and prophecies, false   66–8,
       188–94
Mestre, Venice   13, 19, 33–4, 59
Milan, Ludovico Sforza, Duke of   44
Milton, John   138, 140
Mishneh Torah   90
Modena, Isaac   129–30
Modena, Mordecai   128, 129
Modena, Rabbi Leon   6, 153, 175,
       177
   Accademia degli Impediti   151
   Ari Nohem/'A Lion Roars'   144–5
   disapproval of Kabbalah   126, 143–5
   family   127–34
   gambling   126, 129–30, 131, 133,
       135, 159–60
   Historia de gli Riti Hebraici - the
       Riti   135–7

L'Ester play   156, 160
Magen v'Tzina/'Shield and
       Breastplate'   145–6
   music and poetry   148–9
   preaching   134–5
   public debate with Thomas
       Coryate   139–40
   and Sara Copia Sulam   156, 159
   as synagogue cantor   148–9
Modena, Rachel   130, 133–4, 154
Modena, Zebulun   130–1
Molcho, Solomon   66–7, 68, 69, 76
Molino, Francesco   184
moneylending/banking, Jewish   2–3,
       17–18, 19, 21–2, 30, 44, 45,
       83, 89, 102–4, 109, 110, 119,
       162–3, 175, 178, 196, 202–3
   see also pawnbroking; *strazzaria*/
       second-hand trade
'monstrous otherness', antisemitism
       and   16–17, 38–9
Montaigne, Michel   165, 184–5
Monte di Pietà   45
Montesquieu   182
More, Thomas   185
Moretto, Giorgio   72–3
Moro, Gabriele   59, 80
Morosini, Giulio   181–2, 188
Mortara, Saul Levi   209–10
Moryson, Fynes   166
Moses   16
Münster, Sebastian   58
music and entertainment   147–8,
       159–60
   Accademia degli Impediti   151
   Leon Modena   148–50, 151, 156
   Rabbi Jacob Raphael Saraval's
       libretto   201
   Salamone Rossi   149–50
Muslims/Islam   8, 23, 27, 54, 189,
       192
Mussolini, Benito   211

Nahmias, Moses   192–3
Naples   8, 9, 14, 44
Nasi, Doña Gracia   86–7, 99
Nasi, Joseph   87, 99, 100, 114

Nathan of Gaza 188, 189, 193–4
Nazari, Bartolomeo 202
Nazism 63, 211–12

occult practices/witchcraft 187–8
olive oil trade embargo 204
Oliver, Francesco 72
Orsini, Count Niccolò 97–8
otherness, fear of 15–17, 38–9
Ottolenghi, Rabbi Adolfo 212
Ottoman Empire 7, 81, 82, 84–5, 87,
 124, 168–9, 181
 see also Turkey/Turkish

Padua, University of 4, 19–21, 53, 76,
 124, 143, 159, 176, 200
Palatine of Krakow, Count 36
Palontrotti, Melchiore 181
Paluzzi, Numidio 157
papal bulls, Jewish restriction in 93–5,
 97–8, 117
Papal States 93–4
Papal States and papal bulls 93–4
Paradiso, Marco see Meshullam, Jacob
Path of the Upright (M.H. Luzzatto)
 200
Paul IV, Pope 91, 93–4, 98, 113
pawnbroking 2, 18–19, 21, 30,
 33–4, 42, 71, 83, 89, 162–3,
 179, 196
 see also moneylending/banking,
 Jewish
Pentateuch 63, 148, 206
piracy 168–9, 170
Pires, Diego 66–7
Pius IV, Pope 98
Pius V, Pope 98
Pius VI, Pope 204–5
plagues and disease 13, 59, 80, 124,
 151, 152, 153, 176
Plato 25
Poland 168, 170, 171
Polish Jews 171–2
Ponentine Jews 109, 111, 146, 161–2,
 198
Popes 19, 55, 65, 68, 76, 77, 91, 93–4,
 98, 101, 113, 204–5

Portugal 7–8, 10–11, 14, 24, 45, 66–7,
 82, 84
Posidonius of Apameia 16–17
Possot, Dennis 73
Prague 35
printing and publishing industry 49–54,
 55, 60–1, 63, 75, 77, 90–3, 96–7,
 120, 123–5, 159, 198
prisca sapentia, Renaissance theory 98
prisca theologia 25
processions, city 165–6
Protestant Reformation, English 37,
 38
Protestantism 37, 38, 89–90
Pugliese, Isaac 118–19
Purim festival 72, 160, 167

Quarantia, Venetian 101

Rapaport, Rabbi Abraham
 Menahem 92, 121
Raphael, Marco 77
refugees 22–3, 86, 171–2
Reuveni, David 64–7, 69
Ribiera, Gaspare 112–13
Ribiera, Giovanni and Alumbra
 112–13
Righetto, Abraham 113–14
Riti (Historia de gli Riti Hebraici),
 L. Modena 135–9
ritual bathing 120, 177
Rodriga, Daniel 108–11
Rome 12, 26, 59–61, 72, 91, 94, 99
Rosenzweig, Claudia 54
Rossi, Salamone 149–50, 154
Roth, Cecil 31–2
Rowse, A.L. 142

Sabbatarians 193, 206
Safed, Galilee 124
Saint Jerome 56
Salvador, Joseph 207
Sandella, Caterina 68
Sanudo, Marin 22–3, 30–1, 32, 35,
 37, 65, 71–2, 76, 160
Saraval, Rabbi Jacob Raphael 198,
 200–1

Saraval, Rabbi Solomon Hay   189
Saravel, Graziadio   132
Sarpi, Paolo   144
Sarug, Israel   125–6
Savanarola, Giralomo   188
Savii/ Sages, Venetian   11, 72, 82–3,
        108–11, 205
Savii Grandi   11
Scepticism   184–5
Scholem, Gershom   191
Scuola Canton synagogue, Venice   81
Scuola Tedesca/German synagogue,
        Venice   80, 134, 176
scuole/fraternities, Christian   165–6
Selden, John   137–8
Selim I of Turkey, Sultan   99
Senate, Venetian   11, 12, 14, 19, 22,
        23, 29–34, 44–6, 59, 68, 71,
        76–7, 80, 81, 84, 100, 107,
        108–9, 165–6, 196–7, 198,
        204, 208
Sephardi Jews   120, 170
Serenissima see Venetian Republic
sexual relations, interfaith   72–3
Shakespeare, William   35, 37–8, 41,
        77–80, 103, 140–3, 172–3,
        205–8, 213
Shapiro, James   37–8, 40, 208
Shylock (fictional character)   6,
        35–6, 41, 78–80, 103, 141, 173,
        205–8, 213
Signoria, Venetian   76–7
Simhat Torah festival   148, 151
Skippon, Philip   168–9
slavery   7, 8, 105, 114–15, 168–9,
        170–1
smuggling refugees   86
Society for the Ransoming of Captives
        166, 169, 170–1, 197
Socrates   184
Socrates, Or On Human Knowledge
        (S. Luzzatto)   184–5
Songs of Solomon (S. Rossi)   150
Spain   7, 8–9, 14, 23, 24, 45, 66, 67,
        69, 84, 99, 109
Spalato free port, establishment
        of   108–9, 110, 111

Spanish Synagogue, Venice   148, 151,
        208–9
Spinoza, Baruch   26
Stoicism   179–80, 184
strazzaria/second-hand trade   43, 44,
        46, 71, 83, 175, 210
Sulam, Jacob   154
Sulam, Sara Copia   6
    and Ansaldo Cebà   154–5, 156
    and Leon Modena   156, 159
    salon and salon members   152,
        155–9
Suleiman of Turkey, Sultan   86–7
Sybilline Oracles   144
synagogues   15, 32, 33, 43, 80–1,
        94, 120, 121, 128, 134–5,
        146, 148–50, 151, 160, 176,
        187, 188, 192, 201, 208–9,
        211, 212

Talmud, the   57, 138, 185
    Bomberg and Hiyya Meir ben David's
        (1520)   51, 77
    Talmud, burning the   91–3, 95–6,
        120, 123, 167, 185
Tamari, Moses HaCohen   116–17
Tamari, Tamar   116
Tatars   170
taxes and levies, Venetian   8, 20, 22,
        29–30, 33, 35, 46, 80, 84, 89,
        110, 153, 162, 163–4, 181,
        195–7
Tedeschi/German Jewish settlers   2,
        13–14, 53, 83–4, 109, 110,
        161–3, 175, 176, 196, 198
Ten Lost Tribes of Israel   62, 188
Thomas of Monmouth   39
Thomas, William   73
Titus, Emperor   105
Tofteh arukh/'Hell Made Ready'
        (Zacuto)   167
Toland, John   183
Torah commentary, Rabbi
        Rapaport's   92, 93
trade links, international   10–12, 81–2,
        87, 108–9, 178
Treves dei Bonfili family   203

Treves, Giuseppe   203
Treves, Isaac   202
Treves, Salomon   203
Tron, Andrea   204–5
Turkey/Turkish   2, 10, 81, 86–7, 96, 99,
    108, 111, 114, 168–9, 181, 195
  pirates   168–9
  rabbis   191
  Turkish–Venetian War (1499–1503)
    10
  see also Constantinople; Corfu; Crete;
    Cyprus; Levantine merchants;
    Ottoman Empire
Tuscany, Ferdinando I de Medici, Duke
    of   106
typhus epidemics   59, 80
Tzemach David (D. De Pomis)   106
Tzvi, Shabbetai   145, 188–94

Ukraine   169–70
Università Grande/Large Assembly   162,
    163, 198, 209–10
Usque, Solomon   156, 160
Usury Bill (1571), English   102–3

Venetian Republic   1
  attitude to Jewish population   1,
    2–4, 5, 13–14, 19, 21–3,
    30–5, 44–6, 59, 66, 71–3, 80–4,
    89–90, 92–7, 100, 107–11,
    133, 153–4, 161, 162–3, 175,
    177–80, 195–8, 204–5 (see also
    under Inquisitions)
  Battle of Lepanto (1571)   99–100, 107
  Catholic Church   12, 22–3, 72,
    89–90, 91–5, 96–7, 100,
    117–18, 144, 165–6 (see also
    under Inquisitions)
  city processions   165–6
  Council of Ten   11, 12, 63, 71, 72,
    92, 101, 108, 114, 116, 132–3
  Cyprus, Corfu and Crete   96,
    99–100, 108, 181, 195, 204
  Easter celebrations   30–1
  Esecutori contro la bestemmia   96–7
  financial crisis   195–8, 203–5

ghetto charters   22, 30, 46, 80, 84,
    89, 94–5, 111, 161, 162–3, 175,
    198, 204–5
international trade links   10–12,
    81–2, 87, 108–9, 178
League of Cambrai invasions   19–21,
    54
model of the Republic and the
    Hebrew Bible   100–1
negotiations with Daniel
    Rodriga   108–11
plans to expel the Jewish community
    44–6, 59, 80, 85–6, 87, 100,
    107, 133, 177, 180–1
Senate   11, 12, 14, 19, 22, 23,
    29–34, 44–6, 59, 68, 71, 76–7,
    80, 81, 84, 100, 107, 108–9,
    165–6, 196–7, 198, 204, 208
taxes and levies   20, 22, 29–30, 33,
    35, 46, 80, 84, 89, 110, 153,
    162, 163–4, 181, 195–7
Venetian State Archive   35
Venice, French occupation of   208–9
Ventura (aka Venturozzo), Samuel
    Moses   116–17
Verallo, Cardinal   91–2
Vicenza, Bishop   113
Vulgate Bible   56

Walpole, Robert   207
Wattasid dynasty   8
Way of Faith (G. Morosini)   181–2
William of Norwich, murder of   39
Wilson, Robert   103–4
women writers, Venetian   154–5
World War II   211–12
Wotton, Sir Henry   135, 140

Yates, Dame Frances   78–9, 141–2
yeshiva, Padua   4, 19–20
yeshiva, Venetian   176
Yiddish language   53

Zacuto, Rabbi Moshe   166–7, 169–71,
    191, 193, 194
Zohar   55, 124

A Note on the Author

HARRY FREEDMAN is Britain's leading author of popular works of Jewish culture and history. His best-selling publications include *Leonard Cohen: The Mystical Roots of Genius, The Talmud: A Biography, Kabbalah: Secrecy, Scandal and the Soul* and *Britain's Jews: Confidence, Maturity, Anxiety.* You can follow his regular articles on harryfreedman.substack.com